Gender and Victorian Reform

Gender and Victorian Reform

Edited by

Anita Rose

CAMBRIDGE
SCHOLARS

P U B L I S H I N G

Gender and Victorian Reform, Edited by Anita Rose

This book first published 2008

Cambridge Scholars Publishing

12 Back Chapman Street, Newcastle upon Tyne, NE6 2XX, UK

British Library Cataloguing in Publication Data
A catalogue record for this book is available from the British Library

ISBN (10): 1-4438-0067-8, ISBN (13): 978-1-4438-0067-9

TABLE OF CONTENTS

INTRODUCTION

In October of 2006, The Victorians Institute (VI), a scholarly organization with an international membership,[1] met on the campus of Converse College in Spartanburg, South Carolina.[2] Converse, founded in 1889, is a residential, undergraduate women's college with a strong focus on the liberal and fine arts. Given the history and traditions of Converse, conference organizers agreed that it was appropriate for the conference to address the topic of gender in Victorian England. More specifically, the theme of "Gender and Victorian Reform," addressed the profound influences that women reformers had in nineteenth-century England, but it also acknowledged the subtle and powerful role that gender and gender identity played in a much broader sense. In addition to investigating the more readily apparent instances of gender concerns that shaped reform,[3] participants in this conference examined the structure of charitable organizations, the interpretation of language and literacy, ideas of beauty, and religion through the lens of gender.

Gender, in the nineteenth century as now, was indeed an integral part of identity, providing a lens through which the world is understood, and this more elusive influence of gender on reform provided a rich source of scholarship and discussion at the Converse gathering. Now, in 2008, gender plays a prominent role in the political landscape of America in an election year. Gender and reform are once again linked in politics and the public imagination, and it seems fitting to revisit the nineteenth century to remind ourselves that gender, along with race, and class, has long been a vital part of public discourse about social concerns and reform.

Reform in the Nineteenth century

The reforming spirit was one of the hallmarks of the Victorian era in England (1830 – 1901).[4] Victorian philosophers, politicians, artists, writers and activists of all predilections considered the tremendous changes in physical science, religious thought, ideas about human psychology, economic relationships, education, and technological achievements.[5] New developments on every front of human endeavor very literally changed perceptions of what it meant to be human. This, in turn, led to a great deal of collective, as well as individual, soul searching.[6] Consequently, the impulse to use this newly acquired knowledge to right perceived inequities and injustices was strong; throughout the nineteenth century, there were major legislative reforms for almost every important social institution. Reforms to redress injustices related to limits on suffrage, religious discrimination, abuse of workers – men, women, and children – and wretched sanitary conditions in the cities evolved throughout the century.

Gender and Reform

Social reform by its very definition implies a disruption of the status quo, and wide-ranging reform, such as was seen in the nineteenth century, speaks to a need to "clean house," figuratively as well as literally. A partial breakdown of the social order developed in part as a result of the Industrial Revolution's uprooting of an agricultural England. The safety net provided by the landed aristocracy and the church became frayed as people moved from the countryside into the cities, their rural occupations supplanted by more efficient, mechanized means of farming and production. The only place for unskilled workers seemed to be in the industrial cities of the North – Engels' "Great Towns."[7] Rapid social change, and its attendant problems, demanded serious domestic reforms. Middle-class Victorian women, long charged with the supervision of the moral and physical health of the family— and, it can be argued, by extension the nation—became increasingly active in the public sphere. These women, often celebrated as the "angels in the house," demonstrated a growing political awareness, and gender became both an overt and a covert factor in reform movements. Equally important, women writers were producing respected and respectable works of literature, and perhaps naturally brought a different sensibility to art itself on a national scale.

The essays in this collection are arranged into four parts: Part I considers both historical context for reform and revisits the historical romance through the lens of gender. Daniel Siegel examines the role and function of the "bible woman" of the Female Bible Mission— a uniquely Victorian figure who often provided a link between the lower classes in desperate need of aid, and the upper classes who were in a position to give it. Chad May discusses George Eliot's only historical novel, *Romola,* and suggests that Eliot re-visioned the role of the romantic heroine of the Sir Walter Scott mold, while Laura Fasick compares ideas about the role of women's education in social evolution in Tennyson's *The Princess* and the Gilbert and Sullivan libretto for *Princess Ida.* The second group of essays addresses more specifically the role of women in public life and in the professions. Audrey Fessler, Laura Rotunno, and Andre' DeCuir examine fictional characters from canonical texts in terms of how gender affects both a reforming spirit and the means by which reform is achieved. The essays in Part III, "Genre, Literacy, and Reform," focus even more specifically on the connections among reform, gender, literacy and literary genre in the novels of Wilkie Collins (Bachman and Chernik), Charlotte Bronte (Lorentzen), and Elizabeth Gaskell (McGavran).

Finally, the four essays in the "Expanded Perspectives" section offer readings that are at once diverse and specialized. Margaret Mitchell discusses Charlotte Bronte's treatment of beauty in *Shirley*; Chris Foss introduces the reader to Indo-Anglian writer Toru Dutt and the intersections of western and eastern religion in her writing. Loretta Clayton and Maggie Atkinson consider the politics of dress and ornamentation in late nineteenth century England.

Taken as a whole, the scholarly works in this collection reflect on the more subtle threads of gender as they bind together gender concerns, questions of class and identity, language and education, and the politicizing of the middle-class. The essays offer a serious consideration of the role of gender in art and in public life that spans the Victorian era. Reformist impulses are revealed in a number of Victorian texts that are not generally read as overtly political. In this way, this collection, and the conference that gave rise to it, thoughtfully focuses on the influence of gender on a wide range of social movements, and moves the significance of gender beyond simply the content of Victorian fiction and the identity of the authors and into the more fundamental connection of discourse to reform.

Notes

[1] http://www.vcu.edu/vij/.

[2] http://www.converse.edu.

[3] I think here of "obvious" gender issues, like marriage law reform, suffrage, and women's education.

[4] One of the most accessible and comprehensive sources for a brief history of Victorian reform is on the Victorian Web, http://www.victorianweb.org/history/legistl.html. This timeline of Victorian legislation gives an overview of the major legislative reform acts throughout the nineteenth century, beginning with the 1828 repeal of the test acts, allowing dissenters to participate in national and local government and ending with the 1897 Workmen's Compensation Act.

[5] Consider that the latter half of the nineteenth century was witness to profound changes in the way life was conducted, in both small ways and great. The theories

of evolution (1859), and Marxist economics (1860s), and psychoanalysis (1896), became part of the collective consciousness. Technological wonders like the telegraph (1837), the trans-Atlantic cable (1858), the typewriter (1873), the telephone (1876), and the incandescent lamp (1879), changed the way people lived and communicated.

[6] One of the more famous instances of this Victorian introspection is Tennyson's *In Memoriam.* Tennyson's masterpiece is at once an example of both a public and private search for meaning and purpose.

[7] For further reading, see Engels, http://www.marxists.org/archive/marx/works/1845/condition-working-class/ch04.htm.

PART I

HISTORICAL CONTEXTS
AND THE HISTORICAL IMAGINATION

CHAPTER ONE

CHARITY THROUGH DISSOCIATION:
THE TASK OF THE BIBLE-WOMAN

DANIEL SIEGEL

The Missing Link (1859), Ellen Ranyard's account of the origin and work of the Female Bible Mission suggests, by its title, that something in the machinery of charity has become unfastened. Ranyard's explicit reference is to the gulf between the classes; in hoping to bridge that gulf she was like many other philanthropists of her day, who felt that the task of philanthropy was to restore the organic ties that had once subsisted between rich and poor. The visiting societies sent out lady volunteers to frequent the homes of the poor and offer their advice, their prayers, and their companionship, an office traditionally performed by rural clergy and their families. In a modern urban variation on the country estate, Octavia Hill developed a scheme to purchase and transform slum tenements, binding together tenant, landlady, and rent collector through economic exchanges and community interests. The settlement movement, too, tried to create community between the classes, as educated men and women of the middle class took up residence in East London and engaged their new neighborhoods in a variety of intellectual and practical enterprises. All of these initiatives sought modern, innovative methods to recover what they considered the traditional social purpose of charity. But the modern charity industry gave rise to a new set of polarizations, based on disagreements over the proper methods and legitimate purposes of charity; particularly contentious were the debates over the effects of monetary gifts, and the relationship between spiritual and material help. Here is another way in which Ranyard's Female Bible Mission was to be a missing link: it would incorporate the methods that typified several different, often divergent, approaches to philanthropy. Ranyard's push for reconciliation, then, took place on two fronts: she wished both to build social bridges between rich and poor, and to forge some sort of coherence among the charitable efforts that were increasingly felt, by those involved, to be pulling in different directions.

The first of these aims—to find a new way to "reconnect" rich and poor—is the central idea that underlies the strange constitution of Ranyard's organization. The Bible Mission effectively took the conventional role of the middle-class visitor and divided it in two: a working-class Bible-woman would visit the homes of the poor, and a lady superintendent would manage these operations at a distance.[1] The Bible-woman would provide a needed channel of communication between the classes, helping to weed out the presumption and mistrust that so often poisoned the work of charity. Ranyard created this protocol in 1857 in response to a letter from Marian Bowers, a working woman looking for a way to help her fellow poor. Ranyard decided that in Marian she had found "a missing link," a woman who could gain access to "a class of persons below the decent poor."[2] Marian and other women of her class would be accepted in households where the lady visitor was unwelcome, and in this way they themselves, simply by virtue of their identity, would embody the social bridges that philanthropists often struggled in vain to build. The Bible-woman's job was to sell Bibles to the poor, usually in weekly installments; when inside a poor woman's home, the Bible visitor might help her with her cooking, cleaning, and needlework. Poor families could also subscribe for goods other than the Bible, such as clothes and bedding. The mission was well-funded, and its clothing clubs were enormously popular. Aside from the sheer volume of its transactions, the Bible mission was significant for its organizational structure. Whereas the Bible-women themselves were all to be recruited from the working classes, every Bible-woman was then supervised by a lady volunteer who handled the administrative and economic aspects of the work. This arrangement seemed ideal: philanthropists had what were effectively a corps of ambassadors to the poor, ambassadors who would ensure that the help that was offered in a spirit of good will would be received in the same spirit.

Ranyard also tackled the growing rifts within the charity industry itself, an industry built around a diverse and not always compatible set of principles. Among other issues, philanthropists disagreed whether their first priority should be the eternal or the temporal welfare of the poor— that is, whether it was the bodies or the souls of the poor that needed saving, or whether one might be saved en route to saving the other. Here, too, Ellen Ranyard saw herself as a bridge-builder; her Bible missions would, in a radical way, reconcile the material and the spiritual aspects of charity.[3] Of course the Bible-women traded in both spiritual and physical necessities, providing Bibles on one day and blankets on another, but they went further than this: by requiring poor families to pay for the Bibles by subscription, they tied their religious ministry to their economic regimen. Part of the organization's mission was to teach thrift to the poor, and to encourage poor families to invest in their own spiritual uplift. Hence, if you didn't pay, you didn't get a Bible. To offer spiritual help free of charge was like offering alms: it would put the poor in the position of paupers, dependent for their spiritual welfare on the attentions of the prosperous classes. Better that they should toil and pay for their Bibles, and thus know that they truly owned them. Ranyard's Bible missions, then, linked the pastoral tradition of charity to a modern economic sensibility.

The Bible-women movement was therefore distinctive for its capaciousness, employing different types of worker (rich and poor) and including of different types of mission (spiritual and economic). Frank Prochaska sees its variety as its virtue; he characterizes the mission as "an ingenious mixture of paid and volunteer, working-class and middle-class workers respectively."[4] And yet, while the complexity of the mixture may have been a resource, it was also a cause for self-interrogation. In *The Missing Link*, far from obviating questions of class, the "ingenious" arrangement requires the various workers to become even more conscious of their position within the machine, and to articulate which functions precisely are proper to which workers. Likewise, the Bible-women's multiple missions require untangling; much of *The Missing Link* discusses the need, given the organization's diverse kinds of work, to make sure each type of work happens in its proper time and place. Mary Poovey points out the difficulty that Ranyard and her Bible-women had segregating the Bible work from the domestic work; Poovey sees this difficulty as growing out of a tension between abstract economic rationality and the more immediate experience of poverty that the workers brought to bear.[5] However we account for the tensions within the movement, it is significant that those tensions are so insistently foregrounded within *The Missing Link*, the book where Ranyard attempts to articulate a unified charity. In this, I will argue, Ranyard's treatise has much to say about the barriers that divide charity workers and charity schemes from one another. If anything, the modernity of Ranyard's movement comes not from its success in ironing out the wrinkles of the charity enterprise, but from bringing them to the surface and, largely, making use of them. Notwithstanding her own urgent calls for a unified charity, Ranyard actually created a protocol that accepted and adapted itself to the communication gap between rich and poor and the incoherence of philanthropic missions.

The impulse to differentiate, for instance, comes through in the way the Bible-woman is figured as the "missing link" between the classes. This is a strange way of thinking about class relations. Of course Ranyard, like many other philanthropists, laments the lack of community between rich and poor. But other philanthropists look to restore this community through some kind of social principle, whether sympathy, or duty, or citizenship, or collaboration. Ranyard's idea that she has found the missing link, and that it is in fact a new class of person, is highly unusual to say the least. Ranyard's usage of this term obviously predates the common late-century reference to the evolutionary link between apes and humans, and yet some of the same logic applies. The missing link is both perfectly natural and utterly monstrous. On the one hand, a missing link simply shares the qualities of two other entities that are well known and that are known to relate to one another, so that it is in some sense the most natural thing of all: even before it is discovered, it can almost be extrapolated into existence. On the other hand, precisely because it is theoretical and not real, a missing link is unnatural; it is the thing that should exist but doesn't, and if it were ever encountered, it could only be experienced as "neither this nor that." Abstract as this discussion is, it seems to have some bearing on the Bible-woman, who is in crucial ways like both the middle-class missionary and the poor petitioner, but could never blend in with either group. In some real sense, the relationship that the Bible-woman creates between the classes takes place wholly within herself. She doesn't *create* a link, as other philanthropists wished to do; instead she *is* the link, straddling two worlds, and holding them apart as surely as she holds them together. No matter how successful the Bible missions were, Ranyard's initiative abandoned the idea of class *contact* that was so central to the mainstream charity protocols. If mainstream visiting failed because either the visitor or the visited balked at the sight of the other, the Bible missions could succeed by interposing a proxy in between the classes, one who might productively stand between the contenders.

Despite the idea that the Bible-woman is a sort of "intermediate form," she does not pass for rich among the rich, poor among the poor. It is the opposite: the Bible-woman becomes the sign, both among her philanthropic colleagues and among her destitute neighbors, of the other. In this sense, Ranyard's organization takes for granted a fundamental dissociation of the classes and even embraces this distance, supplying both rich and poor with a new kind of person who can stand in for the alien, uncooperative person at the other end of the charity transaction. The Bible worker would give a new face to middle-class charity, a face in which the poor woman might catch a reflection of her own, a face in which the lady volunteer could always find a welcome reception. Marian's slum expeditions are dramas of identification, where she is repeatedly transformed from an invader to a fellow sufferer. "I am quite as poor as you are," she assures the people that she visits, and they seem to rally around this idea.[6] When someone pours a bucket of filth on Marian from an upper window, the ground-level tenants gather to help her; "on the whole her friends exceeded her foes," Ranyard says, "and from the date of this roughly commenced acquaintance she numbers several of her best friends."[7] When Marian goes into Soho and Whitechapel she hears some people say, "What use is it to come with the Bible here? It is not for such as we are." But others answer, "Ah, let her come; I wish we were like her!"[8] At once a stranger and a neighbor, Marian makes others of her class want to emulate her, a power that the middle-class philanthropist seemed unable to achieve. At the same time, for the philanthropist, the Bible-woman plays the role of the perfect sufferer, the quintessentially deserving poor. For example, Ellen Ranyard notes that the Bible-woman Sarah "is one who herself slept last winter without a blanket, for the sake of others. She is sometimes almost desperate on behalf of the people she sees. God help her in her efforts, and the people in their misery!"[9] The kind of suffering Sarah undergoes is not really available to the middle class volunteer who, no matter how hard she works, will return to a comfortable home. Sarah, by contrast, is exchanging her comfort for that of her neighbor. She has the power of impoverishing herself. And in her admiration, Ranyard offers a benediction for both Sarah and "the people she sees": they together constitute the community of the poor. Sarah is praised not for her philanthropic acumen, but for her nobility in suffering.

Indeed, even the idea that the Bible-woman, as a missing link, has brought rich and poor into contact with one another, is a strange departure from the account Ranyard actually provides of her first exchange with Marian. The exchange certainly emphasizes the question of class contact, but Marian does not emerge as some sort of automatic native ambassador to the slums. Instead, she herself appeals to Ranyard to provide her with some way to interact with her own neighbors. Marian explains that she is interested in helping "the lost and degraded of my own sex, whom, from their vicious lives, no tenderly reared female would be likely to approach" (20). In this sense the philanthropist needs Marian's help to establish contact with the outcast. And yet the fact that Marian writes this petition at all implies that she needs the help of the philanthropist as well. In the petition, Marian simply asks to be told where such sufferers live, but it is clear that Ranyard believes that Marian also needs to be taught how to help them. Marian must go through the middle-class charity establishment in order to reach other women of her own class, suggesting that the rich are implicated even in the way that the poor relate to one another. Indeed, as Marian's petition describes the details of her own religious conversion, it seems that her piety and insight have on the one hand equipped her to help her neighbors, and on the other hand raised her above them. Just as a missionary lifted Marian out of the dens of vice, she needs a missionary to put her back in. In other words, while the success of middle-class charity depends on the working-class agent, there also can't be any kind of successful working-class ministry that doesn't involve middle-class direction. Marian vindicates the importance of differentiation and the power, within the charity enterprise, of the division of labor.

Just as the Female Bible Mission underscored the difficult distance between rich and poor, it acknowledged the ways in which the manifest aims of charity could work at cross-purposes. Take, as an example, an excerpt from one Bible-woman's journal of her work in Clerkenwell.

> "Here, you Bible-woman," called out a young man who had paid a penny for a Bible last week—"here's your penny for the Book, but you never told me you sold shirts. Don't you see, I've no mother, and I want a shirt—the Bible won't clothe me."
>
> "But," I said, "it will teach you to clothe yourself. However, I do not sell shirts at this time; I only sell Bibles. If you want a shirt, you can have one; it is ready made for you—a good strong working shirt; you must send your sixpence by some woman you know, to my clothing-club room on Wednesday nights, and you may get a shirt for 1s. 6d., but I cannot take your money now."
>
> "I think," said an old man, one of his fellow workmen, "you might as well take mine. I was going in for a glass of gin, but I'll give you this twopence for a shirt. I would not give it you for a book." "I hope you will some day," I said, "when you hear more about the Book; but I suppose I must take it for the shirt, to save it from the gin-shop, only it is not my rule. I do one thing at a time."[10]

This is a strange kind of testament to the Bible-woman's effectiveness, or to the coherence of her mission. For one thing, neither man wants the Bibles she's selling; in fact one of them wants to cancel his Bible subscription when he finds out he can have a shirt for the same price. The Bible-woman's various enterprises, in other words, seem to be in competition with one another. As if to keep these parallel missions from impinging on each other, the Bible-woman tries to avoid selling Bibles and shirts at the same time, but, as the Bible is in this scheme a commodity like other commodities, this "rule" of hers cannot hold up. The market is the market, and a sixpence is a sixpence.

Throughout Ranyard's accounts of the Bible missions, the blending of spiritual and temporal aid does not happen very smoothly or easily; indeed, the rules of the organization seem to force the Bible-women to pry these things apart at every point. It turns out that Sarah's rule isn't simply her own; the Bible-women are instructed to do the Bible work on certain days, and the domestic work on others. And they're always to make the same mysterious response: "I do one thing at a time." This cryptic utterance is explained in the constitution of the organization:

> The Bible-woman may be employed for two, three, four, or five days, ONLY IN SELLING BIBLES, according to the needs of the particular district, and for this ONLY the Bible Society can pay her. She must not do any other work at the same time. If the people offer to subscribe for clothing and beds, she will say, "I only do one thing at a time," and "the right thing first. I bring you now the Message from God. I shall be glad also to provide you with clothing, &c., at the lowest prices, and for this you can pay as you do for the Bibles, in small sums weekly; but you must COME TO ME to do this, at a certain hour, in my Mission-room." There would be great evil in mixing the two departments of labor; the Bible Society would never know what they paid for, and mistakes would be made in the accounts . . .[11]

Poovey cites this passage as evidence of "the tension between the conditions of almost limitless need that Bible women encountered in poor homes and a system that sought to rationalize poor women's efforts to help each other."[12] In one sense, we could read this sort of tension as a testament to the inadequacy of such philanthropic rationales, where the careful work of differentiation betrays the real impossibility of creating a system to answer the demands of poverty. And yet the very clumsiness of the accommodation speaks to a sort of hypersensitivity folded into the charity interaction, a way in which rich and poor are awkwardly required to think about the specific character of (respectively) their resources and their needs. In particular, the difference between spiritual and material help is emphasized in a way it wouldn't be for an organization less determined to make those into parallel and equal aims. This emphasis comes out elsewhere in a related rule that requires the Bible-woman to remind the poor that their pennies are not, in reality, covering the costs of the Bibles, which are mainly paid for by the British and Foreign Bible Society. Thus the Bible-work is differentiated from a fully economic exchange; if the Bible is in one sense purchased, it is in a fuller sense bequeathed.

Strangely, in Ranyard's account, the Bible-woman's mixed messages seem to make her more, not less, effective. The Bible-woman is an oddity, a puzzle, and as such she offers an alternative to business as usual. At least this is the feeling one gets from some of the stories the Bible-women tell, stories in which they surprise the cynical poor into attentiveness. Sarah recalls a man who snapped at her, "That's all you religious people think about—if you can thrust a Bible or a tract down our throats, it will do as well as food. Now, I have five children and a wife, and no work." Sarah's response takes the man by surprise: she says, "My good man, you quite mistake me if you think I want you to live on the Bible. I only want you to live by its precepts, that you may be led to call on him who careth for you in all things, and died to save you, that by his stripes you may be healed." The man then relents: "Well, then, put down my name; I'll have a Bible."[13] While it's possible that Sarah's religious message has a touched a chord in the man's heart, his response doesn't seem especially spiritual; he mainly seems grateful for Sarah's unusual concession, her acknowledgment that he is right, that he can't live on the Bible. In Ranyard's book, the Bible-woman's best weapon is that her methods are strange and unexpected. For instance, in her first letter to Ranyard, Marian happily envisions the following scenario: she will attempt to sell the Bible in the morning, she'll be rejected, and she'll then return to the same home in the evening and perform "some kind office," at which point the man or woman of the house will allow her to read from the Bible at last.[14] It's telling that Marian's philanthropic fantasy involves an initial failure and a change of tactic; why not just use the right tactic to begin with? The idea, I would contend, is that this failure, along with all of the awkwardness of the Bible visits, open the door for something new or unexpected. Lest this argument seem too bizarre, I want to point out that the idea of a first failure is common in Victorian narratives of charity. Consider Esther and Ada's first visit to the brickmaker's cottage, or Dinah Morris's early attempts to comfort Hetty Sorrel: in these and other cases, the rituals and conventions of charity fail, and in the ensuing social vacuum, the characters are able to forge authentic connections.

Ranyard's efforts to build bridges can certainly seem less elegant, less innovative, than some of the work of her fellow philanthropists, especially as she seems so often to emphasize the very divisions she wants to reconcile. But there is also something modern about this. Rather than try to reconstitute a bygone age, Ranyard's missions are bound up in the contemporary scene, with all of its problems; they wage their battles within the social world of the present moment, and never imagine a society constructed on different principles. Paradoxically—and maybe to its credit—Ranyard's scheme for social cohesion actually reveals a felt need for a more detached charity, one whose success wouldn't depend on the fraught personal exchanges between rich and poor.

Works Cited

Poovey, Mary. *Making a Social Body: British Cultural Formation, 1830-1864*. Chicago: University of Chicago Press, 1995.
Prochaska, Frank. "Body and Soul: Bible Nurses and the Poor in Victorian London." *Bulletin of the Institute of Historical Research* 60 (1987): 336–48.
—. "Philanthropy." In *The Cambridge Social History of Britain 1750-1950*, edited by F. M. L. Thompson, Cambridge: Cambridge University Press, 1990.
—. *Women and Philanthropy in Nineteenth-Century England*. Oxford: Clarendon Press, 1980.
Ranyard, Ellen. *The Missing Link; or Bible-Women in the Homes of the London Poor*. New York: Carter and Brothers, 1861.

Notes

[1] Frank Prochaska refers to the Bible-woman as "an ingenious variant of the district visitor." Prochaska, "Body and Soul: Bible Nurses and the Poor in Victorian London," 338.

[2] Ranyard, *The Missing Link*, 37.

[3] It should be noted, as Mary Poovey points out, that Ranyard's Bible Mission was not "the only society committed to collecting contributions from the poor." Poovey, *Making a Social Body,* 195 n.57.

[4] Prochaska, *Women and Philanthropy in Nineteenth-Century England*, 128. Elsewhere, Prochaska presents Ranyard's Bible Mission as one of the most extensive examples of charitable cooperation between classes: see Frank Prochaska, "Philanthropy," in *The Cambridge Social History of Britain 1750–1950*, edited by F. M. L. Thompson, 368.

[5] Poovey, 46–51.

[6] Ranyard, 30.

[7] Ibid., 30.

[8] Ibid., 29.

[9] Ibid., 95.

[10] Ranyard, 97–98.

[11] Ibid., 300.

[12] Poovey, 46.

[13] Ranyard, 103.
[14] Ibid., 24–25.

CHAPTER TWO

REFORMING HISTORY: GEORGE ELIOT'S *ROMOLA*

CHAD MAY

At the close of the eighteenth century, the convergence of Enlightenment theories of cultural change, the rise of antiquarian societies, the birth of nationalism,[1] and a sense of the radical distance between past and present produced by the French Revolution, worked to generate a different conception of history. This newly emergent romantic historicism would initiate the creation of the historical novel and the eventual transformation of history into a professional discipline. Perhaps the most important result, however, was the separation of historical writing from the model of political conflict. In place of wars and kings was a definition of history which could potentially "include . . . all aspects of experience."[2] Ultimately, the practitioners of this new movement were interested in those figures that a traditional political history had marginalized. As Nina Baym and Rohan Amanda Maitzen have recently demonstrated, the romantic focus on social and cultural history in both England and America allowed women to become visible as historical subjects. Yet, the opportunity to write about previously unexplored aspects of the past generated difficulties. New subjects and approaches to history required the transformation or abandonment of existing discursive models. As Ann Rigney suggests, "the representability of a particular aspect of the past has its own history. . . . It is constituted over time according to the changing interests of historians . . . [and] the development of new discursive forms."[3] In her only historical novel, *Romola*, George Eliot succeeds in producing an account in which women appear as historical agents. However, to open up a space in which such a history can be told, Eliot adopts and modifies the discursive structures of her predecessor, Sir Walter Scott. Specifically, Eliot employs the romantic figure of loss and suffering so central to the Waverly Novels. However, unlike Scott, who allows such figures to appear in his narratives as symbols of historical trauma, but then expels them through death, Eliot transforms the romantic and suffering female into a site from which social authority and historical agency can emerge.

Whereas most historical fiction places women in the role of marginal figures who lie outside the movement of history, Eliot's title suggests that she intends to do just the opposite, to place a female protagonist at the center of her text. And yet for any reader what is perhaps most striking is Romola's near absence from the first half of the novel. Instead of its heroine, the narrative focuses on two figures: the fictional Tito Melema, who rises from a shipwrecked wanderer to an influential scholar and politician, and the historical monk Girolamo Savonarola, who, at the end of the fifteenth century, attempted to reform both the political system of Florence and the Catholic Church. In other words, despite the suggestion of the title, the texts opens with the type of political and historical narrative that so often excluded women.

Initially, Romola is prevented from emerging as a presence in the narrative due to the influence of her father, Bardo Bardi, a blind scholar who Romola has devoted her life to assisting. Romola's subservient position within her father's home arises from the absence of his son Dino, who has abandoned the family for his religious calling. Romola can only partially fill the space opened up by his departure. Despite his constant belief that "the sustained zeal and unconquerable patience demanded from those who would tread the unbeaten paths of knowledge are [not] reconcilable with the wandering vagrant propensity of the feminine mind,"[4] Bardo hopes that Romola's assistance will allow him to generate a lasting fame through his scholarship and library of ancient texts. Consequently, Romola is dominated by the "lifeless objects [of the library] . . . - the parchment backs, the unchanging mutilated marble, the bits of obsolete bronze and clay" and by the literal and figurative hand of her father "with its massive . . . rings, [which he let] fall a little too heavily on the delicate blue-veined back of [Romola's] hand."[5] Both the task, which is not of her choosing, and her father's belief that she is inadequate ensure that Romola's position is one of inconsequence and futility. It is clear that even as her father demands so much of her, it is only his historical presence as a scholar that is at stake and not the possible contribution of her "wandering . . . mind."[6] Her marriage to Tito represents only a continuation of her self-effacement in the dreams of her father; he is the new son who will allow Bardo to complete his work: "'Yes father,' said Romola, firmly. 'I love Tito – I wish to marry him, that we may both be your children and never part.'"[7] Yet Tito, like Dino, is drawn out into the concerns of the wider world.

These two male figures not only fail to fulfill the role of son that Romola has taken upon herself, they also serve initially to define the two modes by which she comprehends the world outside her father's home. Visiting her brother on his death bed, Romola is given an account of his visionary apprehensions regarding her future. As she later explains to Tito, although never fully reconciled to her brother's betrayal of the family, Romola cannot forget what his death and his faith suggest to her of the world: "The yearning look at the crucifix when he was gasping for breath – I can never forget it. Last night I looked at the crucifix a long while, and tried to see that it would help him, until at last it seemed to me by the lamplight as if the suffering face shed pity."[8] As the narrator informs us, in the sheltered world of her father's library, Romola has "known nothing of the utmost human needs; no acute suffering – no heart-cutting sorrow."[9] Dino's death and his faith, particularly the image of human suffering and sympathy embodied in the crucifix, suggest a new dimension to the world, one which she has never considered before.

Tito provides a counter image. Continually connected through his own words and those of the narrator to Bacchus and the sun-god Apollo, he promises to lock "all sadness away from" Romola.[10] In effect, Tito has done so with his own life, refusing to give up his prosperous position in Florence to find and ransom his imprisoned father, Baldassarre:

> What, looked at closely, was the end of all life, but to extract the utmost sum of pleasure? And was not his own blooming life a promise of incomparably more pleasure, not for himself only, but for others, than the withered wintry life of a man who was past the time of keen enjoyment, and whose ideas had stiffened into barren rigidity?[11]

For Tito, the sorrow of life can be banished, in this case in the form of an old man who had fathered him, but who must suffer in his stead. Unlike the image of the crucifix which offers a public display of the need for sacrifice in a world defined by suffering, Tito believes all sorrow can be hidden away. For this reason, on the day of their wedding, Tito places the crucifix within a triptych decorated with a triumphant image of Ariadne and Bacchus.[12] As he says to Romola, "You have done with sadness now; and we will bury all images of it – bury them in a tomb of joy."[13]

For Romola, the contrast between her brother and Tito is irreconcilable:

> Strange, bewildering transition from those pale images of sorrow and death to this bright youthfulness, as of a sun-god who knew nothing of night! What thought could reconcile the worn anguish in her brother's face-

that straining after something invisible-with this satisfied strength and beauty, and make it intelligible that they belonged to the same world?[14]

Ultimately, both extremes represent a flight from the world. In the latter, suffering is denied and erased. In the former, its contemplation has the potential to conceal all other aspects of existence, as is the case with Romola's brother, who finds himself detached from "human sympathies which are the very life and substance of our wisdom."[15]

It is to the world of sorrow that Romola will be taken. However, in this case suffering will be tied to sympathy and social action. In fact, Romola is only able to emerge as a forceful and active presence in the narrative after becoming the victim of an "acute suffering."[16] When Tito sells her father's library, a collection he had pledged to help maintain, Romola recoils from both the betrayal and her husband. Watching her father's life work slowly being carted away while hearing the celebratory bells of Florence, Romola imagines the sound as "the triumph of demons at the success of her husband's treachery, and the desolation of her life . . . . now the general joy seemed cruel to her: she stood aloof from that common life."[17] The result of this suffering, of this separation from the common life of Florence, is action on Romola's part; she decides to flee and find a place for herself elsewhere. Her flight, however, is arrested by the historical figure Savonarola who convinces her that in her suffering lies a certain kind of strength and, more importantly, a form of agency:

> And now, when the sword has pierced your soul, you say, 'I will go away; I cannot bear my sorrow.' And you think nothing of the sorrow and the wrong that are within the walls of the city where you dwell: you would leave your place empty, when it ought to be filled with your pity and your labor. If there is wickedness in the streets, your steps should shine with the light of purity; if there is a cry of anguish, you, my daughter, because you know the meaning of the cry, should be there to still it.[18]

Romola's own suffering, according to Savonarola, provides her with a possible connection to the sorrows of Florence and it ultimately authorizes and demands her action within the city. Whereas before she had seen her brother's religion as a "groveling superstition,"[19] Romola, through the words of Savonarola, partly accepts his conception of the world, abandoning the joy which refuses to acknowledge pain. Again the crucifix becomes the central symbol: "Conform your life to that image, my daughter; make your sorrow an offering."[20]

Welcoming this role which combines her brother's emphasis on sorrow with a purpose that pulls one into the world instead of away from it,

Romola becomes a central figure in the daily scenes of Florence:

> As usual, sweet womanly forms, with the refined air and carriage of the
> wellborn, but in the plainest garb, were moving about the streets on their
> daily errands of tending the sick and relieving the hungry. One of these
> forms was easily distinguishable as Romola de Bardi.[21]

Not only a figure of maternal comfort, as many critics have argued,
Romola is also one of command. Her selfless devotion provides a moral
strength that is respected by all who encounter her. Her actions stand as a
direct form of participation in the historical struggle of Florence against
the Papacy, the French King, and the other city states of the Italian
peninsula. In fact, it is the moral power of her position that allows her to
disrupt her husband's scheme to deliver Savonarola to his enemies. Forced
by Romola to account for Savonarola's safety in public, we are told that
Tito felt "completely helpless before this woman . . . . Romola had an
energy of her own which thwarted his."[22] Not present when Tito had sold
her father's library, Romola's energy is definitively presented as a product
of her suffering.

In transforming Romola into a historical agent through her suffering,
Eliot is clearly invoking her predecessor in the genre of historical fiction,
Sir Walter Scott. As a result of his central and founding position in the
tradition of the historical novel, Scott is often seen as a key figure in the
progressive and national narratives that excluded women as historical
agents. In part, this characterization is accurate. In telling the history of
England and Scotland from the Middle Ages to the beginning of the
eighteenth century, in giving a continuous history of the birth of the
modern imperial British nation, Scott affirmed his belief in nineteenth-
century narratives of historical progress.

However, there is another dimension to the imaginative recreation of
the past found in his work. Scott's second novel, *Guy Mannering*, provides
a clue to this aspect of his historical vision. The opening of the narrative
presents a familiar and often repeated formula: an English protagonist
journeying through the liminal landscape of Scotland, his gaze
transversing the border between the past and the present. In this particular
moment, the temporal boundary is found in the contrast between the late
eighteenth-century mansion of the Laird of Ellangowan and the adjacent
ruins of his ancestors' castle:

> He now perceived that the ruins of Ellangowan castle were situated upon a
> promontory, or projection of rock, which formed one side of a small and
> placid bay on the sea-shore. The modern mansion was placed lower,

though closely adjoining, and the ground behind it descended to the sea by a small swelling green bank, divided into levels by natural terraces, on which grew some old trees, and terminating upon the white sand.[23]

In this moment of description one is presented with the central themes that Scott's historical fiction will continue to engage over the next fifteen years. The ruined castle and the modern mansion provide a striking visual presentation of Scott's conception of historical transition. In effect, an antiquarian relic provides a concise vision of the historical transition from a world of feudal obligations and bonds to the modern nation state's dependence upon the middle class.

Yet following an impulse of romantic sympathy, Mannering moves within the ruined castle and reveals an aspect of Scott's historical imagination which stands outside this narrative of national and historical progress. Mannering finds

> The gypsy he had seen on the preceding evening . . . . [He] could not help feeling that her figure, her employment and her situation, conveyed the exact impression of an ancient sibyl . . . . Equipt in a habit which mingled the national dress of the Scottish common people with something of an Eastern costume, she spun a thread, drawn from the wool of three different colors – black, white, and gray – by assistance of those ancient implements of housewifery, now almost banished from the land, the distaff and spindle.[24]

Meg Merrilies, the gypsy that Mannering looks upon, is the first of many similar figures in Scott's fiction; in fact, later manifestations of this type were often criticized by contemporary reviewers as simple repetitions of the initial creation. Like the castle she inhabits, Meg is ancient; she is the representative of a past age. However, unlike the castle which prompts and allows for the working of Mannering's romantic imagination, Meg is a living remnant of the past, one that can directly affect the present. Her ability to influence the plot is central to the restoration of Lucy and Harry Bertram as the rightful heirs of Ellangowan. Yet even as she represents a Scottish past and works to return it, she is also a gypsy, an eastern figure of romance, a wanderer without a homeland, crossing national, historical, and gender boundaries ("and in all points . . . [she] seemed rather masculine than feminine").[25] In addition, however, she is marked by a traumatic suffering that has shattered her sanity (a result of her participation in the kidnapping of Harry Bertram as a child). Existing on the margins of any traditional historical account, but absolutely essential to the plots of the novels they inhabit, such romantic figures of suffering represent what Kathryn Sutherland has defined as the Waverley Novel's "unreadable core, . . . [a collection of] social outcasts, gypsies, . . . and madwomen."[26] Marked with the individual suffering brought about by the movement of history, and retaining, despite their marginal status and link to the past, an uncanny ability to influence the present, the figures that make up the unreadable core of Scott's fiction, through their very presence, represent those aspects of history that are not accounted for in progressive and national historical discourses.[27] They are, as Scott envisions them, both a testament to the suffering associated with historical change and a central force in any narrative's forward movement.

It is after a second moment of suffering, the death of her godfather, Bernardo del Nero, at the hands of the Florentine government, a death both her husband and Savonarola are partly responsible for, that Romola again decides to abandon the city. Setting herself adrift in a small boat on the Mediterranean, Romola deliberately imitates Boccaccio's romantic tale of Gostanza.[28] It is this scene and its aftereffects, more than any other, which have contributed to the critical disregard the novel has faced in the past. Romola's emergence from the Mediterranean ocean at a plague stricken town where she will ultimately recover her sense of purpose has been read as an abandonment of realism for romance and the point at which the novel and Romola, herself, lose any claim to historical probability.[29] Yet, Eliot is obviously conscious of the romantic turn of her narrative, the explicit reference to Gostanza makes this clear, as does Romola's sense that she is returning to the dreams of her "early girlhood."[30]

Maitzen, also noticing the deliberate nature of Eliot's turn to romance, argues that this transformation is meant to highlight the failure of contemporary historical accounts regarding women. Such accounts posited an idealized model of a woman's character, an a-historical or trans-historical definition of the feminine that held little relation to specific historical experiences. According to Maitzen, Eliot's goal is to demonstrate that

> as long as essentializing myths constructed women as a-historical beings detached from their context, women would continue to be misfits, out of place in historical representation as Romola is out of place in her novel. And until such a transformation wrote women into history, historiography would continue to be partial, inadequate, and, in its own way, mythical.[31]

In other words, Eliot's novel becomes an elaborate critique or parody of the a-historical woman found in so many of her contemporaries' historical accounts.

Romola's presence in this village is, as the narrator indicates, transformed into a romantic legend "of a blessed lady who came over the sea."[32] However, in invoking the genre of romance Eliot is rewriting, or recalling, the suffering woman of Scott's historical fiction, a being who, despite her romantic connotations, has a historical presence and agency. Ultimately, the journey to the plague stricken village is the means through which Eliot can forge a source of authority for Romola which does not originate in the male figures who have controlled her life up to this point. Finding herself in opposition to Savonarola because of his refusal to spare her godfather's life, Romola considers the question of "where the sacredness of obedience ended, and where the sacredness of rebellion began. To her . . . there had come one of those moments in life when the soul must dare to act on its own warrant."[33] However, initially such a warrant does not come. Romola's drifting across the Mediterranean is both literal and figurative; she believes "she had freed herself from all claims."[34] Yet in denying all claims upon her person, Romola also denies herself a place in the historical world. This suspension within a romantic dream of nothingness cannot last. It is broken by a single "piercing cry . . . . Romola felt sure it was the cry of a little child in distress that no one came to help. She started up."[35] In essence, the child's cry and the pain it represents pulls Romola back into the world of history and action.

However, the narrative does not wholly abandon romance. When Romola finds herself facing the plague stricken village, the religious and cultural symbolism of the Virgin Mary provide her the agency and authority to act.[36] The priest she encounters sees her as both "the holy mother, come to take care of the people who had pestilence" and "a substantial woman."[37] And although the belief in her connection to Mary may disappear to be replaced by what the narrator defines as "the more effective sense that she was a human being whom God had sent over the sea to command them,"[38] it is evident that what we have is not a trans-historical or a-historical vision of a woman's maternal nature, but rather the identification by Eliot of a specific historical and cultural moment in which women were authorized to act and function as historical agents in their own right.[39] This authority depends on a collective use of the romantic imagination, but the conflation of Romola with the Virgin Mary is only possible because of the specific cultural conditions of fifteenth-century Italy.

Romola's success in this moment and her desire to return to Florence and continue her work of charity represents an expansion of her agency. Whereas before it was the strength of Savonarola "who roused a . . . strength within [her]"[40] and allowed her to pursue her work, her return to Florence is fully self-authorized:

If everything else is doubtful, this suffering that I can help is certain; if the

glory of the cross is an illusion, the sorrow is only the truer. While the
strength is in my arm I will stretch it out to the fainting; while the light
visits my eyes they shall seek the forsaken.[41]

No longer dependent on the ethical demands generated by Christ's
sacrifice, for which she no longer has faith, Romola's actions are now the
result of her own perception of sorrow and her own inner conception of
moral behavior. As the third male figure who both dominated and then
disappointed her, Savonarola can stand as an inspiration, but not finally an
authority. Her last words in the text to the illegitimate son of her husband
make this apparent,

> We can only have the highest happiness, such as goes along with being a
> great man, by having wide thoughts, and much feeling for the rest of the
> world, as well as ourselves; and this sort of happiness often brings much
> pain with it, that we can only tell it from pain by its being what we would
> choose before everything else, because our souls see it is good.[42]

Both a condemnation of her husband's preference for the easy path, and a
testament to Savonarola's greatness, the quotation can also easily be read
as an account of Romola's life. In this final statement, Romola and
Savonarola blend into one, both individuals who transformed suffering
into historical agency.

A great deal of critical energy has been directed toward the closing of
the novel in which we learn Romola cares for her husband's mistress,
Tessa, and her two children Lillo and Ninna. The arguments surrounding
this scene can, for the most part, be divided into two camps. On the one
hand, critics see Romola's actions as a retreat from the public and political
sphere, an abandonment of the authority she had gained in both Florence
and the plague stricken village.[43] Yet as Robin Sheets has convincingly
argued,

> By protecting and providing for Tessa and the children, Romola . . . .
> challenges the system that granted the father absolute power over his
> legitimate and illegitimate children . . . . Moreover, at a time when
> illegitimate, orphaned, and abandoned children crowded the streets of
> Florence, she assumes responsibility for a problem ignored by church and
> state . . . . Blurring the distinction between the 'public world' of politics
> and the 'private' world of the home, . . . [Eliot] insists that Romola's
> decision . . . .can be seen as a socially significant action.[44]

In other words, the maternal and domestic aspects of Romola's position
need not be read as an abandonment of social action. As Sheets indicates,

Romola usurps a form of masculine authority and employs that authority to respond to the shortcomings of the social community in which she lives.[45] In forming her life as such a challenge, Romola retains her presence as a historical agent. Her enclosure within the domestic space of the home is not a return to the self-effacement of her previous life under her father, but rather a transformation of her own individual suffering into a sympathetic and active strength.

Turning to Eliot's writings of the present day one can see this search for cultural and historical agency repeated. Within *Middlemarch*, it can be found in the failure of Dorothea to duplicate the influence of St. Theresa:

> Many Theresas have been born who found for themselves no epic life wherein there was a constant unfolding of far-resonant action . . . . With dim lights and tangled circumstance they tried to shape their thought and deed in noble agreement; but after all, to common eyes their struggles seemed mere inconsistency and formlessness; for these later-born Theresas were helped by no coherent social faith and order which could perform the function of knowledge for the ardently willing soul.[46]

Unlike Romola, who can romantically employ the cultural belief in the Virgin Mary to authorize her social activity, Dorothea finds herself in a historical and social context in which no such roles are possible for women. Ultimately, Eliot's turn to history by way of romance does not represent a flaw within her work, but rather a conscious rewriting of her predecessor, who saw in the historical romance the possibility of giving an account of those figures who had been pushed to the margins of historical discourse. Unlike Scott's figures of romantic suffering and loss, however, Eliot's Romola does not perish or disappear, overwritten by an ending which reaffirms the notion of national progress. Instead she becomes the dominant voice of the text which bears her name. In the end, romance stands as the discursive form through which a previously untold history can finally be revealed.[47]

Works Cited

Anderson, Benedict. *Imagined Communities: Reflection on the Origins and Spread of Nationalism*. London: Verso, 1991.

Barrett, Dorothea. Introduction to *Romola*, by George Eliot, vii – xxiv. New York: Penguin Group, 2005.

Baym, Nina. *American Women Writers and the Work of History*. New Brunswick: Rutgers University Press, 1995.

Bonaparte, Felicia. *The Triptych and the Cross: The Central Myths of George Eliot's Poetic Imagination.* New York: New York University Press, 1979.

Booth, Alison. *Greatness Engendered: George Eliot and Virginia Woolf.* Ithaca: Cornell University Press, 1992.

—. "The Silence of Great Men: Statuesque Femininity and the Ending of *Romola.*" In *Famous Last Words: Changes in Gender and Narrative Closure,* Alison Booth,ed., 110-134. Charlottesville: University Press of Virginia, 1993.

Dekker, George. *The American Historical Romance.* New York: Cambridge University Press, 1987.

Eliot, George. *Middlemarch.* New York: W.W. Norton & Company, 2000.

—. *Romola.* New York: Penguin Group, 2005.

Fleishman, Avrom. *The English Historical Novel: Walter Scott to Virginia Woolf.* Baltimore: Johns Hopkins University Press, 1971.

Gezari, Janet K. "*Romola* and the Myth of Apocalypse." In *George Eliot: Centenary Essays and an Unpublished Fragment,* edited by Anne Smith. Totowa, NJ: Barnes & Noble, 1980.

Gosselink De Jong, Mary. "*Romola*: A Bildungsroman for Feminists." *South Atlantic Review: The publication of the South Atlantic Modern Language Association* 49.4 (1984): 75-90.

Greenstein, Susan M. "The Question of Vocation from *Romola* to *Middlemarch.*" *Nineteenth-Century Fiction* 35.4 (1981): 487-505.

Maitzen, Rohan Amanda. *Gender, Genre, and Victorian Historical Writing.* New York: Garland Publisher, 1998.

Paxton, Nancy L. "Feminism and Positivism in George Eliot's *Romola.*" In *Nineteenth-Century Women Writers of the English-Speaking World,* edited by Rhoda B. Nathan. New York: Greenwood Press, 1986. 143-150.

Rigney, Ann. *Imperfect Histories: The Elusive Past and the Legacy of Romantic Historicism.* Ithaca: Cornell University Press, 2001.

Scott, Sir Walter. *Guy Mannering.* London: Macmillan, 1923.

Sheets, Robin. "History and Romance: Harriet Beecher Stowe's *Agnes of Sorrento* and George Eliot's *Romola.*" *Clio* 26.3 (1997): 323-346.

Simpson, Shona Elizabeth. "Mapping Romola: Physical Space, Women's Place." In *From Author to Text: Re-Reading George Eliot's Romola,* edited by Caroline Levine and Mark W. Turner. Aldershot: Ashgate, 1998. 53-66.

Sutherland, Kathryn. "Fictional Economies: Adam Smith, Walter Scott and the Nineteenth-Century Novel." *ELH* 54.1 (1987): 97-127.

Thompson, Andrew. *George Eliot and Italy: Literary, Cultural and Political Influences from Dante to the Risorgimento*. New York: St. Martin's Press, Inc., 1998.

Thurin, Susan Schoenbauer. "The Madonna and the Child Wife in *Romola*." *Tulsa Studies in Women's Literature* 4.2 (1985): 217-233.

Uglow, Jennifer. *George Eliot*. London: Virgo, 1987.

Notes

[1] Nationalism, the establishment of the nation state's historical continuity and organic growth over time, was a method for replacing the lost unties of a prior period, "the large cultural systems that preceded [the nation] . . . the *religious community* and the *dynastic realm*." Anderson, *Imagined Communities*, 12.

[2] Rigney, *Imperfect Histories: The Elusive Past and the Legacy of Romantic Historicism*, 1.

[3] Ibid., 94.

[4] Eliot, *Romola*, 51.

[5] Ibid., 52-53.

[6] Ibid., 51.

[7] Ibid., 128.

[8] Ibid., 177.

[9] Ibid., 158.

[10] Ibid., 200.

[11] Ibid., 115.

[12] Felicia Bonaparte seeing the triptych and the cross as the two central symbols of the narrative argues "that Eliot found the essence of the universal human condition in the eternal conflict between man's spontaneous passion for joy and the experience of sorrow that he discovers to be his human destiny. The conflict is enacted in *Romola* . . . between Bacchus, the god of joy, and Christ, the Man of Sorrow." *The Triptych and the Cross: The Central Myths of George Eliot's Poetic Imagination*, 25. In addition to symbolizing the universal condition of humanity, the two objects are concrete representations of the cultural forces in fifteenth-century Italy (Christianity and Greek/Roman Culture). Andrew Thompson suggests that out of this dialectic emerges Eliot's positivist vision of a religion of humanity. *George Eliot and Italy: Literary, Cultural and Political Influences from Dante to the Risorgimento*, 68.

[13] Eliot, *Romola*, 198.

[14] Ibid., 178.

[15] Ibid., 160.

[16] Ibid., 158.

[17] Ibid., 316.

[18] Ibid., 361.

---

[19] Ibid., 152.

[20] Ibid., 359.

[21] Ibid., 371.

[22] Ibid., 409, 414.

[23] Sir Walter Scott, *Guy Mannering,* 37.

[24] Ibid., 43.

[25] Ibid., 33.

[26] Sutherland, "Fictional Economies: Adam Smith, Walter Scott and the Nineteenth-Century Novel," 121.

[27] Other figures who fall into this category are Ulrica (*Ivanhoe*), Norna (*The Pirate*), Helen Campbell (*Rob Roy*), Margaret of Anjou (*Anne of Geierstein*), Vanda of the Red-finger (*The Betrothed*), Sister Ursula (*Castle Dangerous*), Elspeth (*The Antiquary*), Elspat (*Chronicles of the Cannongate*), Lucy Ashton (*The Bride of Lammermoor*) Magdalen Graeme (*The Abbot*), Fenella, (*Peveril of the Peak*) and Madge Wildfire, (*The Heart of Mid-Lothian*).

[28] Eliot, *Romola*, 502.

[29] Avrom Fleishman sees it as a "flight from the world" that abandons a "historical relationship . . . [for] the eternal sorrows of the human condition." *The English Historical Novel: Walter Scott to Virginia Woolf*, 161. Dorothea Barrett describes it as "an embarrassment" although she qualifies this claim by saying "it is so because in it, as always, George Eliot is trying something new, straining the generous limits of what she can do, rather than repeating or refining her earlier accomplishments." introduction to *Romola*, xvii.

[30] Eliot, *Romola*, 502.

[31] Maitzen, *Gender, Genre, and Victorian Historical Writing* (New York: Garland Publisher, 1998), 131.

[32] Eliot, *Romola*, 559.

[33] Ibid., 468-469.

[34] Ibid., 504.

[35] Ibid., 551.

[36] For a summary of the novel's references to the Virgin Mary see Gezari, "*Romola* and the Myth of Apocalypse," in *George Eliot: Centenary Essays and an Unpublished Fragment*, 99.

[37] Eliot, *Romola*, 554, 556.

[38] Ibid., 558.

[39] Conversely Nancy Paxton has read Romola's actions not as evidence of a trans-historical feminine ideal, but rather as "an allegory of nineteenth-century life . . . that demonstrated the impact of the feminist movement upon the Victorian cult of domesticity." "Feminism and Positivism in George Eliot's *Romola*," 149. Both Maitzen and Paxton's readings which place Romola as a figure out of place in the historical context of the novel, do not acknowledge the way in which Romola's ability to act arises from the cultural and religious beliefs of the period.

[40] Eliot, *Romola*, 374.

[41] Ibid., 560.

[42] Ibid., 582.

[43] For example, Susan Greenstein suggests that Romola fails to "establish a public self" and that "Romola's history dramatizes much more emphatically than Dorothea's the barriers which may prevent the 'modern Theresa' from discovering and entering into her vocation." "The Question of Vocation from *Romola* to *Middlemarch*," 500-01. Discussing the central problem that Romola's final actions presents for a reader interested in seeing the novel as a "feminist bildungsroman," Mary Gosselink De Jong suggests that "despite the heroine's development of a cautiously individualistic moral vision, from first to last she esteems and generally practices the traditional (so called feminine) virtues of charity, service, obedience, passivity, and self-suppression – the bases, according to radical feminists, of the oppressive 'phallic ethic.' Romola's moral radicalism is countered by its social conservatism." "*Romola*: A Bildungsroman for Feminists," 85.

[44] Sheets, "History and Romance: Harriet Beecher Stowe's *Agnes of Sorrento* and George Eliot's *Romola*," 22.

[45] As Jennifer Uglow puts it "a passionate intellectual woman responds to being told what to do all her life by men, and ends by shaking herself free altogether to become the matriarchal head of a household of women, shaping a boy of the next generation of men according to her beliefs." *George Eliot*, 159-160. Susan Thurin concurs, arguing that "the self-sufficiency of this world-almost-without-men challenges the patriarchal paradigm." "The Madonna and the Child Wife in *Romola*," 231. Or as Shona Elizabeth Simpson suggests "but as in the village, she is a stepmother who does not need authority from anyone other than her self." "Mapping Romola: Physical Space, Women's Place," 63. Alison Booth argues that in Romola's "last words we sense that she is still carrying out her duty of rebellion, standing outside the patriarch's kingdom; here she may forgive men because they are absent." *Greatness Engendered: George Eliot and Virginia Woolf*, 194.

[46] Eliot, *Middlemarch*, 3.

[47] Alison Booth comes to a similar conclusion regarding the novel's reforming of historical discourse: "*Romola* suggests that narratives of feminine greatness – of heroines not necessarily famous who perfect an ethic of disinterested kindness – belong among the biographies of great men, and indeed these suppressed narratives force a revaluation of masculine historical achievement." "The Silence of Great Men: Statuesque Femininity and the Ending of *Romola*, 118.

CHAPTER THREE

THE REFORM OF WOMEN'S EDUCATION IN TENNYSON'S *THE PRINCESS* AND GILBERT AND SULLIVAN'S *PRINCESS IDA*

LAURA FASICK

Tennyson's long poem *The Princess* could easily be considered forward-looking in that large portions of it are concerned with explicitly feminist ideals, including discussion of claims that men and women are inherently equal intellectually, with only nurture, not nature, keeping women from developing their potential. Indeed, much of the poem is set in an all-female university designed specifically to allow women to fulfill the potential that patriarchal societies have suppressed. Yet the fact that the university collapses by the end of the poem and that the hitherto obdurate heroine agrees to marry her lovelorn prince are among the reasons why Tennyson's poem has long been subject to attack for allegedly treating the subject of female education with contempt or with a condescension that is only contempt by another name. Tennyson's poem, however, in my view, deserves reconsideration, and the relative complexity and richness of Tennyson's perspective in this poem seems all the more striking when contrasted with the far glibber, less interesting, and less insightful tactics of Gilbert and Sullivan in their operetta *Princess Ida*, loosely based upon Tennyson's poem. The ostensible comedy of the Gilbert and Sullivan operetta obscures the essential pessimism of the work. Tennyson's poem emphasizes human nature and human history as dynamic and evolutionary, with one of education's most beneficial effects being its ability to improve not only the individual but – eventually – the entire human race. By contrast, Gilbert's libretto relies upon a model of human nature that is static and fixed, with immutable laws within which individuals are trapped and limited. Thus, "Nature" is an important figure in both works, significant enough to be considered a character in its own right, yet the ideas about Nature expressed in the two works are diametrically opposed.

Gilbert and Sullivan, of course, wrote decades after Tennyson's original was published, and therefore at a time when the movement for women's education had made considerable advances. Tennyson published his original poem in 1847 with revisions emerging up until 1851. Gilbert, the librettist of the famous team, first launched his "respectful perversion" of Tennyson's poem in play form in 1870. In 1884 he collaborated with composer Arthur Sullivan to transform that play into *Princess Ida*, the eighth Savoy opera.[1] Yet instead of the straightforward progression in attitudes towards women's education that one might expect – or hope – to be the case, just the reverse is true, with Gilbert and Sullivan's parody being far more conservative and unsympathetic to the woman's cause than Tennyson's poem.[2] Just as there is much discussion today of an anti-feminist backlash after the advances of the 1960s and 70s and a renewed interest in popular culture in heavily sexualized depictions of women, so it appears that in the late nineteenth century the decades of improvement in women's social position had led to a backlash of its own. Perhaps our witnessing of this backlash can lead us to appreciate the virtues as well as the limitations of the liberalism that Tennyson's poem embodies: the heartfelt interest in moderation, reconciliation, and harmony. Tennyson appears most deeply interested in what men and women have in common and he strongly suggests that improved education can deepen those commonalities. Gilbert's waspish libretto insists on differences and threatens apocalyptically that to ignore those differences would be to erase human existence. As suggested above, another way of putting this is to suggest that Tennyson's primary metaphoric model for humanity generally and for men and women individually is evolutionary, with education as a key component in an evolutionary movement upward. Thus, by Tennyson's way of thinking, as successive generations of men and women improve themselves individually, the sexes – and the human race – generally will also improve. Gilbert, by contrast, refers to a model of Nature that exists statically, operating by unchanging laws in which men, women, and their behavior remain always the same.

Even the form that Tennyson's poem takes shows the urge to discard rigid and exclusive ideals and to push beyond traditional boundaries. After all, the main story of the poem begins when the poem itself becomes a collaborative tale spun not only by men but by women, too. Men and women join together as story-tellers and singers to fashion the poem that constitutes the bulk of the book, and within that poem, everything operates to show the importance of emphasizing similarity over difference and union over separation and the importance of education as a multi-faced experience affecting the whole individual and, ultimately, all of humanity.

The poem itself is subtitled a "miscellany," since, as pointed out above, it supposedly consists of the juxtaposed and shared voices of a group of both men and women telling a story in incremental sections, passing it from mouth to mouth with each new speaker contributing a new twist. This unusual form was a concern to Tennyson himself, as well as to the poem's main narrator, who doubts the experiment's success in his own comments upon it, and subsequent critics have often agreed with both poet and narrator in their skepticism about the poem's coherence. Yet the form of the poem, which seeks to create unity by embracing variety and which mingles male and female, comic and heroic, past and present, North and South aptly demonstrates the process by which Tennyson dissolves all rigid distinctions, including those between the sexes. Even the fact that poem is supposedly set in a vaguely medieval past and yet anachronistically portrays a female version of a nineteenth-century university in Ida's school reflects the extent to which time itself dissolves in Tennyson's poem. The past is not what one might have thought and neither, Tennyson suggests, is the present. The crux of the poem may indeed be its dissatisfaction with all the alternatives that are currently available for social and individual life, a dissatisfaction mirrored in the dissatisfaction expressed within the poem itself for its own poetic achievement. What hope the poem offers comes not through what is stable and known but through what is evolving and possible.

Tennyson's "Prologue" is especially useful for setting up some of the terms that the poem later develops because it is set in the present day (as opposed to the vaguely medieval period of the poem's body) at another example of a widening of educational opportunities. Sir Walter Vivien has opened his grounds for a show of exhibits for an "Institute" designed to edify and inform the working-class folk of his area. It is easy nowadays to read the long list of displays that Tennyson's narrator jovially describes as mocking trivialities. The narrator himself points out that they range from "sport [that] went hand in hand with Science" to "pure sport."[3] But is that necessarily a bad thing? Let us look at the passage in detail:

> With happy faces and with holiday,
> There moved the multitude, a thousand heads:
> The patient leaders of their Institute
> Taught them with facts. One reared a font of stone
> And drew, from butts of water on the slope,
> The fountain of the moment, playing, now
> A twisted snake, and now a rain of pearls,
> Or steep-up spout whereon the gilded ball
> Danced like a wisp: and somewhat lower down

A man with knobs and wires and vials fired
A cannon: Echo answered in her sleep
From hollow fields: and here were telescopes
For azure views; and there a group of girls
In circle waited, whom the electric shock
Dislinked with shrieks and laughter: round the lake
A little clock-work steamer paddling plied
And shook the lilies: perched about the knolls
A dozen angry models jetted steam:
 A petty railway ran: a fire-balloon
Rose gem-like up before the dusky groves
And dropt a fairy parachute and past:
And there through twenty posts of telegraph
There flashed a saucy message to and fro
Between the mimic stations; so that sport
Went hand in hand with Science; otherwhere
Pure sport: a herd of boys with clamour bowled
And stumped the wicket; babies rolled about
Like tumbled fruit in grass; and men and maids
Arranged a country dance, and flew through light
And shadow, while the twangling violin
Stuck up with Soldier-laddie, and overhead
The broad ambrosial aisles of lofty lime
Made noise with bees and breeze from end to end. (Prologue: 56-88)

This image of educational activity seamlessly combines the physical, the experiential, the theoretical, and the festive in a scene that – most appropriately – takes place during Nature's loveliest and most blooming season. In this festival, learning and dancing exist side by side and bodies become vehicles of insight as the "electric shock" becomes something not only understood theoretically but experienced physically and understood because experienced. Rather than segregation of any kind, along lines of sex, class, marital status, or age, this festival unites all creatures, in a setting in which "bees and breeze" and trees are also included. Sensory experience promotes both knowledge and fellowship, as sounds, sights, and all that is visceral and kinetic lead to learning and conduce to dance: one of the supreme images of harmony.

The presence of games, indeed of physical activity of any kind, and on the buoyant pleasure of the participants, might seem at first glance like a condescending "watering down" of learning to the level of the working class and female "students." Yet the joyful, exploratory, highly creative and participatory exhibits described actually meet the educational ideals of many Victorian writers who pondered the subject of education. One point to keep in mind when considering the movement to expand education for women in the nineteenth century is that many, if not most, commentators on nineteenth century education for males deplored both its methods and its substance. Thus, the unease with what educational opportunities should be given to females is also a reflection of the dissatisfaction with the educational opportunities that actually were given to males.

Against this background of dissatisfaction with much of the formal education of the time, Sir Walter's educational festival is strikingly in tune with what many Victorians hoped education could be. From Charles Kingsley's insistence that the mind and the body must be developed in healthy unison to Charles Dickens's concern for maintaining the child's creativity and for engaging the pupil's interest in what is being studied to John Ruskin's desire for literally "hands-on" experience for all learners of whatever ages, the more sensitive and imaginative among the Victorians understood the appeal of precisely those tactile and immediate learning experiences that Tennyson's narrator lists. By having Sir Vivien host this event, Tennyson also establishes the themes of reconciliation and harmony that run throughout this poem. Here, working-class people previously excluded from education (just as women had been) are beginning to taste it – not through separation or enmity from those who have enjoyed it previously but through cooperation with them.

As for the playful nature of the afternoon's events, in the context of much of the most forward-thinking educational theory of the nineteenth century just as in our own, pleasure and even play could go hand in hand with learning, while education pursued too rigorously as a matter of abstract intellectual training, could only lead to dire results for all. Philip Collins's *Dickens and Education*, still the most comprehensive study of Dickens's treatment of educational matters, accurately points out not only Dickens's holistic vision of education but also his stinging criticism of much of the actual schooling of the day as well as the extent to which "[m]any of the ideas or formulations he expresses were very much in the air."[4] Dickens's horror of over-study, his distrust of abstraction, and his emphasis on the need to consider the whole personality and character of the student were indeed reflective of his time, and to the extent that Tennyson insists upon such concerns in *The Princess*, Tennyson prescribes for female education just what was being prescribed (although not necessarily practiced in) for education for males.

One might note, for example, that Charles Kingsley, in an 1873 essay ostensibly devoted to the education of women, makes his most stinging criticism of women's proposed "higher" education contingent upon the fear that such education will fail to recognize what Kingsley sees as the greatest good of education for young men: its embrace of the physical vitality that underlies all learning and that leads to the formation of good character as well as of a keen mind. The passage is worth quoting in full:

> It is proposed, just now to assimilate the education of girls more and more to that of boys. . . . .[I]f the proposal be a bona-fide one: then it must be borne in mind that in the Public schools of England, and in all private schools, I presume, which take their tone from them, cricket and football are more or less compulsory, being considered integral parts of an Englishman's education; and that they are likely to remain so, in spite of all reclamation: because masters and boys alike know that games do not, in the long run, interfere with a boy's work; that the same boy will very often excel in both; that the games keep him in health for his work; and the spirit with which he takes to his games when in the lower school, is a fair test of the spirit with which he will take to his work when he rises into the higher school; and that nothing is worse for a boy than to fall into that loafing, tuck-shop-haunting set, who neither play hard nor work hard, and are usually extravagant, and often vicious. Moreover, they know well that games conduce, not merely to physical, but to moral health; that in the playing-field boys acquire virtues which no books can give them; not merely daring and endurance, but, better still, temper, self-restraint, fairness, honour, unenvious approbation of another's success, and all that "give and take" of life which stands a man in such good stead when he goes forth into the world, and without which, indeed, his success is always maimed and partial.[5]

This view of education insists, indeed, that education should be the same for both boys and girls. Education for both sexes, however, should eschew the purely abstract and intellectual in favor of the development of the entire individual. Kingsley's reputation as a "Muscular Christian" has sometimes led to assumptions that he gloried male strength at the expense of female but the essay just quoted is one of many in which Kingsley argues passionately for women's capacity for, and right to, the vigorous and pleasurable activity that would facilitate both outward and inward strength. The emphasis on sport as part of the education for both sexes is also, of course, a recommendation of pleasure itself and of play - since sport is certainly that - as part of education. This playfulness, Kingsley argues, is crucial for males and females alike.

Even John Ruskin, whose views on women are often viewed as retrograde in the extreme, argued passionately in 1865 that female education must include "such physical training and exercise as may confirm [girls'] health"[6] and, even more passionately, that Nature itself ordains that such education must be based upon a pleasure that is "vital, necessary to very life."[7] Indeed, drawing upon the same ideal of Nature as the proper pattern for education, Ruskin advocates unrestricted reading for girls on the grounds that, when given free choice in a well-stocked library, girls know how to choose for themselves. His metaphor on this subject is worth looking at in some detail. Ruskin writes:

> Let her loose in the library, I say, as you do a fawn in the field. It knows the bad weeds twenty times better than you, and the good ones too, and will eat some bitter and prickly ones good for it which you had not the slightest thought would have been so.[8]

The animal image might seem demeaning to females at first glance, but as we shall see the emphasis on commonalities between animal and human has in it the potential not to demean the human but to expand the range of sympathy, empathy, and respect for all creation. Indeed, Ruskin uses the image not to insist on the need for females to be controlled and subdued by males but rather on the appropriateness and naturalness of their freedom. "[Y]ou cannot fetter her;" he sternly instructs his readers, "she must take her own fair form and way if she take any."[9] Ruskin, then, like Tennyson in *The Princess*, uses Nature as a touchstone and also as a justification for his educational ideals, and for Ruskin, as we shall see is also true for Tennyson, the result is a degree of female autonomy that runs counter to stereotypes about Victorian gender roles.

   With this in mind, we can see that the male-imitative university Ida proposes is actually only one possibility for female education, and by no means the best one. After all, in Tennyson's poem, the picture that emerges of the classical university education being offered males of the privileged classes is bleak indeed. The narrator and his companions unite in describing a university setting that is intellectually barren and morally corrupt in which so-called students engage in puerile, destructive pranks while their supposed teachers judge them only by their wealth and status, flattering a "lord" while scorning "common men" (111-117). While the unifying and inclusive Institute celebration had taken place in full summer, the paradigmatic description of the all-male university is set in the dead of winter. In this scene of literally and figuratively chill and sterile sexual segregation, the only relief comes from men's immersion in the memory, celebration, and enactment of rituals that feminize them. Walter, one of the students, describes it thus:

> We seven stayed at Christmas up to read:
> And there we took one tutor as to read:
> The hard-grained Muses of the cube and square
> Were out of season: never man, I think,
> So mouldered in a sinecure as he;

For while our cloisters echoed frosty feet,
And our long walks were stript as bare as brooms,
We did but talk you [girls] over, pledge you all
In wassail; often, like as many girls –
Sick for the hollies and the yews of home –
As many little trifling Lilias – played
Charades and riddles as at Christmas here,
And *what's my thought* and *when* and *where* and *how*,
And often told a tale from mouth to mouth
As here at Christmas. (Prologue: 176-189)

In this bleak setting, separation from women is a curse and an affliction, not a sign of men's special privileges, while the celibate tutor, far from a male ideal of intellectual achievement, is a figure to shun. The ideal, rather, is the commonality between male and female as the men console themselves with a collaborative tale that clearly has its origins in nursery games and fantasy, when both boys and girls were under female supervision and before strict sexual differentiation began.

Thus, even before the reader encounters Ida's university, we are prepared for the fact that her greatest mistake, in fact, is her one concession to conservatism. In establishing her university for women, Ida closely follows the forms and traditions of male universities. Yet since the poem has elaborately established male universities as intellectual and social frauds, Ida's university is founded upon a false ideal. As F.E. L. Priestley acerbically reminds the reader,

> It is not long before the question arises in the reader's mind whether a college which excludes every male creature is intrinsically any more ridiculous than one which excludes every female, and whether an education of fact-cramming or of superficial surveys is any more ridiculous for women than for men, and whether history from an exclusively feminine perspective is any more one-sided than from a masculine on. In so far as Ida's college is ridiculous, it may be because it imitates a ridiculous model.[10]

Indeed, any institution that practices strict segregation and separation is both ridiculous and potentially evil in Tennyson's poem. Division between the sexes can only lead to wrong, and – in a fascinating perspective – the same is true for too rigid a division between animal and human. Ida refuses to allow anatomical studies in her university because she abhors the cruelty of vivisection. Some modern critics such as Eileen Tess Johnston[11] and Beverly Taylor[12] have read in this a squeamishness about physicality itself and a virginal terror of male sexuality, here figured by the penetration of the scalpel into a living body. Yet Ida's stand actually identifies her as participating in a debate that was as absorbing to and deeply felt by many Victorians as similar issues are by animal rights activists today. Authors such as Barbara T. Gates in *Kindred Nature: Victorian and Edwardian Women Embrace the Living World* have pointed out that many nineteenth- and early twentieth-century women found common cause with animals and the environment. Perhaps even more striking, this was a humanitarian position that could and did unite both men and women in fellow feeling with other creatures. Indeed, Richard French points out in *Antivivisection and Medical Science in Victorian Society* that anti-vivisectionism was a widespread and important movement that counted Victorian notables including John Ruskin, Wilkie Collins, Frances Power Cobbe, and Tennyson among its supporters. Thus, Tennyson's attribution of this compassionate sentiment to Ida is no sign of frigidity or asexuality but rather an identification of her with a significant philosophical and philanthropic movement to which he himself belonged.

By contrast, one might note that the Prince's father, the single most horrific and incorrigibly callous figure in the poem, consistently uses a predatory and an exploitative model of human/animal relations to characterize relations between men and women. In his reckoning, men are hunters and women are prey; men are horse-breakers and horse-riders, and women the mounts who must be curbed and bridled against their wills. In this scheme of things, the order between the "higher" human and the "lower" animal is fixed and hostile, with no tinge of sympathy or a shared condition to bridge the gap between species. Indeed, the Prince's father is as extreme in his insistence on the opposition between men and women as though the sexes themselves were different species – and as though that species-hood itself were a fixed and unchanging thing.

Of course, the initial publication of *The Princess* in 1847 preceded the 1859 publication of Darwin's *On the Origin of Species* by more than a decade, but the decades prior to Darwin's publication simmered with preliminary speculations about the history of the world and the development of humans within it. Tennyson's own struggles between despair over faith-challenging discoveries and a desperate insistence upon hope have been well-documented by his biographers. Certainly Tennyson, like many Victorians, had to adjust his world view and religious beliefs in the light of scientific knowledge, but the implications of that knowledge did not have to breed hopelessness. Although Barbara Gates claims that "the theory of evolution seemed to have set limits on what humanity could do, learn, say, or be,"[13] Tennyson's poetry is filled with images of evolution as a spiritual movement upward that can lift people as far above what humanity is now as modern humankind is from its prehistoric ancestors The idea of spiritual improvement both for individuals and for humanity in general could, in Tennyson's poetry, co-exist with scientific imagery and context. In this vision, science does not puncture idealism and lower expectations for human behavior but actually heightens them.

These expectations, of course, depend upon the belief that humanity is capable of self-improvement, both consciously and unconsciously achieved. Yet, if humanity is capable of evolving into new forms in the future, then it is also true that what it is today is the result of the experiences that have shaped it in the past Thus it is no accident that history is one of the subjects of which we hear the most at the Princess's university. Learning from the past in order to rise above it is a recurrent theme. Nor does Tennyson undercut the version of history taught there. The history of male mistreatment of women, scathingly detailed and drawing upon an impressive array of cultures and periods, stands as an accurate indictment of what has been. In line with the poem's attentiveness to the malleability and importance of the flesh as a reflection of the mind, the history lesson that describes women's suffering emphasizes the constriction of and disregard for female bodies. Chinese women whose feet are bound, Russian brides who must be prepared for scourging by their husbands, female infants who are exposed to death by their own mothers because female children are not wanted: these are the experiences – the "six thousand years of fear" (4. 486) - that have led to women being, as Ida despairingly concludes in her bleakest moment:

Live chattels, mincers of each other's fame,
Full of weak poison, turnspits for the clown,
The drunkard's football, laughing-stocks of Time . . . .
(4.494-496)

Again, it is important to emphasize that Ida's belief that women's past inculcation with servile and ignoble patterns of thought and behavior have warped women today is directly in line with Victorian ideas about the transmission of acquired characteristics. However unappealing Ida's wholesale denunciation of her female contemporaries might appear to us, her theory as to why the women around her seem (to her) so trivial is one that Tennyson and his peers would have accepted. Likewise, Ida's belief that by educating one generation of women, she can elevate the generations of women to follow them also would ring true, not simply because the educated mother might educate her daughter but because the higher mode of thought induced by education could be considered hereditary as well. Thus John Ruskin, writing in Volume Three of *Modern Painters* (1856), declares

> The sentiments of a people increase or diminish in intensity from generation to generation, every disposition of the parents affecting the frame of the mind in their offspring; the soldier's child is born to be yet more of a soldier, and the politician's to be still more a politician; even the slightest colors of sentiment and affection are transmitted to the heirs of life; and the crowning expression of the mind of a people is given when some infant of the highest capacity, and sealed with the impress of this national character, is born where providential circumstances permit the full development of the powers it has received straight from heaven, and the passions which it has inherited from its fathers.[14]

All minds and all bodies, too, it seems, are capable of surprising changes and variety. Within the walls of Ida's university, the three male intruders enter dressed in female clothes and they are indeed convincingly female. After all, the nameless Prince who woos Ida describes himself in the story's beginning as

> . . . blue-eyed, and fair in face,
> Of temper amorous, as the first of May,
> With lengths of yellow ringlet, like a girl . . . .
> (1.1-3).

Here the Prince might appear, paradoxically, to be an ideal of feminine beauty and grace, yet he is simultaneously the same man who after a rough night is described by his own father as

> ". . . a draggled mawkin, thou,
> That tends her bristled grunters in the sludge" . . . .
> (5.25-26).

Both sex and status dissolve as the Prince, now "disprinced from head to heel" (5.29) appears like a kitchen-wench, a creature that although female has no feminine beauty and none of the protection supposedly allotted to ladies. The King himself, the poem's firmest upholder of rigid gender norms, unwittingly exposes their artificiality, when he instructs his son to "make yourself a man to fight with men" (5.33) in unconscious acknowledgement that manhood is a matter of social construction rather than natural identity.

Yet while the Prince must laboriously equip and armor himself to become a warrior (and even then quickly falls in combat), Ida's university furnishes evidence that "the wrestling sinews that throw the world" (7.266) are not inherently male. Ida's bodyguards are

> Eight daughters of the plough, stronger than men,
> Huge women blowzed with health, and wind, and rain
> And labour. Each was like a Druid rock;
> Or like a spire of land that stands apart
> Cleft from the main, and wailed about with mews.
> (6.260-263)

Small wonder that these "mighty" (6.528) women's "heavy hands" (6.531) carry "[t]he weight of destiny" (6.532) and that the Prince and his male companions are helpless against this female force. The reality of male and female flesh and male and female minds alike is that all are capable of more change, more development, and more adaptation than is admitted by the King's dicta about the nature of manhood or womanhood.

Indeed, the poem's optimistic ending depends for its optimism upon a vision of human evolution, of development beyond what currently exists. The Prince predicts of men and women alike that

> . . . in the long years liker must they grow;
> The man be more of woman, she of man;
> . . . .
> And so these twain, upon the skirts of Time,
> Sit side by side, full-summed in all their powers,
> Dispensing harvest, sowing the To-b,
> Self-reverent each and reverencing each,
> Distinct in individualities,
> But like each other even as those who love.
> Then comes the statelier Eden back to men:
> Then reign the world's great bridals, chaste and calm:
> Then springs the crowning race of humankind.
> (7.263-264, 271-278)

In this vision, both men and women can and do transform themselves, appropriately and desirably, in order to mingle qualities of both sexes within themselves and to mate with each other more harmoniously and completely. It is a triumphant and transcendent vision and it is deeply reminiscent of Tennyson's frequent evolutionary musings in *In Memoriam*, in which he pictures his dead friend Arthur Hallam as a forerunner of a more advanced form of humanity. The final note of Tennyson's *The Princess*, then, is not one of scorn for female educational ambitions but one of optimism for human advancement generally.

Turning to Gilbert's libretto for *Princess Ida*, one finds a very different set of ideas and ideals, although the reliance upon appeals to "Nature" is equally strong. Yet what "Nature" means in *Princess Ida* is far different from what it means in *The Princess*. In Gilbert's libretto, Nature's chief characteristics are an unchanging consistency and an utter fixity of mind and body. Far from the malleable and fluid bodies of which Tennyson writes in *The Princess*, bodies in *Princess Ida* are signs of an unchanging selfhood. Thus, King Gama, one of the operetta's least sympathetic characters, can be immediately recognized as such due to his deformed shape. As King Hildebrand describes him,

> He [is] a twisted monster – all awry –
> As though Dame Nature, angry with her work,
> Had crumpled it in fitful petulance![15]

Yet it is not Nature's anger, but her accuracy, that Gama embodies. His body shows what he is, just as does that of the adder to which he is compared, for "adder-like, his sting lay in his tongue" (1.45). In short, as Cyril points out:

> Nature never errs.
> To those who know the workings of your [Gama's] mind,
> Your face and figure, sire, suggest a book
> Appropriately bound.
> (1.257-260)

Indeed, Gama's malicious nature, like his crooked body, is a constant throughout the play and cannot be altered by any new experiences. When King Hildebrand wishes to subject him to the worst possible torture, he inflicts kindness upon him, providing Gama with every comfort including that of unfailing acquiescence and courtesy from all who surround him. Of course, because it is Gama's nature to be querulous and hostile, it is agony for him to have "nothing whatever to grumble at" (3.226). Rather than adapting and changing in response to this unprecedentedly "confoundedly politeful" (3.222) environment, Gama is reduced to despair and the threat of death because all his natural instincts to "malice spiteful" (3.182) are thwarted.

Clearly, Gama's predicament is comic in the extreme, but all the comedy in *Princess Ida* depends upon the acceptance of the unchanging nature both of individuals and of humanity generally. Gilbert, like Tennyson, includes allusions to evolution in his work, but unlike Tennyson, he uses evolutionary images only to reject their implications of the possibility for further human development. In his scene of a lecture at Ida's university, the lecturer does not remind her audience – and the reader – of the historical record of women's sufferings, as Tennyson's Lady Psyche had. Rather, Gilbert's Lady Psyche improbably offers a story of a female human and a male ape, with the ape in amorous pursuit of the woman. Their mating – their union – would clearly be as unnatural as undesirable for they literally are members of different species and there is neither the prospect of commonality among them nor the prospect of improvement on the part of the ape. As Lady Psyche explains,

> With a view to rise in the social scale,
> He shaved his bristles, and he docked his tail,
> He grew moustachios, and he took his tub,
> And he paid a guinea to a toilet club –
>
> . . . .
>
> [But] the Ape, despite his razor keen,
> Was the apiest Ape that ever was seen!
> (2.444-447, 453-454)

His attempts at self-improvement and at civilization fail woefully to disguise the unchanging reality of his ape-like nature. Gilbert mockingly dubs him "Darwinian man" (2.458), but of course Gilbert's emphasis on stasis entirely negates Darwin's theories. In Gilbert's universe, unlike Darwin's, each entity is trapped in one fixed and unchanging nature that no forces, external or internal, can improve.

Thus, when Gilbert's young males set out to conquer Castle Adamant from within, they mockingly imagine the female scholars setting themselves tasks that, in Gilbert's handling, are clearly designed to be examples of physical impossibility. To Hilarion (as Gilbert names Tennyson's unnamed Prince), the intentions of Ida's scholars are to

> . . . set the Thames on fire
> Very soon – very soon;
> Then they learn to make silk purses
> With their rigs – with their rigs,
> From the ears of Lady Circe'
> Piggy-wigs – piggy-wigs.
>
> . . . .
>
> To get sunbeams from cucumbers,
> They've a plan – they've a plan.
>
> . . . .
>
> And they'll find Perpetual Motion,
> If they can – if they can.
> (2. 227-232, 235-236, 239-240)

In this view, women's education has nothing to do with women's self-improvement, with their elevation of their own intellects and spirits. Rather, it will consist of the futile ambition to shatter physical laws (such as by setting a body of water on fire) rather than to affect the inner and outer state of the individual and, through her, of her descendents.

Even more damningly, Ida's own address to her scholars confirms the accuracy of the men's skepticism. She triumphantly quotes proverbs – again, emblems of a received wisdom that having always been will always be – while misconstruing their meaning. She declares women's superiority on the basis of their ability to make two and two equal any number they like, but in a mathematical system that treats numbers as fixed and unchanging entities, two and two can only equal four: the one, invariable, and eternal answer. Only in a system of growth and change – a system, for example, where one coupling can produce slightly different offspring and a subsequent coupling by those offspring produce different offspring yet – can those rigid mathematical formulae prove inadequate to convey experience.

Hilarian's friend, Florian, aptly sums up the operetta's dismissal of the possibility of educational change when he answers the question of whether he and his friends are "young men" (2.474) by claiming

> Well, yes, just now we are –
> But hope by dint of study to become,
> In course of time, young women.
> (2.475-477)

Not only is such a transformation impossible but it, or any form of it, is also undesirable in Gilbert's world. Immediately recognizing both men's physical difference from women and their superiority to them, Florian's female questioner proclaims

> My natural instinct teaches me
> (And instinct is important, O!)
> You're everything you ought to be,
> And nothing that you oughtn't, O!
> (2.509-512)

Here, Nature instructs all who will listen that there is no need for change in either sex. They are already what they should be and what they will always remain. As for Ida's educational plans, they could only end by annihilating both sexes entirely since Gilbert's Ida, unlike Tennyson's, requires life-long celibacy of her followers. With no "Posterity" 3.362, 368), there could be no improved human race resulting from Ida's efforts.

In conclusion, it is interesting to note that the optimistic and benign vision of human development that Tennyson offers in *The Princess* and which is so sharply contradicted in Gilbert's *Princess Ida* is contradicted as well by the historical developments that made *Princess Ida* possible in the first place. Numerous scholars have pointed out that the nineteenth century, rather than witnessing an unequivocally upward rise in women's status and an increased harmony in relations between the sexes, instead saw several severe setbacks, reversals, and intensified sexual animosities. Elaine Showalter, in *Sexual Anarchy*, has studied the disquieting sexual hostility that was prominent at the end of the nineteenth century. Claudia Nelson, in *Boys Will Be Girls*, has explored the way in which gender roles actually grew more distinct and more opposed to each other throughout the course of the nineteenth century. In our own time, likewise, books such as Susan Faludi's *Backlash* have documented the ways in which advances for women and some tentative softening of gender roles are in danger of being undone. Certainly, if we look at the expanse of time since Tennyson composed his hopeful poem, we can only recognize that we have hardly reached the heights he predicted. But does that mean that we must live without hope altogether? The expansion of educational opportunities across class and sex lines has not yet led to the inward and spiritual improvement that many Victorians believed education could produce. Tennyson's poem itself, however, indicates that the model of university education current in his time could not lead to the new "Eden" Tennyson himself believed was possible. As we can continue to explore what men and women are capable of becoming, let us continue to consider what a wide range of experiences and models can be part of education.

Works Cited

Collins, Philip. *Dickens and Education*. London: MacMillan, 1964.

Faludi, Susan. *Backlash: The Undeclared War Against American Women*. New York: Crown, 1991.

French, Richard. *Antivivisection and Medical Science in Victorian Society*. Princeton: Princeton University Press, 1975.

Gates, Barbara T. *Kindred Nature: Victorian and Edwardian Women Embrace the Living World*. Chicago: University of Chicago Press, 1998.

Gilbert, W.S. "Princess Ida," *The Complete Annotated Gilbert and Sullivan*. Edited by Ian Bradley. Oxford: Oxford University Press, 1996. 449-549.

Johnston, Eileen Tess. "This *Were* a Medley: Tennyson's *The Princess*." *ELH* 51   (1984): 549-574.

Killham, John. *Tennyson and The Princess: Reflections of an Age.* London: Athlone   Press, 1958.

Kingsley, Charles. "Nausicaa in London, or, The Lower Education of Women" *Sanitary and Social Lectures. The Works of Charles Kingsley*. Vol. 18. London: MacMillan, 1880. Reprinted by Georg Olms Hildesheim, 1969.

Nelson, Claudia. *Boys Will Be Girls: The Feminine Ethic and British Children's Fiction, 1857-1917.* New Brunswick, London: Rutgers University Press, 1991.

Priestley, F.E.L. *Language and Structure in Tennyson's Poetry*. London: Andre Deutsch, 1973.

Ruskin, John. *Sesame and Lilies*. Chicago: McClurg, 1889.

—. *Modern Painters*. Vol. 3. Boston: Estes and Lauriat, n.d.

Showalter, Elaine. *Sexual Anarchy: Gender and Culture at the Fin de Siècle*. New York: Viking, 1990.

Smith, Geoffrey. *The Savoy Operas: A New Guide to Gilbert and Sullivan*. New York: Universe, 1983.

Taylor, Beverly. "'School-Miss Alfred' and 'Materfamilias': Female Sexuality and Poetic Voice in *The Princess* and *Aurora Leigh*." *Gender and Discourse in Victorian Literature and Art*. Edited by Antony H. Harrison and Beverly Taylor. DeKalb: Northern Illinois University Press, 1992. 5-29.

Tennyson, Alfred Lord. *The Princess. The Poems of Tennyson*. Vol. 2. 2nd Ed. Edited by Christopher Ricks. Berkeley, Los Angeles: U of California P, 1987. 188-296.

Notes

[1] Smith, The Savoy Operas: A New Guide to Gilbert and Sullivan, 115-116.

[2] John Killham's *Tennyson and The Princess: Reflections of an Age* sets Tennyson's poem in the historical context of the debate over women's education in England.

[3] Tennyson, *The Princess. The Poems of Tennyson*, lines 79-81. Line numbers for further quotations from this poem will be given in the text.

[4] Collins, *Dickens and Education*, 211.

[5] Kingsley, *The Works of Charles Kingsley*, 124-125.

[6] Ruskin, *Sesame and Lilies*, 147.

[7] Ibid, 148.

[8] Ibid, 158.

[9] Ibid, 157.

[10] Priestley, *Language and Structure in Tennyson's Poetry*, 87.

[11] See Johnson, "This *Were* a Medley: Tennyson's *The Princess*, 550.

[12] See Taylor, "School-Miss Alfred" and "Materfamilias": Female Sexuality and Poetic Voice in *The Princess and Aurora Leigh." Gender and Discourse in Victorian Literature and Art*, 11.

[13] Gates, *Kindred Nature: Victorian and Edwardian Women Embrace the Living World*, 1.

[14] Ruskin, *Modern Painters*, Vol. 3, 341.

[15] Gilbert, "Princess Ida," *The Complete Annotated Gilbert and Sullivan*, 1.37-40. Line numbers for further quotations from this play will appear in the text.

PART II:

PATRIARCHY, CLASS, AND PROFESSIONS

CHAPTER FOUR

FEMINIST SOCIAL REFORM
AND THE PROBLEMS WITH PATRIARCHY
IN CHARLOTTE YOUNGE'S
CLEVER WOMAN OF THE FAMILY

AUDREY FESSLER

Charlotte Mary Yonge (1823-1901), the highly conservative author of scores of didactic domestic novels, begins *The Clever Woman of the Family* (1865) with an impassioned indictment of mid-Victorian economic, religious, social class, and gender systems. Many scholars have noted that Yonge achieved what June Sturrock has called a "quiet satire" of feminists[1] by tracing the story of Rachel Curtis, the putative "clever woman," who is morally earnest and unselfishly committed to social reform, but also economically and socially privileged and egotistical. The novel concludes with Rachel acknowledging her need for male guidance in practical and intellectual matters. This essay focuses on a related but as yet unexplored theme of *The Clever Woman*: that the absence and corruption of patriarchal authorities cause the real and awful suffering of Victorian women and children. The novel suggests that these problems in the patriarchy perpetuate the flawed social systems that feminists strive to reform.

The novel opens with a "half-aloud" soliloquy by Rachel indicting *laissez-faire* capitalism for the "wretchedness" it creates for so many Victorian laborers, including children. Rachel broadens her indictment by condemning all charity work—whether motivated by Church affiliation or a sense of *noblesse oblige*—as spotty and insufficient. She then makes mid-Victorian gender norms responsible for the persistence of social ills that circumscribe the actions of those economically and social privileged women who might otherwise have attempted real, systemic reform:

Not a paper do I take up but I see something about wretchedness and crime, and here I sit with health, strength, and knowledge, and able to do nothing, nothing—at the risk of breaking my mother's heart! I have pottered about cottages and taught at schools in the dilettante way of the young lady who thinks it her duty to be charitable; and I am told that it is my duty, and that I may be satisfied. Satisfied, when I see children cramped in soul, destroyed in body, that fine ladies may wear lace trimmings! Satisfied with the blight of the most promising buds! Satisfied, when I know that every alley and lane of town or country reeks with vice and corruption, and that there is one cry for workers with brains and with purses! And here am I, able and willing, only longing to task myself to the uttermost, yet tethered down to the merest mockery of usefulness by conventionalities. I am a young lady, forsooth! I must not be out late; I must not put forth my views; I must not choose my acquaintance; I must be a mere helpless, useless being, growing old in a ridiculous fiction of sweet seventeen that I never had.[2]

Two scholars have recognized this as one of the most impassioned and compelling passages that Yonge ever wrote. Virginia Thompson Bemis wonders in passing "if Yonge had ever felt this way."[3] Having mooted this possibility, however, Bemis in effect dismisses it by immediately redirecting her analysis to another question. Similarly, Myra Stark admits to being "surprised" by the "depth of conviction" with which Rachel's soliloquy "captures the sense of female restlessness" that mid-century feminists had begun to articulate.[4] Nevertheless, Stark reads *Clever Woman* as unequivocal in its condemnation of Rachel's activism on behalf of poor girls and women. Bemis calls it "Yonge's most detailed anti-feminist statement."[5]

One aspect of *Clever Woman* certainly is "anti-feminist": its promotion of the idea that a woman's thoughts and actions should be guided by a man in matters that lie outside of a woman's "proper sphere." But the novel also provides a searing, if less direct, critique of Victorian patriarchy itself, as manifested both within the "female" domestic sphere of the Curtis household and in the broader "male" socioeconomic sphere that Rachel eventually enters in order to reform it. Indeed, social reform work—specifically Rachel's effort to provide girls with alternatives to exploitative lace-making jobs—becomes the novel's central metaphor both for the risks of feminist activism and for the dangers of the patriarchal social order. To make sense of the seemingly conflicting implications of Rachel's social reform work, it is useful to examine two principles of the conservative, high-church Oxford Movement: patriarchalism and the notion that charitable work, as John Keble put it, is "the life of faith."[6]

Yonge acknowledged John Keble (1792-1866), a founder and guiding light of the Oxford Movement, as "the chief spiritual influence of my life."[7] Keble was Yonge's village priest and a close friend of her family. He prepared her for confirmation, instructed her in religious matters, and, like Yonge's own father, guided and edited her work until his death.

Yonge proclaimed Keble "my master [...] in every way."[8] She chose as the motto of her work and life not *pro gloria dei*, but rather *pro ecclesia dei*[9]—and for Yonge, *ecclesia* meant the most conservative faction of the Anglican Church, Keble's Tractarian or Oxford Movement faction. In her old age, she commented, "I have always viewed myself as a sort of instrument for popularizing Church views."[10]

Casting herself as a passive conduit for Keble's or, more broadly, the patriarchal Church's views is consistent with the patriarchal ideology that Yonge intended to convey in didactic novels like *The Clever Woman of the Family*. Keble and other proponents of the Oxford Movement insisted that the patristic formularies, or "Church Fathers," be the intellectual and spiritual guides of Anglican priests, and that the priests in turn guide the laity.[11] I have argued elsewhere that, in her earlier novels, Yonge translated this patristic hierarchy into domestic terms by showing that those who obey not only the Church and its priests, but also their own parents or guardians, earn spiritual and sometimes also material rewards.[12] And Yonge further stratified her fictional domestic hierarchies by factoring in the category of sex. In her early novels, especially, female characters routinely discover the "wisdom" and "benefits" of deferring to the judgment and guidance of their husbands and elder brothers, as well as to that of priests, parents, and guardians. Although Victorians usually justified domestic patriachalism by arguing that women are innately inferior to men, Yonge promoted domestic hierarchialism in her novels because she believed that the organization of the home should mirror that of the God-given, Father-directed Anglican Church. Yonge's strongest statement on women's subordinate status opens her 1872 advice book for females, *Womankind*: "I have no hesitation in declaring my full belief in the inferiority of women." But even here she refuses to concede that women's "inferiority" is innate: "How far [prelapsarian Eve] was [...] on an equality with [prelapsarian Adam] no one can pretend to guess."[13]

It is evident that the dire consequences of Rachel's social reform work symbolically reaffirm the patriarchalist notion that women's thoughts and actions ought to be directed by men. Rachel is acutely aware that, as she puts it, "overwork, low prices, and middle-men perfectly batten on the lives of our poor girls" forced into lace-making.[14] The narrator characterizes this knowledge as "a constant burden on Rachel's mind."[15]

In order to "mitigate the evil," Rachel eventually founds a school to teach girls alternative, more remunerative trades such as woodcutting and printing.[16] She aims "to lessen the glut of the [lace] market, to remove the workers that are forced to undersell one another, and thus oblige buyers to give a fairly remunerative price."[17] Bowing to sex-role "propriety," Rachel employs a man to oversee the enterprise, but, as we shall see below, the school soon collapses under the weight of scandal and disaster. Rachel then begins to reconceive herself as "that object of general scorn and aversion, a woman who [...] step[s] out of her place."[18] She eventually becomes convinced that "many of her errors had chiefly arisen from the want of someone whose superiority she could feel": specifically, the superiority of "a highly educated man."[19]

Remarkably, this strong affirmation of patriarchalism marks the very point at which Yonge's countervailing critique of patriarchy comes into its sharpest focus. Yonge's depiction of the awful exploitation of the lace-making girls powerfully validates Rachel's belief that reform of patriarchal capitalism is urgently needed. But no man within Rachel's social sphere is willing to work toward this end. Her father died when she was a toddler, and she has no other male relatives.[20] Mr. Cox, employed as "Mrs. Curtis's man of business,"[21] refuses Rachel's pleas to redirect a portion of the family's assets toward helping poor girls. The narrator adds that Mr. Cox was an antagonist to every [charitable] scheme Rachel had hatched, ever since she was fifteen years old, [...because] he [...] regarded it as his duty to save the Curtis funds, let the charity sink or swim.[22]

Nor is Rachel's long-time clergyman, Mr. Touchett, of any help. Indeed, he is far too preoccupied by a hopeless flirtation with Rachel's cousin Fanny Temple to attend to his needy parishioners. Moreover, Touchett resents Rachel's efforts to teach his choir boys reading, writing, mathematics, geography, and other subjects at Sunday school.[23] He must be dissuaded from "assert[ing]" his clerical "authority" by "preach[ing a] sermon upon the home-keeping duties of women" for Rachel's supposed benefit.[24]

Yonge makes clear that these representatives of the patriarchal economic and religious order show no desire to reform the society that grants profit and authority to them. Not even the two devout high-church Anglican military men whom Rachel befriends after the novel begins, Colin and Alick Keith, seem to want to change the exploitative conditions that create and perpetuate the suffering of the poor. As Rachel struggles to raise funds for the school she dreams of establishing, Colin and Alick withhold donations. They observe the school's early days skeptically and quietly anticipate its collapse. In patriarchy as Rachel experiences it, men

are absent, hostile, or willfully disengaged from social reform work,
however sorely needed it might be. Rachel therefore chooses to undertake
reform work herself.[25]

Yonge scholar June Sturrock explains the second of the Oxford
Movement principles I mentioned above, Keble's notion that charitable
work is "the life of faith,"[26] as follows:

> Tractarians […] believed that salvation depended not on faith alone, but on
> good works as well. They believed, that is, that all Christians are obliged to
> use *to the full* their talents and energies in the service of God, and that such
> works have a *sanctifying* effect, the deeds augmenting faith and holiness in
> the doer.[27]

From her opening soliloquy, as we have seen, Rachel longs "to task
[her]self to the uttermost" with the work of alleviating "wretchedness."[28]
Even within a patriarchal community where men fail to do such work, a
Christian woman would remain *obligated*—for her own soul's sake—to
engage in such work. The logic of Tractarianism and the increasingly
sympathetic authorial tone in which Rachel and her charitable works are
described seem to converge here. Even high-church readers most hostile to
the gathering wave of feminist activism would surely have appreciated
Rachel's moral earnestness and her energetic, spiritually necessary pursuit
of good works.

And so Rachel "step[s] out of her place."[29] From a patriarchalist
capitalist point of view, her great "transgression" might be characterized as
an attempt to move from the "proper" female domestic sphere into the
"male" world of business ownership and management. In short order, and
"contrary to most expectation,"[30] Rachel amasses the capital resources
needed to launch a re-training school for girls.

Although a female's entrance into business financing would have
seemed radical to Yonge's contemporaries, Yonge tempers Rachel's
radicalism—and presumably the hostility of anti-feminist readers—by
showing that Rachel continues to abide by social conventions for female
behavior, as far as possible, when she ventures outside her "proper"
sphere. First, her purpose in entering into business is altruistic, not
materialistic—and charity work was widely accepted as proper to women.
Second, Rachel senses that it would be socially unacceptable for a woman
to undertake such a project herself; she therefore decides to employ a man
to oversee the day-to-day operations of her business: one Mr. Mauleverer,
a virtual stranger to her. She hires him because he is the only man she has
ever known who expresses a willingness to help her to increase the
autonomy, prosperity, and education of female workers. Unfortunately for

Rachel, Mauleverer is dishonest both in his avowed championship of women's welfare and in his business practices.

Because sexual politics inform Mauleverer and Rachel's alliance, Yonge's portrait of Rachel's entrepreneurial failure takes on the dimensions of a moral allegory for women who long to leave the "safe" domestic environment for the "dangerous" world of business. In the year that Yonge brought out *The Clever Woman of the Family*, 1865, John Ruskin published his essay "Of Queens' Garden." Ruskin distinguishes the "male" world of commerce, politics, and war from the "female" world of the home as follows:

> The man, in his rough work in the open world, must encounter all peril and trial: to him, therefore, must be the failure, the offense, the inevitable error: often he must be wounded, or subdued; often misled; and always hardened. But he guards the woman from all this; within his house, as ruled by her, unless she herself has sought it, need enter no danger, no temptation, no cause of error or offense.[31]

Mauleverer, at home in the "male" world of business, seeks to exploit and profit from the sheltered Rachel and her altruistic objectives. Mauleverer keeps the money that Rachel has raised for the workshop-school, forges woodcuts that he claims the girls have produced, and forces them to make more lace under worse conditions than ever before. His mistress, Maria, beats and starves the students. Her cruel actions seem to express her fury at her own exploitation by Mauleverer, who is the exaggeration *ad absurdum* of Ruskin's "hardened," manly businessman. Rachel's devotion to her charitable mission and her lack of experience with exploitative businessmen keep her oblivious, for a time, to the brutal abuses that her own foundation is perpetrating against the very girls she so much wants to help.

Rachel's friends intervene. But by the time they remove the girls from the workshop-school, Rachel's favorite student—Lovedy Kelland—has become dangerously ill with diphtheria; her condition is aggravated by the starvation and beatings she has suffered. Rachel of course feels responsible for her protégée's condition. She tries to heal the girl with her own homeopathic treatments, but fails; Lovedy dies. Rachel comes to regard herself as "twice [Lovedly's] destroyer": by exposing Lovedy to abuse and by failing to cure her illness.[32] Amazingly, Rachel also comes to believe that her own "credulity may have *caused* [Mauleverer's] dishonesty."[33] The local magistrate agrees that Rachel is, indeed, "accountable for all this."[34]

These passages leave readers wondering whether Rachel and the judge have gone too far in placing all of the guilt and responsibility on her. Mauleverer, after all, is a witting agent of real evil, whereas Rachel "only want[s] to do right."[35] And Yonge by no means presents Rachel's sex as the reason she becomes Mauleverer's fool. For one thing, Yonge shows that male characters are as prone as Rachel is to being duped by Mauleverer.[36] For another, the school's catastrophic collapse is due not so much to Rachel's "womanly" naïveté as to her socially mandated reliance on male aid. Ironically, the very society that requires Rachel to rely on male guidance to accomplish her indisputably worthy goals cannot furnish a single man who will publicly and honestly help her to reach those goals. Rachel's only alternatives seem to be to abandon her plans or to turn to society's most deceitful type: the businessman who will lie to and abuse others without compunction if doing so will promote his own interests. Rachel's social reform work therefore functions as a metaphor for the dangers of the patriarchal socioeconomic and gender systems that Rachel contends against, even as the failure of the workshop-school and Lovedy's death prompt the "full surrender of herself" to the judgment and guidance of Alick Keith–when he proposes to marry her. Thus at last Yonge brings her feminist protagonist to, in the narrator's words, a "meek submission, very touching in its passiveness and weary peacefulness."[37] Rachel abandons all thoughts of systemic social reform, and the novel closes on a scene of Rachel caring exclusively for her and Alick's two children.

The failure of Rachel's reform campaign has one further noteworthy consequence. It sparks charitability in some of the men who had previously refrained from helping her. Indeed, Alick Keith goes so far as to appropriate, and present as his own, Rachel's longtime belief in the urgent need for social reform. In the tale's crowning irony, Alick tries to entice the psychologically shattered Rachel to marry him by offering her an auxiliary role in reform efforts that *he* wants to lead. Speaking broadly of the English populace, Alick observes, "Our women and children want so much done for them, and none of our ladies are able or willing." Then he gathers up for himself the work that the newly submissive Rachel had once been so ardently willing to do—and proposes, "Will you not come and help *me*?"[38]

If she is to realize her faith, now that she is debarred from taking a primary role in good works, Rachel must accept an auxiliary role. Her access to that role is solely through marriage. Rachel laments that, because she cannot "live without [Alick...,] then all the rest of it [viz., wifehood and motherhood] must come for his sake. [...] I did think I should not have been a commonplace woman."[39] Rachel's regretful tone indicates that

Yonge was aware of the pain some women felt at being forced into marriage and motherhood. And yet Yonge seems intent on showing, through Rachel, that there were no viable alternatives to these "commonplace" Victorian roles.[40]

In the novel's final chapters, Yonge may be suggesting through Alick and two other male characters—Colin Keith and the blind priest Mr. Clare—some prospect of a morally re-enlivened, newly worthy patriarchy.[41] Perhaps she intends readers to take it quite literally on faith that Alick, Colin, and Mr. Clare will someday accomplish broad social reform. Alick and Colin do set up a convalescent home that will train poor girls as domestic servants. Unlike Rachel's workshop-school, however, this enterprise will return young women to their "proper" milieu: the home. The pupils will direct their attention to caring for others, not to developing skills that would enrich themselves.

Similarly, Rachel herself is returned to the domestic sphere. It is a resigned, not a joyous, return. On meeting, in London, a female social reformer, Rachel sighs: "I am not fit to be anything but an ordinary woman with an Alick to take care of me; but I am glad some people can be what I meant to be."[42] This passage suggests that, in the end, Yonge could not altogether ignore the real-world achievements of women's social reform movements, although she certainly withholds any such achievement from her fictive feminist reformer. A further implication of this passage is also striking. Having given up hope of personal achievement, Rachel comes to think of herself only in terms of a socially constructed gender role: the generic "ordinary woman." Rachel's sense of individuation has succumbed to the totalizing influence of patriarchal gender norms. Further, by calling her husband "*an* Alick" (emphasis mine), Rachel in effect robs him of individuality too. The indefinite article suggests that this man is just one of many who would identically play out the social script of caring, confining patriarch of the family. When Rachel accepts confinement to the sphere supposedly proper to her *quâ* woman, both she and Alick are reduced to generic gender role performances.

The air of melancholy is unmistakable at the novel's end. The world of "properly" subordinated feminists is one in which Rachel, for all her efforts at systemic change, will continue to "see children cramped in soul [and] destroyed in body, that ladies may wear lace trimmings."[43] In this world, patriarchy, though contested, prevails despite the absence, hostility, strategic silences, or corruption of most men. Even thus degraded, patriarchy remains powerful enough to socially re-form Rachel, not the other way around. For Rachel, privileged and circumscribed, the world has become melancholy. For poor women and children, it remains menacing.

Works Cited

Auerbach, Nina. *Romantic Imprisonment: Women and Other Glorified Outcasts*. New York: Columbia University Press, 1986.

Banks, James A., and Olive Banks. *Feminism and Family Planning in Victorian England*. New York: Schocken, 1964.

Battiscombe, Georgiana. Afterword to *The Clever Woman of the Family*, by Charlotte Mary Yonge. New York: Virago, 1985. 368-372.

Bemis, Virginia Thompson. *The Novels of Charlotte Yonge: A Critical Introduction*. PhD diss., Michigan State University, 1980.

Coleridge, Christabel R., ed. *Charlotte Mary Yonge: Her Life and Letters*. London: Macmillan, 1903.

Delafield, E. M. Introduction to *Charlotte Mary Yonge: The Story of an Uneventful Life*, edited by Georgina Battiscombe. London: Constable, 1943.

Fessler, Audrey. "Intellectuality and Female Sexuality in the Novels of Charlotte Yonge." PhD diss., University of Michigan, 1995.

Foster, Shirley. *Victorian Women's Fiction: Marriage, Freedom, and the Individual*. Totowa, NJ: Barnes and Noble, 1985.

Greg, William Rathbone. "Why Are Women Redundant?" *National Review* 14 (April 1862): 434-60.

Keble, John. *The Christian Year: Thoughts in Verse for the Sundays and Holydays throughout the Year*. 1827. Reprint, London: Church Literature Association, 1977.

—. "Adherence to the Apostolical Succession the Safest Course." 1833. Reprint, *Tracts for the Times* Vol. 1. London: Rivington and Parker, 1940.

Ruskin, John. "Of Queens' Gardens." In *Sesame and Lilies*. 1865. *The Works of John Ruskin*. Vol. 10. New York: Crowell, 1905. 76-105.

Stark, Myra C. "The Clever Woman of the Family—and What Happened to Her." *Mary Wollstonecraft Journal* 2, no. 1 (1979): 13-20.

Sturrock, June. *"Heaven and Home": Charlotte M. Yonge's Domestic Fiction and the Victorian Debate over Women*. Victoria, B.C.: Univ. of Victoria, English Literary Studies Monograph Series, no. 66, 1995.

Yonge, Charlotte Mary. "Autobiography." In *Charlotte Mary Yonge: Her Life and Letters*, edited by Christabel R. Coleridge. London: Macmillan, 1903. 1-119.

—. *The Clever Woman of the Family*. 1865. Reprint, New York: Virago, 1985.

—. *Womankind*. 1872. Reprint, New York: Macmillan, 1877.

Notes

[1] Sturrock, *"Heaven and Home": Charlotte M. Yonge's Domestic Fiction and the Victorian Debate over Women*, 49.

[2] Yonge, *The Clever Woman of the Family*), 3.

[3] Bemis, *The Novels of Charlotte Yonge: A Critical Introduction*, 179.

[4] Stark, "The Clever Woman of the Family—and What Happened to Her." 17.

[5] Bemis, *The Novels of Charlotte Yonge*, 178.

[6] Keble, *The Christian Year: Thoughts in Verse for the Sundays and Holydays throughout the Year*, vii.

[7] Yonge, *Autobiography* 116.

[8] Ibid., 119.

[9] Coleridge, *Charlotte Mary Yonge: Her Life and Letters* , 132.

[10] Delafield, "Introduction," 14.

[11] See especially Keble's 1833 essay "Adherence to the Apostolical Succession the Safest Course," which became Tract 4 of the Oxford Movement's *Tracts for the Times*.

[12] Fessler, "Intellectuality and Female Sexuality in the Novels of Charlotte Yonge," 27-32.

[13] Yonge, *Womankind*, 1.

[14] Yonge, *Clever Woman*, 136.

[15] Ibid.

[16] Ibid.

[17] Ibid., 135.

[18] Ibid., 253.

[19] Ibid., 337.

[20] Yonge may have intended Rachel's lack of male relatives to symbolize and problematize a demographic trend that Victorians had identified and begun to discuss in the popular press just as Yonge was drafting *Clever Woman*. Many Victorians were convinced, with William Rathbone Greg, author of the widely read *National Review* article "Why Are Women Redundant?" (1862), that females had come to outnumber males in England by the "hundreds of thousands—not to speak more largely still—scattered through the ranks, but proportionately more numerous in the middle and upper classes" (435), and that the disproportion was fast leading England into a socioeconomic crisis. A century later, James and Olive Banks explored the reasons for and consequences of this supposed demographic imbalance and critiqued the remedies that Victorians proposed. *Feminism and Family Planning in Victorian England*, 27-41. Recent scholars are more skeptical of Greg's contentions; nonetheless, the important point here is that Victorians themselves believed there was an enormous and growing dearth of males in England. In a patriarchal society this is intriguingly problematic, as Rachel's closing statement makes clear: "I should have been much better if I had had either father or brother to keep me in order." Yonge, *Clever Woman*, 367.

---

[21] Yonge, *Clever Woman*, 236.

[22] Ibid., 243.

[23] Ibid., 46.

[24] Ibid., 47.

[25] Before she launches her business, Rachel tries to effect social reform through activities that her society deems 'proper' for women. First she takes up, as a "most sacred office," the "domestic mission" of educating her sickly cousin Fanny's children—even though she acknowledges to herself that she would "far rather become the founder of some establishment that might relieve women from the oppressive task-work thrown on them in all branches of labour" (3). She hopes to inspire and prepare Fanny's sons to "ameliorate [...] the condition of the masses" (7). But the boys reject her tutelage. Then she reasons, "If I can make myself useful with my pen, it will compensate for the being debarred from so many more obvious outlets" (52). But her pseudonymously written journal articles advocating social change are rejected by publishers. Personified by domestically powerful, if physically frail and intellectually vacant, 'womanly women' like Fanny, and politically powerful men such as journal editors, 'society' prevents Rachel from performing what she sees as her moral duty. Only thereafter does she launch into the 'male' realm of business. As Bemis notes, Yonge is careful not to grant Rachel any solid achievements. *The Novels of Charlotte Yonge*, 180.

[26] Keble, *The Christian Year*, vii.

[27] Sturrock, *"Heaven and Home,"* 53 (emphasis mine).

[28] Yonge, *Clever Woman*, 3.

[29] Ibid., 253.

[30] Ibid., 145.

[31] Ruskin, "Of Queens' Gardens," 87.

[32] Yonge, *Clever Woman*, 231.

[33] Ibid., 223 (emphasis mine).

[34] Ibid., 233.

[35] Ibid.

[36] In a complicated subplot, a brilliant inventor named Edward Williams is bilked by Mauleverer and must flee the country, abandoning his baby daughter Rose.

[37] Yonge, *Clever Woman*, 284.

[38] Ibid., 269 (emphasis mine).

[39] Ibid., 283.

[40] This 'lesson' might sound especially odd, perhaps even hypocritical, coming as it does from a successful author who herself never married, had no children, and worked diligently to 'improve' her society. But, as Shirley Foster notes, many female Victorian writers were unwilling or unable to imagine fates for their heroines other than wifehood or motherhood. Foster concludes that because Victorian society at large attached "so much importance [...] to the roles of wifehood and motherhood, marriage was deemed the apotheosis of womanly fulfillment, alternatives to which were regarded as pitiable or unnatural." *Victorian Women's Fiction: Marriage, Freedom, and the Individual,* 6. Nina Auerbach cautions that "this vacuum where the adult female should be, this paradox whereby

her existence is defined only in reference to children, explains much of our difficulty not only in creating our own lives, but in assessing the lives of women in the past. This difficulty is compounded when we look at the lives of childless women in the nineteenth century, struggling against universal approval of large families and paeans to the holiness of motherhood. For the nineteenth-century popular imagination, motherhood was not merely a biological fact, but a spiritual essence inseparable from pure womanhood." *Romantic Imprisonment: Women and Other Glorified Outcasts*, 173-174.

[41] Georgiana Battiscombe, Yonge's foremost biographer, remarks that, although "Charlotte was far too good an artist ever to copy a portrait exactly from life, [...] the holy and learned country parson, Mr. Clare, is in many ways reminiscent of Keble." Afterword to *The Clever Woman of the Family,* 370.

[42] Yonge, *Clever Woman*, 345.

[43] Ibid., 3.

CHAPTER FIVE

WRITERS OF REFORM AND REFORMING WRITERS IN *AURORA LEIGH* AND *A WRITER OF BOOKS*

LAURA ROTUNNO

Upon meeting the budding novelist, Cosima Chudleigh of "George Paston's" (Emily Morse Symonds's) *A Writer of Books*, a fellow lodger sums her up: "A stupid little thing, like most of your clever women."[1] This description is apt. It is one that would also go far to describe many heroines (and heroes) of Victorian novels of development, or more specifically, Victorian novels that chart the development of authors, *Künstlerromane*. Victorian *Künstlerromane* are noted for their attention to the artist's recognition of his/her muse, the artist's acknowledgement of his/her own unique nature and subsequent ability to understand and interact with others, and ultimately, his/her capacity to balance artistic vision with the business realities of the Victorian literary marketplace.[2] All of these elements are in place in Elizabeth Barrett Browning's *Aurora Leigh* (1856) and Paston's *A Writer of Books* (1898).[3]

Aurora Leigh and Cosima Chudleigh reach their artistic maturity in similar ways. Both are the daughters of fathers with libraries in which their own authorial visions take flight. Buoyed with such visions, both women work not primarily towards popular success in the periodicals and bookstands, but rather towards creating texts that show literary merit and, especially in Aurora's case, social significance. Moreover, both women attempt to help those suffering under the brutal realities of marital abuse, mental instability, and rape. Those interactions shape Aurora's and Cosima's ideas about the types of people and events that need to be represented in their writings, and their abilities to explore artistically these sensitive issues mature throughout the course of these novels. Both female artists thus end at points where their duty to their art, themselves, and those around them appears more balanced than it was at the onset of their careers.

The development described in Aurora's and Cosima's stories also fit with the expectations surrounding the female version of the Victorian *Künstlerroman*. The female Victorian *Künstlerroman* is most often differentiated from the male *Künstlerroman* in two ways. First, the female Victorian *Künstlerroman* focuses on how women's struggles to fit into the literary marketplace were made more difficult through social expectations and family obligations. Second, it emphasizes the worth of women's visions; in other words, its attests to women's deserved place in political and artistic debates. Correspondingly, family and suitors who fail to understand or fully support the women's writings repeatedly enter *Aurora Leigh* and *A Writer of Books*. While Cosima saddles herself with a husband who fails to appreciate literature, Aurora faces Romney, her cousin and later her love interest, who claims that, as a woman, she does not have sufficient knowledge or sympathy to be a successful poet; bluntly he declares "We get no Christ from you—and verily / We shall not get a poet."[4]

Adding to the trials to be overcome, Aurora's and Cosima's initial entries into the literary world do not yield the type of respect they seek, but, in *Künstlerroman*-style, the belief in a woman's capacity to contribute actively and innovatively to Art motivates the women and brings relative success. For example, Aurora's first publications are met with remarkable public acclaim. The acclaim, however, is deceptive. As Aurora puts it, "I did some excellent things indifferently, / Some bad things excellently. Both were praised, / The latter loudest."[5] As she is in this passage so she is throughout her career: her own best critic who forces herself to give the public not just what they want but what she and they need artistically and intellectually. Cosima starts in a less lucrative position; the initial sales of her first novel were just "sufficient to cover expenses," and the reviews contained a hodgepodge of extreme praise and extreme censure.[6] However, the support of Quentin Mallory, a writer/historian friend, who deems her first book just "good in patches," yet argues passionately for the value of "female writers who possess[] ideas of their own, and dare[] to express them," combined with Cosima's willingness to hone her literary talent and use it for substantive projects—ideals that also inspire Aurora—lead to a number of subsequent articles and novels that gain serious notice and well-earned acclaim.[7]

Not surprisingly, Barrett Browning's and Paston's novels themselves were viewed as instruments of reform, and contemporary reviews identified their novelists as reformers. *The Academy's* review of *A Writer of Books* described George Paston as "pre-occupied by the general injustice of man's attitude towards woman, and so she writes about that injustice."[8] Similarly, in *The Athenaeum, Aurora Leigh* was described as Barrett Browning's

> contribution to the chorus of protest and mutual exhortation, which Woman is now raising, in hope of gaining the due place and sympathy which, it is held, have been denied to her since the days when Man was created, the first of the pair in Eden.[9]

These and similar reviews emphasized the novels' and novelists' focus on women as victims of injustice at the hands of men or society in general. While such injustice is definitely found in these texts, the novels also examine their heroine's actions, exposing a need for reform in these women's ideals and endeavors. This paper's focus is the call for female reform voiced in these novels. This reform is unique for it is a reform of the women themselves, specifically one that asks the female authors to question their goals as authors and to consider how female authors should be positioned within the Victorian literary marketplace.

Some of the most memorable portions of each of these seemingly representative female *Künstlerromane* overtly display Aurora's and Cosima's unrealistic visions of authorship. Early in *Aurora Leigh,* the heroine poet admits she "drew a wreath . . . across [her] brow" and positioned herself "arms up, like the caryatid, sole / Of some abolished temple."[10] In an equally memorable scene of *A Writer of Books,* Cosima considers her initial lodgings in London this way:

> She was really rather glad that this temporary abode was not more luxurious. . . . A period of real privation, nights spent on the Embankment, furtive visits to the pawnbrokers, these experiences seemed to be among the most effectual fertilizers of literary genius.[11]

Cosima goes so far as to save letters written to her, visit restaurants, attend plays, and approach marriage as a way of gaining material for her novels, rationalizing that if

> she were to resolve never to marry until she fell passionately in love, it seemed likely that she would be doomed to remain a spinster all her life, and so lose an experience that must be valuable to any woman, and practically indispensable to a novelist.[12]

Although these visions of the female artist's life become somewhat tempered as the novels progress, the *Künstlerromane* offer frequent and significant portrayals of their heroines as women swept up in romanticized visions of what it means to be a writer.

Exploiting Aurora's and Cosima's naively imagined visions of the Victorian literary professional, Barrett Browning's and Paston's novels ostensibly offer support for the theory that young women's reading can be dangerous. Aurora's and Cosima's ideas of what it means to be a writer indeed echo nineteenth-century rhetoric concerning the dangers of reading, especially the dangers facing women who read. British readers of the mid to late nineteenth century were audience to a considerable amount of rhetoric concerning the too-often degenerate or degenerating state of readers and reading. The sheer mass of reading materials available to the public was of paramount concern. The 1874 article "Vice of Reading" put it this way: reading

> has become a downright vice,—a vulgar, detrimental habit, like dram-drinking . . . a softening, demoralizing, relaxing practice, which, if persisted in will end by enfeebling the minds of men and women, making flabby the fibre of their bodies, and undermining the vigour of nations.[13]

It was asserted that too much reading produced people who lived in dream worlds and who would, necessarily, fail to focus on the important issues and events of their own lives. Of such people, it was written, "Their minds, their whole natures, have become subdued to what they work in. They have become of the books, booky."[14] Authors' seemingly supreme power over readers assumed a prominent role in the 1859 "Cheap Literature" an article in which the author asserted that a story ". . . is entirely in the hands of the author, and is at his absolute disposal for good or evil" and concluded that

> it is easy to see that the author can conduct us to any given conclusion with the greatest possible certainty; but it is equally clear that his conclusion, whatever it may be, is mere smoke.[15]

Not surprisingly, women were seen as most prone to such imprudence as explained in an article entitled "What Should Women Read?":

> There is something in the feminine nature which finds comfort and solace in words of imagination, but to pander too much to the imaginative and emotional side is to create the morbid. So the perusal of too many novels, particularly of the more modern school, is gravely injurious to young girls whose imagination is immature and too easily biased.[16]

Implicitly, and sometimes explicitly, these articles argued that such flights of imagination led to a weakening of the intellect and a waning of interest in anything serious or substantial.

And then, of course, there was the moral and sexual danger. *The Wesleyan-Methodist Magazine* defined the "harm of novel-reading" by telling the story of a young girl too taken with the pastime. The story of that girl, ultimately a destitute mother of two, concluded this way: "Golden dreams of sinful pleasure—the creation of novel-reading—ended in disgrace, ruin, disease, a broken heart, and an untimely grave."[17] When women read the works of other women, the results were cast as even more dire. William Rathbone Greg, writing of the "False Morality of Lady Novelists" claimed that when young women read novels written by female novelists they were sure to suffer, for the

> experience [of the female novelists] affords no criterion whereby to separate the true from the false in the delineation of life, and the degree of culture is as yet insufficient to distinguish the pure from the meretricious, the sound from the unsound.[18]

As if channeling *Aurora Leigh*'s Romney whose invective against Aurora was inspired by her superficial knowledge of the "real" world, Greg concludes that those who take up these female-authored novels

> are constantly gazing on inaccurate pictures, constantly sympathizing with artificial or reprehensible emotions, constantly admiring culpable conduct, constantly imbibing false morality.[19]

Albeit already a slim possibility in the minds of the above quoted critics, the potential that a novelist would offer ideas that could guide readers' understandings and actions to positive ends is eliminated in Greg's scenario.

Rather surprisingly, especially for novels ostensibly supportive of female authors, *Aurora Leigh* and *A Writer of Books* portray Aurora and Cosima as having fallen victim to the dangers of reading and potentially becoming purveyors of dangerous writings themselves. While the moral and sexual dangers of reading are not a central issue in either novel, they are not foreign to the story lines. Aurora initially rejects Romney's marriage proposal and supports Marian Erle in her pregnancy and life as a single mother. Cosima interacts with men with whom she has not been "properly" introduced, can be read as largely responsible for her miserably failed marriage, and fraternizes with a woman who brings about a man's death and who is sexually pursued by Cosima's own husband. All of these experiences place Aurora and Cosima in positions of questionable morality and potential sexual danger. At the very least, then, these women are versed in issues dealing with the underbelly of romantic relationships, issues unbecoming to good Victorian women.

The vices bred by reading that occupy a more prominent place in Barrett Browning's and Paston's texts are those that focus on the dangerous encroachment of fictional worlds on factual. Both Aurora and Cosima are cast as avid readers, so avid in fact that they become separated from their "real" lives and the lives of those surrounding them. That Aurora is initially unable to understand that Marian's pregnancy was not the result of Marian's fallen nature, but rather the result of a brutal rape, can be read as Aurora's lack of interaction with such a true-to-life "narrative." Upon first seeing Marian in Paris, Aurora quickly "recalls" a story explaining what she sees:

> as truly as that was Marian's face,
> The arms of that same Marian clasped a thing
> . . . .
> A child. Small business has a castaway
> Like Marian with that crown of prosperous wives
> . . . .
> A child's too costly for so mere a wretch;
> She filched it somewhere, and it means, with her,
> Instead of honour, blessing, merely shame.[20]

Notably, Aurora admits a potential for error in her story—". . . I go too fast; / I'm cruel like the rest—in haste to take / The first stir in the arras for a rat"—and yet almost immediately after this admission, she continues the story and her plans: ". . . we'll find her, have her out, / And save her, if she will or will not—child / Or no child—if a child, then one to save!"[21] Similarly, upon Cosima's arrival in London, she pigeonholes new acquaintances. In her boarding house, she finds Miss Phelps who "was evidently a doctor," and immediately she starts her planning: Miss Phelps's

> conversation should be full of instruction to the novelist. Cosima recalled
> the useful information that the De Goncourts had gained from their friend,
> Dr Robin, and determined to cultivate this new acquaintance.[22]

Instead of talking with the American girl who moves into her boarding house, Cosima composes a "character note" about her.[23] Likewise, in respect to Sargent, whom she meets on the street and ultimately dines with, she desires

> to continue her study of this type of youth, and, as a scientific spectator, to
> see something of a phase of life which is mostly shuttered off with jealous
> care from the knowledge of the girl from whom the wife is bred.[24]

She assumes all are either types with which she is already familiar because
of her extensive reading or those from whom she can make "good copy."
The tenet that a good artist sees through another person's eyes so as to
understand and then create does not naturally enter Aurora's or Cosima's
ideas, because real people appear to them as characters already present in a
novel or ready-made for one, rather than as human beings with whom they
might personally interact.

Such an immersion in books can affect the artist's vision of herself as
well. For example, when Cosima arrives in London, she undergoes a
strange sort of identity crisis. When she steps off the train,

> a few moments she stood apart, and watched the jostling crowds, finding it
> almost impossible to realize that this tired, lonely, frightened girl was
> really she, and not some heroine of romance, whose adventures she was
> reading by the light of the station lamps.[25]

Cosima's tendency to see her life as following an already-written narrative
of "the writer" also determines her ideas about the submission of her first
manuscript, for she believes that

> Immediate acceptance of her work would be positively alarming; it would
> be so entirely out of accord with the best literary traditions. Success
> without a long and heartbreaking struggle would be almost proof positive
> that her work was only destined for an ephemeral popularity.[26]

This mindset continues late into the novel when Cosima finds herself at
night on the Embankment:

> This, she reflected, was an experience which, to judge by the biography
> books, the majority of successful authors had gone through. A night on the
> Embankment, or in Hyde Park, seemed almost a necessary prelude to
> celebrity.[27]

And so she spends a cold, lonely night, and the novel records no great
story that comes of this time.

Notably, *Aurora Leigh* and *A Writer of Books* self-consciously present
these connections between their heroines and those whom the periodical
press drew as victims of contemporary fiction and poetry. Notably too,
most of the instances I've discussed are presented to readers ironically, if
not comically. A lightness of presentational tone, however, should not be

mistaken for a lack of seriousness in these texts' examination of their heroines' ideas about the role of female authors in the Victorian literary marketplace. The final images of both novels—images that can be read as heavily romanticized visions of the power and purpose of the artist— underscore the seriousness with which these female visions of literary professionals are presented. *Aurora Leigh* ends with Aurora accepting the now-blind Romney's marriage proposal. Upon accepting the proposal, Aurora describes herself this way:

> I flung closer to his breast,
> As a sword, that, after battle, flings to sheath;
> And, in that hurtle of united souls,
> The mystic motions which in common moods
> Are shut beyond our sense, broke in on us.[28]

Further on, Aurora and Romney share a vision of their union as one capable of bringing a New Jerusalem. *A Writer of Books* concludes with Cosima, inspired by the relatively positive critical reception of her just-published novel, sitting down to begin her next work:

> She would take a year, two years, to write this new book. She would live on crusts but she would write it well. Heart-ache, anger, bitterness, fatigue, for the moment all were forgotten. The ink-craving was upon her, and her fingers involuntarily crooked themselves round an imaginary pen. The new work was going to be *the* book, the flawless masterpiece that every author is always going to write.[29]

Consistent in both novels' conclusions is the fact that the women are relatively secure in their social and professional worlds. While Cosima is separated from her husband, she has sufficient financial security and has attained enough professional respectability that she can undertake her authorial plans. Aurora looks forward to a forthcoming marriage and can also rest securely on her professional reputation. Even more importantly, these women have thoroughly considered and extensively discussed with others what women can contribute to the literary tradition. They have put forward visions—literally articulated visions—of how female writers could reform the literary marketplace. For Aurora, she recognizes the need for literature to be "epic" but to

> represent the age,
> Their age, not Charlemagne's—this live, throbbing age,
> That brawls, cheats, maddens, calculates, aspires,
> And spends more passion, more heroic heat
> Betwixt the mirrors of its drawing-rooms,

Than Roland with his knights at Roncevalles.[30]

Bucking tradition from another angle, Cosima comes to believe that "the greatest mistake a woman writer can make" is to write and think like a man; instead, the best goal to follow is to "give [readers] a study of manners and character from the woman's point of view."[31] She concludes that "the ideal novel of the future will surely be the true and faithful history of a character," one that focuses on that character's growth.[32] She moves away from her early dependence on stock characters (and even stock tales) and towards the idea that a novel could explore a female individual, one like herself who has witnessed and experienced the injustices and opportunities afforded Victorian women.

Such declarations from Aurora and Cosima have led critics to assert, in the case of *A Writer of Books*, that the "strong polemic" against women's reading and writing common in New Woman novels is overcome, for Cosima

> progresses from a concept of "experience" as something to be acquired by coming in contact with the wide world . . . to the realization that her own "individual sensations and experiences" may act as "the sun and the rain that fertilise one's mind."[33]

Even greater growth is attributed to Aurora; as SueAnn Schatz asserts

> Aurora is now mature enough to realize not only that art and love are compatible, but also mature enough to take on the creation of two "New Jerusalems": the writing of socially-beneficial poetry and partnership in an egalitarian marriage.[34]

The fact that the sword image can actually be read as a repetition with meaningful revision of an earlier line in which Aurora declares her disgust with her own early artistic forays—"I played at art, made thrusts with a toy-sword, / Amused the lads and maidens"—supports such assertions of growth.[35]

I agree that these female characters have made significant progress beyond their earliest visions of the Author and Art. Such arguments accord well with my own assertion that these novels accentuate the reforms that these women—not the male characters, not the communities in general— undergo throughout the course of these *Künstlerromane*. These women reform their visions of what women can uniquely contribute to the literary marketplace. Extended examinations of the novel's final images of Aurora as a sword and Cosima taken by the "ink-craving," however, reveal the calls for further reforms put forth by these novels, reforms that would make it possible for Aurora and Cosima to make those unique contributions to the Victorian literary marketplace.

The pen as the sword and the almost feverish, physical urge to write, these images return Aurora, Cosima, and readers to romanticized visions of authorial genius. The sword image, while it fits the epic requirements that Aurora has set out for contemporary literature, is presented in a way far from contemporary. Following the previously quoted lines, Aurora claims that she and Romney

> we felt the old earth spin,
> And all the starry turbulence of worlds
> Swing round us in their audient circles, till
> If that same golden moon were overhead
> Or if beneath our feet, we did not know.[36]

Invoking the music of the spheres through the "audient circles" and suggesting not only Romney and Aurora but the whole world has somehow been turned head over heels, these lines and those introducing the sword are ones of high romance, not those of the "live, throbbing age" of Victorian Britain. Similarly, Cosima's desire to write the "flawless masterpiece that *every* author is always going to write" and the subsequent war terminology used to describe the onset of her writing—she

> went to the writing-table, to prepare the materials of war. But before sitting down to begin her campaign, a campaign, in which she hoped to conquer heart-sickness . . .[37]

—separate Cosima from the particularly feminine and uniquely individual vision of character development and growth that she put forth as her artistic ideal. The disjunction between all of these images and Aurora's and Cosima's earlier proclamations about art thus suggest that, while these women possess specific instruments of power, it is not certain that they will use them to those proclaimed ends. They leave readers with a sense of, in Schatz's words, "guarded optimism" in respect to the women's ability to achieve truly significant literary success.[38]

A dramatic break in my connections between *Aurora Leigh* and *A Writer of Books* is now essential. There are significant differences between Barrett Browning's and Paston's final images and thus also the reform that they suggest is necessary if their heroines are to embody the visions of the novelists upheld in these texts. *Aurora Leigh* presents its heroine as more capable than Cosima to speak to large audiences about socially significant issues. Throughout the text, Aurora strives to make her work socially and spiritually fulfilling for herself and readers. The sword and the attendant

religious references point to such capabilities; they are also literally
followed up by Aurora's declaration that she and Romney must "stand
upon the earth" if they are to help any fellow humans.[39] Moreover, because
this text connects the sword with Biblical references, this sword stands in a
tradition different than Charlemagne's or the Arthurian legends to which
so many of Aurora's and Barrett Browning's contemporaries were turning
in their works and against which this novel-poem positions itself.

However, even after these qualifications are taken into consideration, I
maintain that the weight of responsibility placed on Aurora is purposefully
exaggerated by the sword image. Swords are quick, precise, powerful.
Simultaneously, swords are heavy. Swords are unwieldy, especially when
maneuvered by an unpracticed hand. And, swords are double-edged. Thus
the challenge put to Aurora by this image is not one that questions her
writing skills or intellectual vision. It pinpoints the paramount need for a
controlled, strategic use of her skills. It intimates that such use of her
power could change the world, and it reminds all that such power could be
turned against her. Aurora's final declarations that invoke grandiose
visions of art's power but quickly place them in a very worldly setting
suggest she is ready and willing to undertake this reform of her visions of
the challenges facing the female Victorian writer.

Commitment to one's vision of what a female artist can best
accomplish is the requirement—the "reform" called for—in the final
images of *A Writer of Books*. Such commitment is presented as much more
elusive to Cosima than is the balance and control asked of Aurora.
Alternating between images associated with artistic genius, authorial
madness, and war, the final descriptions of Cosima's attempts to compose
her masterpiece undermine her description of what a female novelist
should strive to create: a character study told from a woman's point of
view. The war imagery and the linkage of herself with "every author"
position her in a male dominated field that does not necessarily celebrate
or investigate female individuality.[40] The intimation that she is writing to
"conquer heart-sickness and win forgetfulness and peace" also suggests a
personal motivation that could interfere with her attempt to record
accurately or insightfully a character's development within the complex
Victorian society.[41] While Paston's novel certainly shows Cosima's
growth, *A Writer of Books* ends by suggesting Cosima's fight against
romanticized visions of novelists has not yet been won. Realistic
achievable goals have been defined, but they have not shouldered out
idealized images from traditions to which Cosima does not fully belong.

Aurora Leigh and *A Writer of Books* do not question whether women
can significantly contribute to the Victorian literary world. They

unequivocally support women's presence and power within that world. However, Barrett Browning's and Paston's novels, by refusing to unequivocally sever these female artists' connections with literary fantasies of struggling but brilliant artists, spur continued reevaluation of what women can contribute. These novels call for social reform beyond that which introduces women's voices into political and artistic debates. They insist that female authors reform their own ideas about literature and their position as writers.

At a pivotal point within *A Writer of Books*, Cosima concludes that "the true reformer is seldom an artist, nor the true artist a reformer."[42] Previous readings of this line assert that Cosima is here defining "true reform" as a proactive, literally interactive, intervention within society. The question I raise in response to such readings is: does *A Writer of Books* uphold that separation? Does Paston's novel support the belief that an artist or author could not also be a reformer? This novel's often damning critique of Cosima suggests that the novel cannot wholeheartedly support such a division. Rather, the novel should be read as using Cosima's words to foreground a separation between the artist and reformer so that the female artists who read this novel feel impelled to evaluate— repeatedly and frequently—their aims and actual contributions to the Victorian literary world. Barrett Browning's *Aurora Leigh* made way for such injunctions, voicing a similar challenge through Aurora's sword, symbol of both artistic precision and socially incisive action.

Works Cited

Abel, Elizabeth, Marianne Hirsch, and Elizabeth Langland. *The Voyage In: Fictions of Female Development.* Hanover: University Press of New England, 1983.

Ablow, Rachel. "Labors of Love: The Sympathetic Subjects of *David Copperfield.*" *Dickens Studies Annual* 31 (2002): 23-46.

Barrett Browning, Elizabeth. *Aurora Leigh.* 1856. Oxford: Oxford University Press, 1998.

Beebe, Maurice. *Ivory Towers and Sacred Founts: The Artist as Hero in Fiction from Goethe to Joyce.* New York: New York University Press, 1964.

Chorley, H. F. Review of *Aurora Leigh*, by Elizabeth Barrett Browning. *Aurora Leigh*, edited by Margaret Reynolds. 403-07. New York: Norton, 1996. Originally published in *Athenaeum* 22 Nov. 1856.

Ellis, Lorna. *Appearing to Diminish: Female Development and the British Bildungsroman, 1750-1850*. Lewisburg: Bucknell University Press, 1999.

Fraiman, Susan. *Unbecoming Women: British Women Writers and The Novel of Development*. New York: Columbia University Press, 1993.

Greg, William Rathbone. "False Morality of Lady Novelists." *Victorian Print Media: A Reader*, edited by Andrew King and John Plunkett, 50-54. Oxford: Oxford University Press, 2005. Originally published in *National Review* 8 (Jan. 1849): 144-67.

Martino, Maria Carla. "Woman as Writer/Writer as Woman: George Paston's *A Writer of Books*." *Victorian Literature and Culture* 32 (2004): 223-38.

Mays, Kelly J. "The Disease of Reading and Victorian Periodicals." *Literature in the Marketplace: Nineteenth-Century British Publishing and Reading Practices*, edited by John O. Jordan and Robert L. Patten. *Cambridge Studies in Nineteenth-Century Literature and Culture 5*. Cambridge: Cambridge University Press, 1995. 165-94.

McSweeney, Kerry. Introduction to *Aurora Leigh*, by Elizabeth Barrett Browning, ix-xxxv. Oxford: Oxford University Press, 1998.

Paston, George. *A Writer of Books*. 1898. Chicago: Academy Chicago Publishers, 1999.

Review of *A Writer of Books*, by George Paston. *Academy*, 12 Nov. 1898, 246-47.

S. "What is the Harm of Novel-Reading?" *Victorian Print Media: A Reader*, edited by Andrew King and John Plunkett, 48-49. Oxford: Oxford University Press, 2005. Originally published in *Wesleyan-Methodist Magazine* 78.2 (Oct. 1855): 932-34.

Schatz, SueAnn. "*Aurora Leigh* as Paradigm of Domestic-Professional Fiction." *Philological Quarterly* 79, no. 1 (Winter 2000): 91-117, *MLA*, ProQuest, Penn State Libraries, <http://proquest.com> (accessed October 1, 2006).

Notes

[1] Paston, *A Writer of Books*, 15.

[2] Consult Beebe's *Ivory Towers and Sacred Founts: The Artist as Hero in Fiction from Goethe to Joyce* for background concerning the *Künstlerroman* in general, and Abel, Hirsch, and Langland, eds., *The Voyage In: Fictions of Female Development*, Fraiman's *Unbecoming Women: British Women Writers and the Novel of Development,* and Lorna Ellis's *Appearing to Diminish: Female*

Development and the British Bildungsroman, 1750-1850, for investigations of novels focused on female development, oftentimes the development of female artists.

[3] *Aurora Leigh* is often treated as a novel-poem; Barrett Browning made way for such treatment herself when describing her early intentions for this work in 1844: "a true poetical novel—modern, and on the level of the manner of the day—might be as good a poem as any other, and much more popular besides" (qtd. in Kerry McSweeney, introduction to *Aurora Leigh*, xiii). Most significantly, this paper treats *Aurora Leigh* as a *Künstlerroman*, a categorization also in line with Barrett Browning's description of this work, this time from 1853: "written in blank verse, in the autobiographical form; the heroine, an artist woman" (Ibid., xiv).

[4] Barrett Browning, *Aurora Leigh*, 2.224-25.

[5] Ibid., 3.205-07.

[6] Paston, *Writer,* 92.

[7] Ibid., 127, 144.

[8] Review of *A Writer of Books*, by George Paston, *Academy,* 12 Nov. 1898, 246.

[9] H. F. Chorley, Review of *A Writer of Books*, by George Paston, in *Aurora Leigh*, edited by Margaret Reynolds, 403.

[10] Barrett Browning, *Aurora Leigh*, 2.56-57, 2.61-62.

[11] Paston, *Writer*, 14.

[12] Ibid., 110.

[13] Qtd. in Kelly J. Mays, "The Disease of Reading and Victorian Periodicals," in *Literature in the Marketplace: Nineteenth-Century British Publishing and Reading Practices,* 170.

[14] Ibid., 172.

[15] Qtd. in Rachel Ablow, "Labors of Love: The Sympathetic Subjects of *David Copperfield,*" 32.

[16] Qtd. in Maria Carla Martino, "Woman as Writer/Writer as Woman: George Paston's *A Writer of Books*," 226.

[17] S., "What is the Harm of Novel-Reading?" in *Victorian Print Media: A Reader*, edited by King and Plunkett 48.

[18] Greg, "False Morality of Lady Novelists," 51.

[19] Ibid., 54.

[20] Barrett Browning, *Aurora Leigh*, 6.344-55.

[21] Ibid., 6.366-68, 6.387-89.

[22] Paston, *Writer*, 17.

[23] Ibid., 82.

[24] Ibid., 41.

[25] Ibid., 12-13.

[26] Ibid., 19-20.

[27] Ibid., 165.

[28] Barrett Browning, *Aurora Leigh*, 9.833-37.

[29] Paston, *Writer*, 258.

[30] Barrett Browning, *Aurora Leigh*, 5.202-07.

[31] Paston, *Writer,* 144, 145.

---

[32] Ibid., 208.

[33] Martino, "Woman as Writer," 225, 230.

[34] SueAnn Schatz, "*Aurora Leigh* as Paradigm of Domestic-Professional Fiction," 114, http://proquest.com (accessed October 1, 2006).

[35] Barrett Browning, *Aurora Leigh*, 3.240-41.

[36] Ibid., 9.838-42.

[37] Paston, *Writer,* 258, 259.

[38] Schatz, "*Aurora Leigh* as Paradigm," 114.

[39] Barrett Browning, *Aurora Leigh*, 9.854.

[40] Paston, *Writer*, 259.

[41] Ibid., 259.

[42] Ibid., 196.

CHAPTER SIX

GENDERED SPHERES AND IDEAL REFORMERS: ESTHER SUMMERSON AND ALLAN WOODCOURT IN *BLEAK HOUSE*

ANDRE' L. DECUIR

A long list of examples can be given of Dickens's interest in reforming the ideologies behind the actual practices of institutions governing the lives of 19th-century Londoners. Bruce Robbins writes for example that Dickens cheered "when imprisonment for debt was eliminated" and sneered "at those who resisted the extension of the state's social welfare efforts"[1]. In *Hard Times*, we read Dickens's relentless criticism of utilitarianism, the philosophy which perhaps hindered the reforms he would have liked to have seen proceed at a quicker pace; Dickens was offended by "a philosophy, and by extension an economic system, which militated against the proper, and often spontaneous, practice of humane charity"[2].

This novel has given us memorable portraits of utilitarians in Mr. Bounderby and Thomas Gradgrind and their victims in the Gradgrind children and Stephen Blackpool, and in *Bleak House*, Chancery, yet another pervasive, victimizing entity is personified in the characters of Tulkinghorn and Vholes, with their victims being Lady Dedlock and Richard Carstone respectively. The characters in this novel, however, who seem to receive a heavy dose of Dickens's criticism are those who should be near and dear to his heart—reformers. In *Bleak House*, Mrs. Jellyby and Mrs. Pardiggle serve as representations of a misguided sense of reform. Both are neglectful of the domestic arena, obsessed with the livelihoods of those far removed from London to the degree that their own household situations and an abundance of ills within their city are ignored. Dickens does offer a corrective to their "telescopic philanthropy" through Esther Summerson as many have written, but I contend that Dickens goes a step further, knowing that Esther, because of societal, gender-based codes, is limited in performing active, "face-to-face philanthropy."[3] Rather, Esther's union with Allan Woodcourt completes what seems to be for Dickens the portrait of the ideal reformer. Woodcourt, because of the *mobility* afforded him by his gender, can carry Esther's and his equal shares of empathy, compassion, and drive to the darkest corners of Tom-all-Alone's and possibly to all areas of disorder and disease.

Esther is known for two major acts of philanthropy in *Bleak House*: her compassion toward Jenny and her dead baby at the brickmaker's cottage, and of course, her sheltering of Jo, the ill street sweeper. Laura Fasick believes that "Esther is a more successful reformer" than Mrs. Pardiggle, because of her "sensitivity," and "her own self-effacement."[4] Unlike "the institutionalized abstractions of Mrs. Jellyby and . . . Mrs. Pardiggle,"[5] Esther embodies what Dickens believes to be the true spirit of reform; Dickens sees "the possibility of redemption arising only out of activity of sympathetic and responsible individuals responding to individuals."[6] Mota stresses that "activity is the key word . . . ; in this novel one must act,"[7] but I would suggest that Dickens realized that gender and class limited the mobility and thus the subsequent activity of potential reformers such as Esther.

Bleak House is a novel concerned with physical movement or the lack of it, a theme echoed in the words of the constable to Jo: "'My instructions are that this boy is to move on'"[8] and in the observation of the narrator of the seemingly free-flowing nature of the world: "There he [Jo] sits, the sun going down, the river running fast, the crowd flowing by him in two streams—everything moving on to some purpose and to one end—until he is stirred up, and told to 'move on too.'"[9] Much has been written on the narrator's ironic tone, which is not diminished on the topic of movement, for the most free-flowing agent in the novel is bred in the stagnant squalor of Tom-all-Alone's. As Michael Gurney points out, "The spread of the infection . . . is used as a symbol to emphasize the connection between social classes . . . the corruption could reach out and touch them all, in every walk of life."[10] The irony of the narrator's image of constant flux in "everything moving on to some purpose"[11] is brought into focus against Esther's, the counter-narrator's, observation, after visiting the brickmaker's cottage, that "between us and these people there was an iron barrier, which could not be removed,"[12] an image of obstruction, not fluidity.

Esther's realization may of course be read as a comment on class boundaries, but after examining her situation more closely, one can see that the "iron barrier" can prevent contact of those in need and those who can offer assistance on the basis of gender. When we are first introduced to

Ada Clare, she and Esther are in the Lord Chancellor's chambers, and we learn that Esther is to be "'a very good companion for the young lady [Ada], and the arrangement altogether seems the best of which the circumstances admit.'"[13] Because of their youth, gender, and status (being raised in an upper-class household), Esther and Ada "suffer," as Virginia Woolf explains, "in the narrowness of life that was imposed . . . . It was impossible for a woman to go about alone. She never traveled, she never drove through London . . . or had luncheon in a shop by herself."[14] Further, Helena Michie implies that a 19th-century woman could perhaps have been alone if she had had a contagious disease. Esther, in her travels is always accompanied by either Ada or Charley, but when she becomes ill, "her removal of herself from Ada's presence creates a space in which she can focus, narratively and psychologically, on her own interior life."[15] Recognizing the period's adherence to such gender-based behavioral codes should bring forth the question: would Esther have been able to exercise the compassion for which she is known if Mrs. Pardiggle, an older woman who would have been considered a suitable chaperone by the Victorians, had not escorted her to the brickmaker's cottage? When Mrs. Pardiggle asks, "'Miss Summerson, I hope I shall have your assistance in my visiting rounds immediately, and Miss Clare's very soon?'", Esther is reluctant and makes excuses: "At first I tried to excuse myself, for the present, on the general ground of having occupations to attend to which I must not neglect."[16] Esther may not have even learned of Jo's illness if not for Jenny and Charley, women of the lower classes, who yet have greater physical mobility. Charley learns of Jo's condition from Jenny who is on an errand to the doctor's shop to get medicine for Jo. Dickens then seems to construct a curious scenario based on gender and class. Poor women such as Jenny and Liz appear to have more freedom of movement within society than upper-class women who could "move" to these women to provide assistance. Jenny and Liz have the ability to move in and out of a neighborhood as they "'come back to where [they] used to live'" after "'tramping high and low.'"[17] Even the aristocratic Lady Dedlock covers much ground in her flight, alone, dressed as Jenny, the poor wife of a brickmaker.

Dickens, I believe, realizes that benevolent actions can be limited by gender and class and could be better propelled toward those in need with the assistance of one allowed to be more ubiquitous such as Allan Woodcourt who appears sporadically and mysteriously throughout the first part of the novel. He is the "dark young surgeon" who examines Nemo, the "gentleman of a dark complexion—a young surgeon"[18] Esther notices at Mr. Badger's home, and is introduced by name while attending on Miss

Flite.[19].He leaves the country as a ship's surgeon but then returns as a more established character with seemingly reformist tendencies. On one level, he functions as a potential romantic interest for Esther, but a close examination of the parallels in the crises in their lives reveals that Dickens is trying to forge together not only a portrait of a proper Victorian marriage but a version of his ideal reformer.

Much has been written about Esther's illness which she contracts from Charley, who contracts it from Jo after their compassionate mission of bringing Jo to Bleak House for recovery. Not much attention has been placed however upon the immediate after-effects of her convalescence on herself and on those around her, and the imagery could guide us to see Esther more clearly as a component of Dickens's portrait of the effective reformer.

Esther's narrative of illness and recovery can be read as a saint's life of good works, suffering, and beatification. The scene in which Esther is made comfortable after the return of her sight and senses may remind one of the "worship" of some iconic goddess.

The first sight Esther describes upon the strengthening of her vision is "the glorious light coming every day more fully and brightly on me."[20] She then is "raised in bed with pillows" and basks in "divine sunshine" while being *appeased* with *offerings* (italics mine) of "little delicacies," "white cloth," and "flowers."[21] In the role of devotee / suppliant, Charley lays her head on Esther's bosom, fondles her, and cries "with joyful tears," but when Esther tells her that she is still too weak for her physical affection, Charley calmly obeys the "command" of the beatified Esther and becomes "quiet as mouse."[22]

Significantly, Dickens has Esther incorporate Miss Flite's account of Woodcourt's shipwreck, just pages after Esther's own story of near-death illness and recovery. Esther may foreshadow her marriage to Woodcourt for the reader through this juxtaposition of the experiences, but I believe that Dickens, by having Esther structure her narrative in this way is composing this image of the ideal reformer by joining gendered spheres, the feminine / domestic, represented by Esther, "Dame Durden," "little Housewife," and the masculine / public / global sphere of Woodcourt, ship's surgeon.

To further emphasize this point, Dickens likens Esther's sensations caused by her illness to a voyage over water. Esther describes, "I seemed to have crossed a dark lake, and to have left all my experiences, mingled together by the great distance, on the healthy shore."[23] She visualizes the much-analyzed "flaming necklace, or ring, or starry circle of some kind of which *I* was one of the beads!" in "great black space."[24] The tale of

Woodcourt is one of shipwreck, heroism, and survival, and coincidentally is also characterized by "'Fire'" and "'darkness.'"[25] Miss Flite narrates:

'Don't be agitated, my dear. He is safe. An awful scene. Death in all shapes. Hundreds of dead and dying. Fire, storm, and darkness. Numbers of the drowning thrown upon a rock. There, and through it all, my dear physician was a hero. Calm and brave, through everything. Saved many lives, never complained in hunger and thirst, wrapped naked people in his spare clothes, took the lead, showed them what to do, governed them, tended the sick, buried the dead, and brought the poor survivors safely off at last![26]

Paralleling Esther's elevation to "pseudo sainthood" because of her self-sacrifice in tending to the contagious Jo, Woodcourt is also ascribed a deified status: "'My dear, the poor emaciated creatures all but worshipped him. They fell down at his feet, when they got to the land, and blessed him. The whole country rings with it.'"[27]

Dickens appears to allow Woodcourt to become more of a reoccurring character in the rest of the novel as his experiences at sea have stirred up more of a "reformist spirit," one equal to Esther's but again with a chief difference—mobility to seek out those in need. A young woman such as Esther, ward to the gentleman John Jarndyce, would never have been able to ramble alone through slums. Allan, unable to sleep, "rather than counting the hours on a restless pillow," "strolls" through Tom-all-Alone's.[28] Quite similar to Esther's realization of the iron barrier between classes, Allan notices that there is much to be done to relieve those who must call places like Tom-all-Alone's home: "he often pauses and looks about him, up and down the miserable byways. . . . in his bright dark eye there is compassionate interest; and as he looks here and there, he seems to understand such wretchedness, and to have studied it before."[29]

While Esther is taken to the brickmaker's cottage by Mrs. Pardiggle where she is able to comfort the grieving Jenny, Allan, as he traverses Tom-all-Alone's by himself, "sees the solitary figure of a woman [Jenny] sitting on a doorstep. He walks that way."[30] He speaks to her "avoiding patronage of condescension, or childishness" which "had put him on good terms with the woman easily."[31] Again, while Esther learns of Jo's illness through Charley, Allan, when he "walks away" after assisting Jenny, personally encounters the emaciated Jo. After he discovers that Jo was taken from Bleak House, Allan patiently listens to Jo's story, buys him breakfast, and procures a place, George's shooting-gallery, for Jo to "'lie down and hide in.'"[32]

We should by no means deduce that Dickens's successful reformers should be candidates for sainthood. The narratives of sacrifice and implied heavenly status are meant to emphasize that Esther and Allan have equal, elevated levels of what is needed in those who could initiate true reform— "a strong sense of relationship to others. Throughout the novel, they act responsibly through love for those around them."[33] Dickens is careful to include in both characters however the human tendency to become frustrated at the overwhelming need of their fellows and lack of means to assist them. Michael Gurney for example argues that when Esther, in her delirium, sees herself as one of the beads in the flaming necklace and prays "to be taken off from the rest, . . . when it was such inexplicable agony and misery to be part of the dreadful thing,"[34] she recognizes "the perils held by society and futility of laboring against them"[35] and is ready to reject her society. Similarly, this frustration is noticed by Jarndyce in Allan: "'I doubt if he expects much of the old world. Do you know I have: fancied that he sometimes feels some particular disappointment, or misfortune, encountered in it.'"[36] Again, the chief difference between Esther and Woodcourt, mobility, is implied as Woodcourt, "'a sea-going doctor'" can, according to Jarndyce, "'give a long trial to another country'" where his humanitarian endeavors may not yet hindered by a tangled system of self interest.

Esther's facial scarring I believe is yet another way of emphasizing her humanity, fallibility included, as she is so eager to help that she does not think of the risk to herself, but like her altruism, it sets her apart physically from her acquaintances. Esther's scars are branded evidence of her own "permeation" of the iron barrier despite gendered and economic limitations. Her "face-to-face philanthropy" is opposed of course to the "telescopic philanthropy" of Mrs. Jellyby and Mrs. Pardiggle and allows her to suffer as those she seeks to help.

Esther does not seem that upset when she first sees her face in the mirror after her recovery. As she gazes into the mirror, her face becomes "more familiar."[37] She says, "Heaven was so good to me, that I could let it go with a few not bitter tears."[38] She puts up her hair herself, which would certainly expose her face more and is ready to become active: "Wishing to be fully re-established in my strength and my good spirits before Ada came, I now laid down a little series of plans with Charley for being in the fresh air all day long."[39]

Yet another overlooked parallel connecting Esther to Allan vocationally is Woodcourt's altered appearance through sunburn after his heroism at sea, which sets him apart physically. On a visit to Richard at Deal, Esther recognizes Allan in "one of the sun-burnt faces" of the sailors from the great Indianman, and the narrator designates him as "the brown sunburnt gentleman"[40] who walks solitarily through Tom-all-Alone's, as he would certainly stand out from the pale, sickly residents of the slum. While Esther's illness should certainly not be placed in the same category as a sunburn, one should still realize that Woodcourt's sunburn is definitely a "casualty" of a sea-going vocation and that he contracted it while suffering "'hunger and thirst'" as did his fellow passengers without complaint. Allan's sunburn and Esther's scars serve as "badges of honor" resulting from their fortitude and a willingness to connect, not only emotionally, but physically with fellow human beings in an attempt to reform their dire situations.

At the end of the novel, Dickens has united two characters, who throughout the novel, have been presented as risking their lives through hands-on alleviation of the suffering of others while still entertaining those basic human qualities of doubt and skepticism. He does not, however, call for a loosening of those societal codes which govern the lives of women as he presents the marriage of Esther and Allan as the ideal Victorian marriage, with the adoring wife praising her hard-working husband. Within the parameters of such a marriage, however, Dickens seems to suggest that a marriage of equals or near-equals might actually allow a woman to have a more active life. In her marriage to Woodcourt rather than the older, more fatherly John Jarndyce, Esther gains a title for which she is praised, "the doctor's wife," and which apparently allows her to "go about" "into a house of any degree"[41] much like Allan is "allowed" to go about in an area such as Tom-all-Alone's and administer to those in need. With the marriage of Esther and Allan, Dickens's portrait of the ideal reformer is complete as the compassionate drive to reform physically the situations of the suffering is doubled and enhanced in the case of Esther by the ability to move into and brighten the most squalid areas until sweeping reforms can be made.

Works Cited

Dickens, Charles. *Bleak House*. 1853. New York: Penguin, 2006.

Fasick, Laura. "Dickens and the Diseased Body in *Bleak House*." *Charles Dickens Bloom's Major Novelists*. Edited by Harold Bloom. Broomfield, PA: Chelsea House, 2000. 65-68.

Gurney, Michael. "Disease as Device: The Role of Smallpox in *Bleak House*." *Literature and Medicine* 9 (1990): 79-92.

Michie, Helena. "'Who is this in Pain?': Scarring, Disfigurement, and
    Female Identity In *Bleak House* and *Our Mutual Friend*. " *Novel: A
    Forum on Fiction* 22, no.2 (1989): 199-212.
Mota, Miguel M. "The Construction of the Christian Community in
    Charles Dickens's *Bleak House*." *Renascence: Essays on Values in
    Literature* 46, no. 3 (1994): 187- 198.
Robbins, Bruce. "Telescopic Philanthropy: Professionalism and
    Responsibility in *Bleak House*." *New Casebooks: Bleak House*. Edited
    by Jeremy Tambling. New York: St. Martin's P, 1998. 139-162.
Sanders, Andrew. *Charles Dickens*. Oxford: Oxford University Press,
    2003.
Woolf, Virginia. *A Room of One's Own*. San Diego: Harcourt, 1929.

Notes

[1] Robbins, "Telescopic Philanthropy: Professionalism and Responsibility in *Bleak House*," 147.
[2] Sanders, *Charles Dickens*, 138.
[3] Robbins, "Telescopic," 153.
[4] Fasick, "Dickens and the Diseased Body in *Bleak House*, 66.
[5] Ibid., 65-66.
[6] Mota, "The Construction of the Christian Community in Charles Dickens's *Bleak House*," 3.
[7] Ibid., 3.
[8] Dickens, *Bleak House*, 308.
[9] Ibid., 315.
[10] Gurney, "Disease as Device: The Role of Smallpox in *Bleak House*," 79, 82.
[11] Dickens, *Bleak House*, 315.
[12] Ibid., 133.
[13] Ibid., 46.
[14] Woolf, *A Room of One's Own*, 71.
[15] Michie, "'Who is this in Pain?': Scarring, Disfigurement, and Female Identity in *Bleak House* and *Our Mutual Friend*," 205.
[16] Dickens, *Bleak House*, 128.
[17] Ibid., 487.
[18] Ibid., 214.
[19] Ibid., 233.
[20] Ibid., 556.
[21] Ibid., 557.
[22] Ibid., 557.
[23] Ibid., 555.
[24] Ibid., 556.

[25] Ibid., 568.
[26] Ibid., 568-569.
[27] Ibid., 569.
[28] Ibid., 710.
[29] Ibid., 711.
[30] Ibid., 711.
[31] Ibid., 711.
[32] Ibid., 718.
[33] Gurney, "Disease," 84.
[34] Dickens, *Bleak House*, 556.
[35] Gurney, "Disease," 88.
[36] Dickens, *Bleak House*, 776.
[37] Ibid., 572.
[38] Ibid., 572.
[39] Ibid., 573.
[40] Ibid., 710.
[41] Ibid., 986.

PART III

GENRE, LITERACY, AND REFORM

CHAPTER SEVEN

WILKIE COLLINS, MASCULINITY, AND THE PERILS OF DOMESTICITY

MARIA K. BACHMAN

Talking of hostility reminds me of marriage . . .
—Wilkie Collins to Charles Collins, 12 August 1853[1]

. . . I can't resist Priapian jesting on the marriages of my friends. It is such a dreadfully serious thing afterwards, that we ought to joke about it so long as one can.
—Wilkie Collins to Edward Pigott, 2 July 1855[2]

Among Victorian male novelists, Wilkie Collins has been long recognized as one of the most prominent crusaders of women's rights. While Collins's close friend and mentor Charles Dickens makes it apparent in the concluding pages of *Bleak House* that the battle for women's rights—the new "mission" of Mrs. Jellyby—is a complete waste of time, Collins's diatribe throughout his major fiction against the inequities of middle-class marriage, the plight of the fallen woman, and limited employment opportunities is unmistakable. Moreover, Collins creates female characters who defy Victorian myths of femininity: his "equivocal" heroines are independent, bold, assertive, manipulative, and, perhaps most important, willing to act on their own desires, which is why, as Winifred Hughes has pointed out, they were regarded as dangerous threats to the "social and moral fabric of Victorian England."[3] Dorothy Sayers, in fact, claimed that Collins was the "most genuinely feminist of all the nineteenth-century novelists, because he is the only one capable of seeing women without sexual bias and of respecting them as human individuals in their own right and not as 'the ladies, God bless them.'"[4] While Collins's discourse of reform is apparent in his novels, the feminism that Sayers assigned to Collins is called into question in several of his early essays and short stories.

During the nineteenth century, an all-pervasive domestic ideology elided the public, economic function of women and championed their private, biological function as perfect wives and mothers. Women were expected to not only find virtue and reward in fulfilling the practical needs of their husbands and children, but with the middle-class home's new "function" as a safe haven from the ills of the outside world, women were also expected to serve as domestic angels, providing nurturance, inspiration, and spiritual regeneration. This cult of domesticity (and concomitant separate sphere ideology) bolstered by the assumption of an immutable biological difference between the sexes, also served to justify the legal subjection of women in both the public and private realms. Throughout the nineteenth century, sociologists such as Herbert Spencer and biologists such as Patrick Geddes and J. Arthur Thomson sought to delineate and justify gendered social spheres through the application of biological principles. Such scientific explanations, according to Jill Conway negated any "guilt to be felt over the inferior position of women. It was a function of natural laws which operated well beyond the boundaries of human society."[5] In fact, at mid-century, a married woman's body was in theory the property of her husband. Under the law of coverture, married women had no rights or existence apart from their husbands: the Common Law of England sanctioned a husband's control of his wife's property, income, and body, and his absolute custody of their children. Sir William Blackstone explained in his *Commentaries on the Laws of England* that in marriage, "the very being or legal existence of the woman is suspended or at least incorporated or consolidated into that of the husband, under whose wing, protection, and cover she performs everything, and she is therefore called in our law a feme covert."[6] While attitudes toward divorce began to change throughout the nineteenth century, marriage (at least among the middle class) was considered a public and indissoluble contract which could only be terminated by death, although ironically, under common law, a woman died "a kind of civic death" when she married.[7]

It was not until the 1850s, when many cases of domestic abuse became a matter of public record, that public debates and attempts to reform the laws governing married women's property and laws pertaining to divorce took place. Despite the efforts of Victorian feminists, including Caroline Norton, Barbara Leigh Smith, and some of the more liberal Ministers of Parliament, the promise of any kind of legal autonomy for wives remained far on the horizon. The Married Woman's Property Bill was defeated in 1856[8] and the Divorce and Matrimonial Causes Act, which did, in fact, become law in 1857, did not mark any kind of significant advance; rather, the law simply transferred jurisdiction over divorce from the Church of England to the civil courts and established more specific grounds for the procedure. The basis for a husband's petition could simply be adultery, while a wife who sought a divorce had to prove more aggravating matrimonial offenses in addition to adultery. While there was a clear double standard working here, the social stigma and exorbitant costs associated with divorce proceedings prevented most middle-class men and women who were trapped in unhappy marriages from pursuing any kind of legal action.

It was only following the defeat of the married women's property bill that Wilkie Collins brought attention to the appallingly compromised status of married women. In *The Woman in White* (1859-50) and *No Name* (1862), for example, Collins dramatizes how women not only lose their property, but their very identity, when they marry. Indeed, marital strife, domestic horror, and the wrongs of English wives are the centerpiece of most of Collins's sensation novels. Yet, in the 1850s, at the very height of the public debates over the institution of marriage and the respective legal rights of husbands and wives, Collins would appear to have remained silent. But he did not. Collins in fact had much to say about the institution of marriage in the essays and short stories he contributed to Dickens's journal *Household Words* during this time.[9] However, unlike his later novels where he focuses his attention (and sympathies) on the victimization of wives by their husbands, Collins instead lashes out against the victimization of husbands by their wives. In doing so, albeit anonymously,[10] he offers another dimension to these public debates by exploding the myth of conjugal felicity and exposing the domestic sphere as the site of diminished masculinity.

For all the legal advantages that church- and state-sanctioned marriage offered Victorian men, their commitment to domestic life was far more problematic than historically presumed. Though "it was entirely accepted by the vast majority of the population that the central event in any woman's life was marriage,"[11] it was considered a man's "duty" to marry, to support and protect his home, and to superintend his family. Unmarried men were to be just as pitied as unmarried women in Victorian England because, according to Judith Flanders, they were "living only half a life."[12] Indeed, John Tosh argues that not only was domesticity "essentially a nineteenth-century invention," but the domestic sphere was seen as absolutely central to masculinity. For men, "to form a household, to exercise authority over dependants, and to shoulder the responsibility of maintaining and protecting them – these things set the seal of a man's gender identity."[13] This was, in fact, corroborated by the 1851 Census

Report which stated: "The possession of an entire house, is, it is true, strongly desired by every Englishman; for it throws a sharp, well-defined circle round his family and hearth – the shrine of his sorrows, joys, and meditations This feeling, as it is natural, is universal."[14] Despite its professed "naturalness" and "universality," domesticity demanded a complicated and not necessarily uncontested code of conduct for men.

Collins not only takes issue with the widespread belief that a complete transition to manhood depended on marriage, but views compulsory marriage and domesticity as compromising, rather than constructing, a masculine ideal. In his varied contributions to *Household Words*, Collins calls attention to the ways in which masculinity was under siege within the domestic sphere. In his critique of the Victorian marriage imperative (and the social construction of manliness), Collins unveils the hitherto unacknowledged figure of the *homme covert*: the man who loses his freedom and autonomy within the institution of marriage. In "Bold Words by a Bachelor," an article that appeared in Dickens's weekly in 1856, Collins wrote "the general idea of the scope and purpose of the Institution of Marriage is a miserably narrow one."[15] While Collins begins his article by good-naturedly chastising wives for estranging husbands from their old male friends, his accusations gradually take on a more serious tone and with more far-reaching implications. The domestic sphere, according to Collins, is the site of insularity and estrangement, which not only alienates men as husbands and fathers, but also wrongly prioritizes familial responsibility over social responsibility. Once a man marries and becomes "settled"—"a model of all the virtues of life, in the estimation of some people"[16]—he suffers, in effect, a different kind of coverture or social incarceration. His "best virtues"—his love, care, and protection of humanity—are "selfishly" enclosed (or covered over) within the bourgeois domestic sphere. In other words, the masculine ideal in the public sphere was fundamentally opposed to the masculine ideal in the private sphere.

According to Tosh, "[b]y elevating the claims of wife and mother far above other ties, domesticity undermined the tradition of a vigorous associational life with other men, and imposed a new constraint on men's participation in the public sphere."[17] To be a paragon of domestic masculine virtue—to provide for his family and set an example as a capable, dependable husband and father—often meant sacrificing one's responsibilities to the larger, public good, thus engendering a kind of social emasculation. Collins demands readers to consider whether "there [can] be a lower idea of Marriage than the idea which makes it, in fact, an institution for the development of selfishness on a large and respectable scale."[18] Such an assault on humanistic potential is a grave offence: it is a "mischievous error in principle of narrowing the practice of social virtues, in married people, to themselves and their children" only. Instead of "depriv[ing] the bachelor of the sole claim he has left to social recognition and pre-eminence,"[19] marriage, according to Collins's narrator must be reconstituted to a higher ideal:

> The social advantages which it is fitted to produce ought to extend beyond one man and one woman, to the circle of society in which they move. The light of its beauty must not be shut up within the four walls which enclose the parents and the family, but must flow out into the world.[20]

While "Bold Words" calls for a reappraisal of man's duties within the home, Collins articulates highly ambivalent feelings toward middle-class wives, those so-called angelic beings, in his 1857 *Household Words* article "Mrs. Badgery." Masquerading as entertaining satire, this litany of complaints by a cranky old bachelor who is insensitive to a grieving widow is soon revealed as ill-tempered misogyny. Tosh points out that "for most of the nineteenth century home was widely held to be a man's place, not only in the sense of being his possession or fiefdom, but also as the place where his deepest needs were met" by his wife.[21] Consider, for example, the following lines from Coventry Patmore's poetic celebration of the angel in the house:

> Man must be pleased; but him to please
> Is woman's pleasure; down the gulf
> Of his condoled necessities
> She casts her best, she flings herself.
> How often flings for nought, and yokes
> Her heart to an icicle or whim,
> Whose each impatient word provokes
> Another, not from her, but him;
> . . . . .
> At any time, she's still his wife,
> Dearly devoted to his arms;
> She loves with love that cannot tire.[22]

Collins's sympathies, however, do not lie with the wives who are expected to live up to such an impossible ideal. For Collins, the idealized wife, whose sole purpose in life is to minister to her husband's every need, emotional and practical, is no helpmate at all, but rather a domestic oppressor. In "Mrs. Badgery" Collins issues a dire warning to single men of the dangers of such wives in his desperate plea for reform of "an entirely new kind"—legal protection for both married and unmarried men from society's "Gorgons": "Is there any law in England which will protect me from Mrs. Badgery?"[23]

As Collins's bachelor-narrator recounts the particulars of his unrelenting persecution by the widow who formerly occupied his new house, he implicitly holds those grotesque angelic helpmates—"young or old, dark or fair, handsome or ugly"—responsible for killing their husbands. His bachelor is quick to dispel any notion that Mrs. Badgery might have marital designs on him: "she should not think of marrying me, even if I asked her," he explains. Despite his "large circle of acquaintance," the bachelor-narrator claims that not only had he never met Mr. Badgery, he had "never heard of him in [his] life."[24] Marriage apparently had completely subsumed Mr. Badgery in both life and death. And even though we are never informed directly of the nature of Mr. Badgery's death, Collins suggests that in Mrs. Badgery's complete and overwhelming devotion to her husband, her attentions were the unwitting cause of his death. Indeed, the bachelor describes how in his involuntary role as surrogate husband, he can find neither freedom nor autonomy in his own home. Rather, he is reduced to state of paralysis, suffocation, silence: "I could go nowhere, look nowhere, do nothing, say nothing, all that day, without bringing the widowed incubus in the crape garments down upon me immediately."[25]

While Mrs. Badgery insists on making the bachelor "as well acquainted with Mr. Badgery's favorite notions and habits as [he was] with my own," details such as he "was singularly particular about his shaving-water" and "was difficult to please about his linen"[26] reveal that the angel-wife proved far from adequate to her husband's needs. No matter how much she tries to comfort him, she is in danger of failing. In casting Mrs. Badgery as a domestic grotesque, rather than a paragon of moral virtue, Collins exposes the dangers that lurk behind the promise of marital bliss. Indeed, "Where is the man to be found who can lay his hand on his heart and honestly say that he ever really pitied the sorrows of a Gorgon? Search through the whole surface of the globe, and you will discover human phenomena of all sorts; but you will not find that man."[27]

Collins continues his diatribe against the angel myth in "A Shockingly Rude Article" (1858) in which he assumes the persona of a "charming woman" who challenges male writers to completely dispense with the depiction of overly sentimentalized female characters in their fiction. With the disclaimer that she is *not* an advocate of the rights of women—presumably, that is part of her charm[28]—the narrator calls upon those writers to kill the angel in the house (and the prevailing domestic ideology) and represent women as they actually are: "What in the world, do they mean by representing us as so much better, and so much prettier, than we really are?"[29] While Collins's inclination to kill the idealized angel in the house long preceded Virginia Woolf's dictum, his intention (his striving for authenticity and verisimilitude) is not as liberating as we might be inclined to think. In attacking the prevailing stereotypes of women in fiction (and encouraging fellow writers to do the same), Collins takes a misogynistic turn in substituting the myth of feminine virtue for the "reality" of feminine vice.

Three years earlier, in fact, at the height of the marriage debates, Collins presented his version of the "killer-angel" in his short story "The Dream Woman." Originally published in the special Christmas issue of *Household Words* in 1855, [30] "The Dream Woman" is a cautionary tale warning men of the dangers of marriage. It is the story of unlucky Isaac Scatchard, an honest and humble ostler who has never had the "good fortune" to marry or to secure stable employment, the two primary markers of Victorian manhood. On the eve of his fortieth birthday, he is forced to seek lodging at an isolated roadside inn. That night Isaac is abruptly roused from his slumber by a "strange shivering" that courses through his body and by "a dreadful sinking pain at the heart." At the foot of his bed stands a fair, flaxen-haired woman staring intently at him with a knife clasped in her hand. While her physical appearance deliberately connotes Victorian innocence and purity, Collins disrupts the prevailing stereotype of feminine virtue by presenting a figure suggestive of monstrous feminine depravity. "Stricken speechless with terror" and cowering in his bed, Isaac manages to evade her repeated attempts to stab him. As the flame on his candle flickers out, so does Isaac's manhood; though the apparition of the woman disappears Isaac is left screaming out for help in the dark.[31] The next morning, Isaac is left wondering whether the fair woman with the knife was "the creature of a dream, or that other creature from the unknown world called among men by the name of ghost?"[32]

Upon his return home the next day, Isaac recounts his dream to his mother who insists on recording every detail, including the date and time of the vision (which just so happens to be the exact date and time of his birth). Seven years later, Isaac literally and figuratively encounters the woman of his dreams. Though purportedly a woman of "lost character," the naïve Isaac is captivated her false charms: "she was kindness itself with him. She never made him feel his inferior capacities and inferior manners. She showed the sweetest anxiety to please him in the smallest trifles."[33] Like the late Mr. Badgery's wife, Rebecca Murdoch is similarly depicted as an incubus, a female monstrosity who "takes possession, not only of his passions, but of his faculties as well. All the mind he had he put into her keeping. She directed him on every point . . ."[34] The so-called "bewitching" of Isaac (a phrase that appears repeatedly in subsequent revised versions of the story), speaks to the ways in which men are coerced into marriage and subsequently rendered powerless. When Isaac introduces his wife-to-be to his mother, Mrs. Scatchard immediately points out (with great alarm) Rebecca's uncanny resemblance to the dream woman. Against his mother's violent protestations, Isaac gives in to his "fatal passion" and marries Rebecca. Isaac's experience of domesticity certainly bears no resemblance to Tosh's description of the Victorian home which was supposed to provide "feelings of nurture, love, and companionship, as well as 'natural forms' of authority and deference."[35] After a brief period of marital bliss, Isaac "wakes from his delusion" to discover his wife—the woman who should embody the ennobling values of home—to be strangely altered in nature: "She grew sullen and contemptuous; she formed acquaintances of the most dangerous kind in defiance of his objections, his entreaties, and his commands; and, worst of all . . . she had grown to be a drunkard."[36] Though Isaac becomes a despondent, "spirit-broken man" in the face of his wife's degradation, he refuses to heed his mother's deathbed advice to escape from the woman who means him mortal harm. Weeks after the funeral of Isaac's mother, Rebecca fulfils the dream prophecy by attacking him in his bed with a knife:

> His eyes opened toward the left-hand side of the bed, and there stood—
> The Dream-Woman again? No! His wife; the living reality, with the
> dream-specter's face, in the dream-specter's attitude; the fair arm up, the
> knife clasped in the delicate white hand.[37]

This image of a woman wielding a knife over her husband while he lies defenseless (a traditionally feminine position) in the bed is evocative of the vagina dentata myth, which highlights the threat that sexual intercourse poses for men. Exposing the horror of the conjugal bed, the "dream woman" is the embodiment of the vagina dentata, which threatens to devour its unsuspecting male victim. She disappears, but Isaac is left in a state of perpetual anxiety that the dream woman will one day return to complete her fatal purpose. While the most dominant images of feminized masculinity in the nineteenth-century have been those of the male aesthete and the homosexual, the emasculated husband, perhaps less visible because of his heterosexual normativity, further challenges the belief that masculinity and manliness are ultimately affirmed in marriage.

Collins's short story "A New Mind," which appeared in *Household Words* in January 1859, presents another depiction of an imperiled husband.[38] While the story appears to register Collins's "first protest against the injustice of the English marriage laws for women,"[39] it also casts an unmistakable pall over the promise of wedded bliss for men. Alongside Collins's sympathetic portrait of the divorced Englishwoman is the somewhat ambiguous story of the wronged husband, the "parson's scruple." The tale opens with a marriage announcement: "On the third instant, at the parish, the Reverend Alfred Carling, Rector of Penliddy, to Emily Harriet, relict of the late Fergus Duncan, Esq., of Glendarn, N. B."[40] It is the first marriage for the middle-aged rector,[41] "a shy, nervous man by nature" and the second for the widow Mrs. Duncan. As a bachelor Mr. Carling had had a very limited social circle, however, after his marriage, he finds that those friends gather round him more "closely and affectionately" than ever before owing to the influence of his new wife:

> Her refinement and gentleness of manner; her extraordinary accomplishments as a musician; her unvarying sweetness of temper, and her quick, winning, womanly intelligence in conversation, charmed every one who approached her.[42]

While this description of the new Mrs. Carling unmistakably draws upon popular definitions of the womanly ideal, her status as "model wife" is compromised by certain "peculiarities of conduct." First, her reaction to Mr. Carling's marriage proposal is completely bereft of love and happiness, Mrs. Duncan responds to the offer of marriage "with an agitation which was almost painful to see." Though she does accept Mr. Carling's hand, she immediately dictates the terms of the wedding and demands that the marriage "be as private as possible." Mr. Carling, "the gentlest and most yielding of men," readily acquiesces to her will and in doing so unwittingly embarks upon his "fatal future." Rather than arousing suspicion, the rector finds his future wife's demand to forego the "ceremony and publicity of a wedding" to be a "positive relief" and following their secret courtship and private nuptials, husband and wife settle into the "enjoyment of their new life." Though "a happier and more admirable married life [had] seldom been witnessed," Collins's "marriage plots" however always revolve around secrecy, duplicity, and criminality. In one scene the rector's wife is seen "working industriously by the blazing fire," the apparent embodiment of the domestic ideal:

> She looked so happy and comfortable—so gentle and charming in her pretty little lace cap, and her warm brown morning-dress, with its bright

cherry-colored ribbons, and its delicate swan's down trimming circling round her neck and nestling over her bosom, that he stooped and kissed her with the tenderness of his bridegroom days.[43]

Despite the image of the domesticated wife at the hearth, the rector's wife harbors a secret that threatens to bring moral and social ruination to her husband. Throughout the narrative, we see the desperate measures that Mrs. Carling takes to prevent her husband from discovering her scandalous secret—that she is not a widow, but in fact, a divorcee. "Since the day when they had first met,

> she had shrunk from the disclosure which she knew but too well would have separated them even at the church door; how desperately she had ought against the coming discovering which threatened to tear her from the bosom she clung to, and to cast her out I to the world with the shadow of her own shame to darken her life to the end.[44]

Her secret is further complicated by the fact that because "she was indebted to the accident of having been married in Scotland, her subsequent divorce—her "release from the tie that bound her to the vilest of husbands"[45]—cannot be recognized under English law. On the one hand, the narrative seems to elicit sympathy for Mrs. Duncan/Carling as the victim of a capricious and unjust law.[46] The rector himself acknowledges, "the deception of which his wife had been guilty was the most pardonable of all concealments of the truth."[47] However, the rector is also cast as another kind of victim. His oppressor is not the Law, but his unlawfully-wedded wife—the duplicitous woman who willfully deceived him and left him vulnerable to moral and social disgrace. Though she wears a "white dress, with a white shawl thrown over her shoulders" the rector now sees in the dark hair that hangs "tangled about her colourless cheeks" his false angel. The woman who should be the moral exemplar of his home "has stained his soul with a deadly sin."[48] Believing, according to his religious precepts, that he has committed adultery, he becomes a kind of fallen man. And like his counterpart, the fallen woman, his abasement is not complete without either being banished from society or being killed off.[49] Collins gives us both: the disgraced rector embarks on a missionary expedition to the South Pacific for the purpose of "separat[ing] him[self] from home and from all its associations," but dies shortly thereafter at sea, a man "broken in body and spirit." His wife meanwhile lives in on "happy oblivion" having reassimilated into a respectable middle-class life "under the tender care of the friends who now protect her."[50]

Thus, although for much of the nineteenth century, marriage was considered to be "a natural progression from youth to manhood," Collins' early texts present an alternate view. And while marriage was assumed to be voluntary, the bachelor, however envied he might be for his freedom from responsibility, was "always in danger of being regarded as less than a man because he had renounced the office of patriarch."[51] Yet as portrayed in "Mrs. Badgery," "The Dream Woman," and "The Parson's Scruple," marriage is not necessarily the guarantor of masculine identity. Rather, these works reveal deep anxieties about the culture of domesticity, representing marriage not only as the destroyer of man's freedom and autonomy, but sometimes even the destroyer of his very life. In "Awful Warning to Bachelors"[52] Collins's renunciation of domesticity is far more pronounced. "The business of courting and marrying," according to his bachelor-narrator is the epitome of masculine degradation; it is "a system of social persecution" that compels the single man to relinquish all that is sacred to him:

> My affectionate tendencies, my grey trousers, my comfortable shooting jacket, my appreciation of time, distance, or fatigue, my bachelor letters, my few connections, my bachelor friends—all must disappear before this devouring Moloch in petticoats. Nothing is left me—nothing but my evening costume and the prospect of being married! [53]

Although this bachelor-narrator is unable to adequately convey in words the extraordinary degree of sympathy he has for the married man, he sounds an optimistic note in his observation that "the new Divorce Court occupies the ground beyond me."

In one of his first non-fiction contributions to *Household Words*, "The Cruise of Tom-tit," Collins emphasizes the drawbacks of domestic life for men and presents a Utopic alternative: bachelorhood. This quasi-travel narrative chronicles a sailing trip to the Scilly Islands that Collins took with a friend in September 1855, and explicitly reprioritizes two longstanding aspects of masculinity: homosociality (regular association with other men) and adventure.

> No man in particular among us is master – no man in particular is servant. The man who can do at the right time, and in the best way, the thing that is most wanted, is always the hero of the situation among us . . . We have no breakfast hour, no dinner hour, no time for rising or going to bed. We have no particular eatables at particular meals. We don't know the day of the month, or the day of the week; and never look at our watches, except when we wind them up . . . We wear each other's coats, smoke each

other's pipes, poach on each other's victuals. We are a happy, dawdling, undisciplined, slovenly lot.[54]

That Collins describes their boat, the "Tomtit," as a "floating castle" has particular import. The adage "an Englishman's home is his castle" enjoyed widespread currency in the 1850s and conveyed a double meaning of possession against all comers, and a place of retreat or refuge. During the course of their adventure, Collins openly rejects the conventions of Victorian manhood with its emphasis on self-control, hard work, responsibility, and resolve. Rather, Mr. Jollins (Collins's persona) proclaims triumphantly, "We have no principles, no respectability, no business, no stake in the country, no knowledge of Mrs. Grundy." Indeed, it is only when men are free from the web of domestic obligations that they can reclaim masculine agency. This point is punctuated in one of the epigraphs to the piece by a "prudent" friend who laments, "If I were only a single man, there is nothing I should like better than to join you. But I have a wife and a family . . ."[55]

In his own life, Collins was emphatically opposed to the stifling conventions of Victorian domestic life and much like his own bachelor-narrators who claim to "have the strongest antipathy to being settled in life,"[56] he retained the social and sexual freedom of a bachelor. Collins lived with two women and chose to marry neither of them, simultaneously maintaining two independent households; in his later years, he circulated the polite fiction that one mistress, Caroline Graves, was his "housekeeper" and when he visited his second mistress, Martha Rudd, with whom he had three children, he assumed the persona of "William Dawson, Barrister." Collins's decision to remain unmarried and not participate in what he regarded as a corrupt social system may have been liberating for him personally. However, even though he stipulated in his will that Caroline Graves and Martha Rudd were to receive an independent income, as mistresses they had no real social standing and the "Dawson" children, born out-of-wedlock as they were, were technically illegitimate. In other words, a flight from domesticity did not hold the same promise of social liberation for women as it did for men. Nevertheless, Collins's professional and personal renunciation of patriarchal privilege was radical, particularly at a time when the avoidance of marriage was not a recognized option for men, nor was bachelorhood an acceptable pattern of life.

Collins continues his celebration of "unprincipled" bachelor life in "The Bachelor Bedroom" an essay he contributed to Dickens's journal *All the Year Round* in 1859.[57] Here Collins takes issue with fictional representations of bachelors as objects of pity, whose so-called misery can only be assuaged in married life:

> The bachelor has been profusely served up on all sorts of literary tables;
> but the presentation of him has been hitherto remarkable for a singularly
> monotonous flavour of matrimonial sauce. We have learned of his
> loneliness, and its remedy, or his solitary position in illness, and its
> remedy; of the miserable neglect of his linen, and its remedy.[58]

As shown in "The Cruise of the Tom-tit," there is another side to
bachelorhood as Collins takes us behind the sacrosanct doors of "the
bachelor bedroom" to show the single man in "a new aspect." Collins's
narrator explains that the "bachelor bedroom" is "the one especial sleeping
apartment in all civilized residences used for the reception of company
which preserves a character of its own." Though these temporary quarters
for single male guests are part of the "civilised residence," a mere glimpse
into this singular habitat reveals a complete disregard for Mrs. Grundy.
Noted for an atmosphere thick with tobacco smoke, contraband bottles and
gasses, and regular midnight parties, the bachelor bedroom unashamedly
"sticks immutably to its own bad character."[59] In his entertaining
descriptions of the "remarkable bachelors" who have "corrupted" Coolcup
House, the hospitable country-seat of Sir John Giles, Collins implicitly
celebrates this scandalous chamber for the freedom and autonomy that it
offers to its occupants. Mr. Bigg, for example, is one bachelor-guest who
to all outward appears is "a man of the world, who can be depended on to
perform any part allotted to him in any society, . . . who has lived among
all ranks and sorts of people." However, once safely ensconced within the
walls of the Bedroom, he becomes the "most incorrigible bachelor on
record. Not only does "a kind of gorgeous slovenliness pervade him from
top to toe" but he becomes "fanatical character, a man possessed of one
fixed idea . . . the real authorship of Junius letters."[60] Mr. Smart is another
single man who finds refuge from the suffocating pretence of middle-class
respectability in the "loose atmosphere of the Bachelor Bedroom." With
the assistance of his fellow bachelors (and a healthy supply of whisky and
water), the man who singularly impressed the other houseguests with "the
serene solemnity of his gentleman[ly] voice, look, manner and costume"
slips easily out of his "close-fitting English envelope": "His moral
sentiments melted like the sugar in this grog; his grammar disappeared
with his write cravat. Wild and lavish generosity suddenly became the
leading characteristic of this once reticent man."[61]
 Another type in the "Bachelor species" is presented in the distinguished
German poet Herr von Muffe who, owing perhaps to his unfamiliarity with
English custom (and institution of the Bachelor Bedroom), does not seek
asylum in this sacred chamber of masculinity, but launches an all-out
assault on the civilized Home.[62] Oblivious to all notions of restraint, the

eminent poet indecorously bear-hugs his startled host and further scandalizes the other dinner guests in a boorish display of excessive drinking, eating, and talking. Collins, however, does not condemn Herr von Muff or his other bachelors for their "uncivilised" behaviour, but instead suggests that the conventions of bourgeois domesticity compel men to a wholly unnatural and suffocating way of life. The excesses of Herr von Muff and the countless other bachelors do, in fact, degrade the gentlemanly ideal and debase the Home as the harbinger of respectability, However, their behind-closed-door exploits actually reaffirm a masculinity that bourgeois domesticity has kept under siege. Like so many modern-day sitcom, "The Bachelor Bedroom" underscores the ways in which domesticity constrains man's "true nature." For Collins, this phenomenon is no cause for alarm, but rather part of his larger commitment to "violate some of the conventionalities of sentimental fiction" in pursuing the "light of Reality."[63]

Clearly Collins's sympathy for the plight of the domesticated male in these early essays and short fiction is a far cry from the feminist agenda that he is lauded for in his later novels. At the same time, we might question how univocal Collins's call for male liberation really was. As a *Household Words* contributor, Collins was required to not only publish anonymously, but also to submit to the strict editorial authority of Dickens.[64] According to Harry Stone, the journal functioned as an instrument of Dickens's will and he "rigidly controlled what was written and how it was written particularly with his "inner staff" (which included among others, Wilkie Collins, John Hollingshead, Percy Fitzgerald, and George Sala).[65] Since the journal was to publish only wholesome fiction and journalism, Dickens insisted that all contributions conform to his strict standards for "family reading." In "A Preliminary Word"[66] which opened the first issue, Dickens described the "mission" of his journal:

> We aspire to live in the Household affections, and to be numbered among the Household thoughts, of our readers. We hope to be the comrade and friend of many thousands of people, of both sexes, and of all ages and conditions, on whose faces we may never look.[67]

According to Catherine Waters, "the purpose and form of the nineteenth-century family magazines [including *Household Words*] was to promote the values of Home: "Women [were] defined as domestic creatures, responsible for creating and maintaining the home, and rearing their children; [while men were] associated with the public sphere, the world of industry and business."[68]

Furthermore, Dickens had conceived of his weekly as a vehicle for middle-class opinion and values and called upon his contributors specifically to embrace "the spirit of reform."[69] To ensure that *Household Worlds* "contained what he desired," Dickens would commission articles by "suggesting topics, distributing source materials, or outlining how particular pieces should be written."[70] The purpose of this policy was "to express the general mind and purpose of the Journal, which is the raising up of those that are down, and the general improvement of our social condition."[71] Given the nature of these editorial policies, Dickens's decision to publish—if not commission—pieces that repeatedly *challenge* the cherished belief in the sanctity of Home in *his* family magazine adds another layer of complexity to his reputation as the prophet of domestic bliss.[72] Throughout his fiction, Dickens was well known for extolling the virtues of domestic life and severely criticizing its absence; however, the disenchantment with the false comforts of home and the marked retreat from marriage that we see in Collins's various contributions calls into question the journal's (and Dickens's) commitment to extolling the "Household affections." At the same time, this discrepancy invites a re-evaluation of the presumed ideological differences between the two men. Though Nayder argues that Collins was always "more willing to challenge the status quo than Dickens,"[73] it is likely that this assault on the virtues of home and hearth was not the entirely the brainchild of Dickens's younger contributor, but rather the "sly scheme" of the "Conductor" himself.[74]

During the 1850s, Dickens was very admiring of his protégé's literary talents and was particularly enthusiastic about the various kinds of contributions Collins might make to his journal.[75] In a letter to his assistant editor W. H. Wills, Dickens remarked

> there are many things, both in the inventive and descriptive way, that [Collins] could do for us if he would like to work in our direction. And I particularly wish him to understand this, and to have every possible assurance conveyed to him that I think so, and that I should particularly like to have his aid.[76]

Dickens was especially pleased when Collins agreed to sign on as a salaried staff writer in 1856, and again noted to Wills how valuable Collins was to *Household Words*: "he is very suggestive, and exceeding quick to take my notions."[77] At that time, Collins also began to collaborate regularly, and almost exclusively with Dickens on several pieces for *Household Words* and *All the Year Round*.[78] Though Dickens did not elaborate on what his "notions" might be, it is entirely possible that Collins's anti-marriage campaign was a collaborative endeavour of another variety. While Dickens was "conducting" the journal in the 1850s, he was in the throes of his own domestic turmoil and was likely quite envious of Thomas Idle's inclination in *The Lazy Tour of Two Idle*

Apprentices[79] to "eat Bride-cake without the trouble of being married, or of knowing anybody in that ridiculous dilemma."[80]

As eyewitness to Dickens's own profound domestic unhappiness, Collins may simply have been attempting to curry favour with his mentor by sympathetically exposing the myth of marital bliss in his contributions.[81] This, however, would be too simplistic a conclusion particularly since Dickens "considered himself personally responsible to the public for the truth and authenticity of every article that went into his periodicals."[82] Indeed, it was Dickens's expressed desire to "circulate the Truth" that compelled him to announce to his readers in 1858 that he was separating from his wife:

> Some domestic trouble of mine, of long-standing, on which I will make no further remark than that it claims to be respected, as being of a sacredly private nature, has lately been brought to an arrangement, which involves no anger or ill-will of any kind.[83]

Though his marriage had been disintegrating for years, Dickens printed this statement in order to squash rumours of his relationship with the young actress Ellen Ternan as well as end speculation about the nature of his relationship with his sister-in-law Georgina Hogarth."[84] Despite Dickens's plea to his readers to respect his privacy, the fallout of this very public disclosure was scandalous. According to one observer, Dickens, the man who was so well known for extolling the redemptive power of Home in his fiction, "committed a grave mistake his telling his readers, how little, after all, he thought of the marriage tie."[85]

However, if the writings of *Household Words* were more "monoymous" than "anonymous" as Douglas Jerrold suggested,[86] then Dickens's opinion of the "marriage noose" had already been hinted at on numerous occasions, in a variety of formats, and with no public outcry. The one contribution to the journal that registers perhaps the greatest antipathy towards marriage is the inset story that Dickens himself contributed anonymously to the fourth part of *The Lazy Tour*. "The Bride's Chamber" is a revenge story in which a diabolical husband holds his unloved wife hostage in her bedroom room ("the bride's chamber") and literally wills her to die until she is no more "than a white wreck . . . with wild eyes." [87] Though the story features a victimized wife, it highlights Dickens's obsession with the ways in which one spouse can be the instrument of another's selfish and destructive will.[88]

It would appear that under the cloak of anonymity, Dickens and Collins could launch their assault on the cult of domesticity that dominated bourgeois Victorian society at mid-century with no public backlash whatsoever. The extent to which their male liberation campaign was in keeping with *Household Words*'s commitment to "the raising up of those that are down, and the general improvement of our social condition"[89] is, however, debatable. Nevertheless, at a time when the majority of men dutifully and unquestioningly embraced marriage, any challenge to the presumed merits of domestic life for men and a call for a reappraisal of bachelorhood as an acceptable lifestyle choice was progressive. In fact, it was not until the later decades of the century, an era marked by imperialism and legal and social gains for women, that a "much keener sense of the drawbacks of domestic life for men was articulated" and middle-class society began to reassess the "advantages" of domesticity.[90] Beyond offering a prescient counter discourse to the ideology of bourgeois domesticity, Dickens and Collins also provided a new context in which to consider the idea of a crisis in masculinity, a crisis which historically has been associated with *fin-de-siècle* Britain and the cultural challenges posed by the New Woman and the homosexual.[91]

Works Cited

Ashley, Robert. *Wilkie Collins.* London: Arthur Barker, 1952.

Auerbach, Nina. *Woman and the Demon: The Life of Victorian Myth.* Cambridge, MA: Harvard University Press, 1982.

Baker, William and Clarke, William C., eds. *The Letters of Wilkie Collins.* 2 vols. New York: Macmillan, 1999.

Collins, Philip. *Dickens: The Critical Heritage.* London: Routledge, 1971.

Collins, Wilkie. "Awful Warning to Bachelors," *Household Words*, 27 March 1858 *http://www.web40571.clarahost.co.uk/wilkie/etext/AwfulWarning.htm.*

—. "The Cruise of the Tom-tit." *Household Words*, 22 December 1855. *http://www.web40571.clarahost.co.uk/wilkie/etext/cruise_plain.htm*

—. "Letter of Dedication," *Basil.* Edited by Dorothy Goldman. Oxford: World Classics, 1990.

—. *My Miscellanies.* New York: Peter Fennon Collier, 1895.

—. *The Queen of Hearts.* New York: Peter Fennon Collier, 1895.

Cook, E.T. and Wedderburn, Alexander, eds. *Works of John Ruskin.* Vol. 14. London 1904.

Dickens, Charles. "A Preliminary Word." *Household Words*, 30 March 1850. http://www.lang.nagoya-u.ac.jp/~matsuoka/CD-HW-Preliminary.html.

—. "The Lazy Tour of Two Idle Apprentices." *Christmas Stories*, edited by Margaret Lane. Oxford: Oxford University Press, 1992.

Davidoff, Lenore and Hall, Catherine. *Family Fortunes: Men and Women of the English Middle Class, 1780-1850.* Chicago: University of Chicago Press, 1987.

Flanders, Judith. *Inside the Victorian Home: A Portrait of Domestic Life in Victorian England.* New York: W.W. Norton, 2004.

Grubb, Gerald. "The Editorial Policies of Charles Dickens." *PMLA* 58.4 (1943): 1110-1124.

Hughes, Winifred. *Maniac in the Cellar: Sensation Novels of the 1860s.* Princeton: Princeton University Press, 1980.

Johnson, Edgar. *Charles Dickens: His Tragedy and Triumph.* 2 vols. New York: Simon and Schuster, 1952.

Nayder, Lillian. *Unequal Partners: Charles Dickens, Wilkie Collins, and Victorian Authorship.* Ithaca and London: Cornell University Press, 2002.

Patmore, Coventry. *The Angel in the House: The Betrothal.* New York: E.P. Dutton, 1876.

Peters, Catherine. *The King of Inventors.* London: Secker and Warburg, 1991.

Sayers, Dorothy L. Introduction to *The Moonstone,* by Wilkie Collins. London: Dent, 1944.

Schlicke, Paul. *Oxford Companion to Charles Dickens.* Oxford and New York: Oxford University Press, 1999.

Showalter, Elaine. *Sexual Anarchy: Gender and Culture at the Fin de Siècle.* New York: Viking, 1990.

Smith, Susan Kingsley. *Sex and Suffrage in Britain, 1860-1914.* Princeton: Princeton University Press, 1987.

Stone, Harry. *The Night Side of Dickens: Cannibalism, Passion, Necessity.* Columbus: Ohio State University Press, 1994.

Stone, Harry, ed. *The Uncollected Writings of Charles Dickens, Household Words 1850-1859.* Bloomington: Indiana University Press, 1968.

Storey, Graham and Tillotson, Kathleen, eds. *The Letters of Charles Dickens.* Vols. I-XII. Oxford: Clarendon Press, 1965-2002.

Thomas, Deborah. *Dickens and the Short Story.* Philadelphia: University of Pennsylvania Press, 1982.

Tosh, John. *A Man's Place: Masculinity and the Middle-Class Home in Victorian England.* New Haven and London: Yale University Press, 1999.

Vicinus, Martha. *Suffer and Be Still: Women in the Victorian Age.* Bloomington: Indiana University Press, 1972,

Waters, Catherine. *Dickens and the Politics of the Family*. Cambridge: Cambridge University Press, 1997.

Wullschlager, Jackie. *Hans Christian Andersen: The Life of a Story Teller*. Chicago: University of Chicago Press, 2002.

Notes

[1] Baker and Clark, eds., *The Letters of Wilkie Collins*, 1:95.

[2] Ibid, 1:140.

[3] Hughes, *Maniac in the Cellar: Sensation Novels of the 1860s*, 46. Dickens invariably removes his fallen women from society, transporting them to Australia (as he does Little Em'ly), or killing them off brutally (as he does Lady Dedlock).

[4] Sayers, introduction to *The Moonstone*, viii.

[5] Vicinus, *Suffer and Be Still*, 141.

[6] Quoted in Smith, *Sex and Suffrage in Britain, 1860-1914*, 27.

[7] Davidoff and Hall, *Family Fortunes: Men and Women of the English Middle Class, 1780-1850*, 200.

[8] It was not until the Married Women's Property Acts of 1870 and 1882 that personal property was gradually extended and granted to married women.

[9] *Household Words* was a weekly family magazine which published from 1850-1859, topical journalism, essays, short fiction, and poetry and later, novels in serial.

[10] All contributors to *Household Words*, including Collins, were required to publish anonymously. None of the pieces were signed but instead published under the masthead "Conducted by Charles Dickens" for the purpose, Dickens claimed, of representing the collective opinion of the staff.

[11] Flanders, *Inside the Victorian Home*, 214.

[12] Ibid., 214

[13] Tosh, *A Man's Place: Masculinity and the Middle-Class Home in Victorian England*, 4.

[14] Census 1851: Report, *British Parliamentary Papers*, Population, VI, xxxvi.

[15] Collins, "Bold Words by a Bachelor," *My Miscellanies*, 530. Hereafter cited as "Bold Words." *My Miscellanies* is the only collection of Collins's non-fiction to be published during his lifetime. The volume, which first appeared in 1863, contained a preface and twenty-five essays drawn from his contributions to *Household Words* and *All The Year Round*.

[16] Ibid.

[17] Tosh, *A Man's Place*, 5.

[18] Collins, "Bold Words," 530.

[19] Ibid., 531.

[20] Ibid., 531.

[21] Tosh, *A Man's Place*, 1.

[22] Patmore, *The Angel in the House: The Betrothal*, 135. The poem was first published in 1854 and then underwent several revisions through 1862.

[23] Collins, "Mrs. Badgery," in *My Miscellanies*, 252.

[24] Ibid.

[25] Ibid. 262.

[26] Ibid., 63, 261.

[27] Ibid. 258

[28] Sayers notes that Collins "disliked what he knew of [feminist movements]" (viii).

[29] Collins, "A Shockingly Rude Article," 127.

[30] Collins later expanded this supernatural story for inclusion in *The Queen of Hearts* (1859) as "Brother Morgan's Story of the Dream Woman." Collins then significantly lengthened the story as a public reading text for his American Lecture Tour of 1873-74 and reprinted yet another revised version of "The Dream Woman" in *The Frozen Deep and Other Stories* (1874).

[31] In *Woman and the Demon: The Life of Victorian Myth*, Nina Auerbach explores the counter myth of woman as demonic, polymorphous, and dangerous. In Collins's second novel, *Basil* (1852), two women—one fair, one dark—appear before Basil in a dream. Though the fair woman beckons to him, he is drawn into the arms of the dark woman. It is this dark woman—whose "eyes were lustrous and fascinating, as the eyes of serpent," rather than the fair one, who becomes his wife and the source of his degradation.

[32] Collins, "Brother Morgan's Story of The Dream-Woman," 146. Hereafter cited as "The Dream-Woman."

[33] Ibid. 154. In fact, the narrator warns against the "tyranny of the new ruling passion," particularly for those men "previously insensible to the influence of women [and who] form attachments later in life" (153).

[34] Collins, "The Dream-Woman," 154.

[35] Tosh, *A Man's Place,* 33.

[36] Collins, "The Dream-Woman," 159.

[37] Ibid. 165.

[38] Collins republished this story under the title "Brother Owen's Story of The Parson's Scruple" in *The Queen of Hearts* (1859).

[39] Ashley, *Wilkie Collins,* 56. Catherine Peters suggests that the story was based on the ten-year-long "matrimonial wrangle" of Frances Dickinson a friend of Collins and actress who performed briefly in *The Frozen Deep* in 1857. Dickinson had left her husband in 1845 on grounds of adultery and cruelty and though she obtained a divorce in the ecclesiastical Court of Arches, she lost custody of her children and was prevented from remarrying. It was not until 1855 that Dickinson was granted a Scotch divorce and became "an entirely free woman." *The King of Inventors,*" 173).

[40] Collins, "Brother Owen's Story of The Parson's Scruple," 351. Hereafter cited as "The Parson's Scruple."

[41] He thus invites some comparison with Isaac Scatchard who found "his heart [sic] opening unworthily to a new influence at that middle time of life" ("The Dream Woman," 153).

[42] Collins, "The Parson's Scruple," 356.

[43] Ibid., 358.

[44] Ibid., 373.

[45] Ibid., 371.

[46] Collins explores the victimization of wives and the injustices of existing marriage laws in *The Woman in White* (1860), *Man and Wife* (1873), and *The Black Robe* (1881).

[47] Ibid., 375.

[48] Ibid., 372. According to Tosh, "Victorian men expected their homes to stand for a moral vision of life which would affect their own sensibilities for the better . . . [and] custodians of this moral flame were the women of the home . . . most often the wife, who was seen as owing a sacred duty to her husband in this respect" (55).

[49] Interestingly, the year before Collins published "A New Mind" ("The Parson's Scruple"), his good friend, the artist Augustus Egg exhibited a trilogy of paintings, *Past and Present* at the Royal Academy depicting the domestic havoc brought on by a fallen wife. The moment in Collins's story when the rector discovers his wife's secret seems to echo the first painting in Egg's triptych in which the husband sits in shock holding in his hand a letter revealing his wife's infidelity. Collins registers the same kind of mortal dread in Mr. Carling as he reads the newspaper article that betrays his wife's secret: "his mind reeled back; and a deadly faintness came over him. There was water on a side table – he drank a deep draught of it – roused himself – seized on a newspaper with both hands, as if it had been a living thing that could feel the desperate resolution of his grasp – and read the article through, sentence by sentence, word by word." Both painting and story cast the husband as the ultimate victim of his wife's transgressions. As John Ruskin described Egg's triptych, "In the central piece the husband discovers his wife's infidelity; he dies five years afterwards. The two lateral pictures represent the same moment of night a fortnight after his death." (See *Works of John Ruskin*, Cook and Wedderburn eds, vol.14, 166).

[50] Ibid., 376.

[51] Tosh, *A Man's Place,* 172, 108.

[52] Collins, "Awful Warning to Bachelors," *Household Words*, http://www.web40571.clarahost.co.uk/wilkie/etext/AwfulWarning.htm.   Hereafter cited as "Awful Warning," n.p.

[53] Ibid.

[54] Collins, "The Cruise of the Tom-tit," *Household Words,* http://www.web40571.clarahost.co.uk/wilkie/etext/cruise_plain.htm.

[55] Ibid.

[56] Collins, "Awful Warning."

[57] *All the Year Round* was Dickens's successor journal to *Household Words*.

[58] Collins, "The Bachelor Bedroom," in *My Miscellanies*, 295.

[59] Ibid.

[60] Ibid., 298-300.

[61] Ibid., 306-7.

[62] Herr von Muff is a parody of Hans Christian Anderson who "was as perfectly regardless of the ordinary forms of social life; his personal habits were exceedingly careless, not to say repulsive; he was not agreeable as a next neighbor; or as observed from over-the-way, at a dinner-table, for he ate voraciously, and was decidedly a dirty-feeder" (Quoted in Jackie Wullschlager, *Hans Christian Andersen: The Life of a Story Teller*, 423).

[63] Collins, "Letter of Dedication," *Basil*, xxxvi.

[64] As a writer who was coming up in the literary world, Collins always resented the fact that he was not credited with authorship.

[65] *The Uncollected Writings of Charles Dickens, Household Words 1850-1859*, Stone, ed., 2 vols., 1:15. Only in the case of fiction, Stone notes, did Dickens occasionally allow for some "deviation from his own agenda."

[66] *Household Words*, 30 March 1850 (http://www.lang.nagoya-u.ac.jp/ ~matsuoka/CD-HW-Preliminary.html. Accessed January 31, 2008.

[67] Paul Schlicke estimates that *Household Word's* normal weekly circulation was somewhere in the number of 38,500, although its initial numbers sold over 100,000 copies and the Extra Christmas Numbers sold over 80,000. *Oxford Companion to Charles Dickens*, 282.

[68] Waters, *Dickens and the Politics of the Family*, 21,18.

[69] Paul Schlicke notes that at least one-third of *Household Words* was dedicated to publicizing and debating urgent social issues. The journal actively participated for example "in campaigns to improve urban sanitation and housing, establish free elementary and industrial schools for the poor, reduce preventable factory accidents, establish a feasible system of urban burial, and bring about changes in penological practice" in addition to call for the reform of other myriad abuses and corruption (284).

[70] Stone notes that staff members particularly (and this would have included Collins) were constantly receiving books, pamphlets, clipping, and digests, together with a note from Dickens suggesting they might find an article therein . . . . [or] on still other occasions he dashed off lists of subjects with suggestions for assignment and treatment (35). At times, Dickens even went so far as to censor submissions that he felt were not appropriate for his middle-class readership. In 1852 Dickens refused to publish Collins's story "Mad Monkton" because he felt that the story's treatment of "the horrible affliction of hereditary insanity" was not suitable for a family magazine. In another case, Dickens asked his assistant editor W.H. Wills to review one of Collins's articles for "anything in it that may be sweeping and unnecessarily offensive to the middle class. [Collins] has a tendency to overdo that—and such a subject gives him a fresh temptation" (Dickens to W.H. Wills, 24 September 1858 (*The Letters of Charles Dickens*, 8:669; hereafter cited as *Letters of Charles Dickens*.)

[71] *Letters of Charles Dickens*, 6:22.

[72] The *Saturday Review* for example lauded Dickens's "unvarying respect for the sanctity of home and the goodness of women" ("The Death of Mr. Dickens,"

Saturday Review, 11 June 1870; reprinted in Philip Collins, *Dickens: The Critical Heritage*, 539). A number of critics, however, have since noted that there is a clear discrepancy between Dickens's image as "the quintessential celebrant of the hearth" and his fictional preoccupation with dysfunctional families" (See Waters for an examination of this disjunction and well as a probing discussion of the complexities of the ideology of domesticity, 1-27.)

[73] Nayder, *Unequal Partners: Charles Dickens, Wilkie Collins, and Victorian Authorship*, 6.

[74] "A Shy Scheme" is the title of an essay that Collins wrote for *Household Words* (20 March 1858) describing the unease—"the loss of self-possession"—a man faces in proposing marriage. The narrator calls for a reform of "the oppressive Laws of Courtship" and for a "Bachelor's Handbook" to alleviate partially the disease of proposing.

[75] Dickens was already well-established as a major novelist and the editor of *Household Words* in 1851 when he met Collins, who was himself just embarking on his career as a serious writer. At that time, Collins had written only the *Memoirs of William Collins, Esq., R.A.*, *Rambles Beyond Railways*, and the unpublished novel, *Antonina*. Collins soon became a good friend and traveling companion of the older author, and wrote for *Household Worlds* and then *All the Year Round*, contributing short stories and articles on a wide variety of subjects from 1852-1861.

[76] Dickens to W.H. Wills, February 1853 (*Letters VII*, 23).

[77] Dickens to W.H. Wills, 16 September 1856 (*Letters VIII*, 188).

[78] These include *The Wreck of the Golden Mary* (1856), *The Lazy Tour of Two Idle Apprentices* (1857), *The Perils of Certain English Prisoners* (1857), *No Thoroughfare* (1867), as well as several essays and reviews. In her study of the Dickens-Collins partnership, Nayder points out that these collaborative works are particularly noteworthy for the ways in which the privilege male bonding (6). Nayder specifically places their working relationship within the context of the Victorian publishing industry in within the context of Victorian labor and political debates.

[79] *The Lazy Tour* was a five-part travel narrative composed jointly by Dickens and Collins was published in *Household Words* in 1857.

[80] Dickens, *The Lazy Tour of Two Idle Apprentices*, in *Christmas Stories*, 721.

[81] In *The Lazy Tour*, Thomas Idle (Collins's persona) admonishes Francis Goodchild (Dickens's persona) to avoid falling in love: "It's trouble enough to fall out of [love], once you're in it, ... so I keep out of it altogether. It would be better for you if you did the same" (665).

[82] Grubb, "The Editorial Policies of Charles Dickens," 1110.

[83] [Charles Dickens], "Personal," *Household Words*, 12 June 1858; reprinted in *The Uncollected Writings of Charles Dickens, Household Words 1850-1859*, 2:586.

[84] Stone writes, "[Dickens] was convinced that the whole world was gossiping about his difficulties and wanted desperately to justify himself before the world. He felt he must publicly acknowledge his separation and at the same time scotch all rumors" (23).

[85] Quoted in Edgar Johnson, *Charles Dickens: His Tragedy and Triumph*. 2 vols., 2: 924. Furthermore, Dickens was greatly angered when his publishers, Bradbury and Evans, refused to reprint his statement in their journal *Punch*. After a successful suit in the Court of Chancery over control of the journal, Dickens discontinued *Household Words* and incorporated it into his new weekly *All the Year Round*.

[86] Ibid., 704. Jerrold, who was described by Collins as "the first and dearest friends of my literary life," refused to be a contributor to *Household Words*.

[87] Just a few weeks after Dickens wrote "The Bride's Chamber," he separated from his wife Catherine by ordering the door that connected his dressing-room to her bedroom be boarded up. Stone and others have noted that "The Bride's Chamber" is the literary manifestation of Dickens's decision to end his marriage. See Harry Stone, *The Night Side of Dickens: Cannibalism, Passion, Necessity*, 286-300 and Deborah Thomas, *Dickens and the Short*, 113, for the biographical implications of "The Bride's Chamber."

[88] Stone similarly describes the story as demonstrating "the havoc that destruction wreaks in the soul of the wilful destroyer" and finds this theme prototypical in Dickens's subsequent novels Although Stone sees the "misuse of the human will" in Dickens's male characters, clearly a case can be made for many of his female characters (See *The Night Side of Dickens*).

[89] *The Letters of Charles Dickens*, 6: 22.

[90] See Tosh, *A Man's Place*, 72-94.

[91] See Showalter, *Sexual Anarchy: Gender and Culture at the Fin de Siècle*, 1-18.

CHAPTER EIGHT

READING THE INSTITUTION: CHARLOTTE BRONTË'S VISUAL LITERACY AND SITES/SIGHTS OF RESISTANCE IN *SHIRLEY*

ERIC G. LORENTZEN

Shirley is a book about books. More specifically, Brontë's novel deals with the different varieties of marginalizing pedagogy and patriarchal literacy that were deployed in the nineteenth-century to discipline, contain, and compartmentalize women. Brontë's treatments of traditional education and literacy, in fact, reflect her serious trepidation about the ways in which these socializing forces work to situate female readers. Her primary fear of the dangers that accompanied book-learning was the problematic socialization of women by male systems of education and the dominant literary narratives that supported such systems. She noticed, in particular, how fictional texts had real-world consequences for women, by legislating passivity, meekness, silence, and male-authored definitions of virtue, morality, and the "woman's place." In response, Brontë experimented with an alternative literacy that allowed women ways of knowing that might circumvent the hegemony of more conventional textuality. In each of her novels, and especially in *Shirley*, she developed a self-fashioning pedagogy through visual literacy which consisted of reading the institutions at the center of patriarchal society, in order to learn how dominant ideology (and, hence, power) was produced and maintained. Brontëan heroines perfect the literacy of reading society and its members, and develop a new epistemology based on a course of watching, seeing, and knowing.

Throughout *Shirley*, Brontë develops the theme of conventional education as a dangerous tool employed for the purposes of social disciplining, an especially limiting tactic which ensured the marginalization and subordination of Victorian women. Perhaps the most obvious target for these disciplinary tactics in the novel proves to be Caroline Helstone.

During her lessons with her "preceptress," Hortense Moore, she constantly is subjected to narratives that seek to keep her in her place, in terms of her gender, her class, and her age. As Hortense explains the curriculum to her brother, the normalizing function of her lessons becomes palpable:

> I sometimes, you are aware, make her read French poetry by way of practice in pronunciation. She has, in the course of her lessons, gone through much of Corneille and Racine, in a very steady, sober spirit, such as I approve. Occasionally she showed,   indeed, a degree of languor in the perusal of those esteemed authors, partaking rather of apathy than sobriety, and apathy is what I cannot tolerate in those who have the benefit of my instructions; besides, one should not be apathetic in studying standard works.[1]

No wonder that Caroline's very steady, sober spirit remains apathetic to these esteemed authors; Brontë makes it clear that Hortense narrowly defines the Canon which will constitute proper reading for her young charge, guarding against any "substandard" works that might in some way challenge these patriarchal "standard works." Above all, Hortense conceives of herself and her pedagogical mission as a guardian of proper feeling, as a transmitter of proper values.

Brontë punctuates the rote quality of this civilizing educational activity by leaving no room for Caroline to pursue any measure of originality or free thought in her lessons. As Hortense remarks about her own pedagogical praxis, "she is fortunate in a preceptress. I will give her a system, a method of thought, a set of opinions; I will give her the perfect control and guidance of her feelings."[2] This kind of cultural hegemony is quite common in the era in which Brontë is writing, and perhaps even more prevalent in the earlier time period in which the novel is set. (Today, we might equate this model with Paulo Freire's banking concept of education.) In the early nineteenth century, this corrective philosophy of education predominated when teaching readers such as Caroline; already marginalized by other social markers, her lessons police and contain any possible deviance through the most blatant disciplining. *Shirley*'s omniscient narrator leaves no doubt about Hortense's corrective philosophy in this case, allowing readers to pursue their own visual literacy with glances both over the shoulder and into the mind. We find ourselves

> now looking over Caroline's exercise or hearing her repetition-lesson. However faultlessly these tasks were achieved, she never commended: it was a maxim with her that praise is inconsistent with a teacher's dignity, and that blame, in more or less unqualified measure, is indispensable to it.

> She thought incessant reprimand, severe or slight, quite necessary to the maintenance of her authority; and if no possible error was to be found in the lesson, it was the pupil's carriage, or air, or dress, or mien, which required correction.[3]

In this "intellectual" process authority is maintained via correction, and with Hortense as preceptress, *Shirley* also "critiques the female subject's complicity in a system that both marginalizes and contains her."[4]

Along with the dangerously disciplinary functions of Caroline's education, Brontë questions the payoff of female "accomplishments." Robert Moore asks an apt question of his cousin: "What life are you destined for, Caroline? What will you do with your French, drawing, and other accomplishments when they are acquired?"[5] Caroline knows all too well for what kind of life she is destined—the domestic kind of life void of any active possibility, the type which Jane denounces in Brontë's earlier novel. As in *Jane Eyre*, we find the pedagogy of the catechistic method surface as a constant reminder of the connection between power and instruction. Helstone's use of this method with his niece contributes to the network of lessons that push Caroline unwillingly into a particular subject position she neither values nor desires:

> "And have you learned your lessons?"
> "Yes."
> "And made a shirt?"
> "Only part of one."
> "Well, that will do: stick to the needle—learn shirt-making and gown-making, and pie-crust-making, and you'll be a clever woman some day."[6]

As in the earlier novel, this educational method seems omnipresent, with even the sympathetic Mr. Hall catechizing the Farren children after he has done their parents a charitable service. Helstone, on the other hand, relishes his role as moral guardian, seeking to extend his pedagogical and political influence beyond his own niece to a number of women in his parish. When Shirley arrives at Briarfield, he attempts to assume the role of her master: "you shall be my pupil in both politics and religion: I'll teach you sound doctrine on both points."[7] Of course, he has had someone anticipate him in this endeavor; Mrs. Pryor has done the "prior" teaching of Shirley in ways that sound remarkably similar to Caroline's course of study with Hortense Moore. As Shirley recognizes, her own educational experience has been a matter of discipline as well: "my governess . . . of all the high and rigid Tories, she is queen; of all the staunch churchwomen, she is chief. I have been well drilled both in theology and history, I assure you, Mr. Helstone."[8] To a certain extent, both Caroline and Shirley do find strategies of reading that allow them to resist this disciplinary education, as we will see in the final section of this discussion of *Shirley*.

Brontë, however, provides the ultimate foils for these resisting young women, and her treatment of the creatures that this conventional education produces, when successful, is absolutely scathing. Her portrayal of the Sympson daughters reads like a summary list of the dangerous effects of a conventional female education:

> The daughters were an example to their sex. . . . They had been educated faultlessly. All they did was well done. History, and the most solid books, had cultivated their minds. Principles and opinions they possessed which could not be mended. More exactly-regulated lives, feelings, manners, habits, it would have been difficult to find anywhere. They knew by heart a certain young-ladies'-school-room code of laws on language, demeanour, &c.; themselves never deviated from its curious little pragmatical provisions; and they regarded with secret, whispered horror, all deviations in others. The Abomination of Desolation was no mystery to them: they had discovered that unutterable Thing in the characteristic others call Originality. Quick were they to recognize the signs of this evil; and wherever they saw its trace—whether in look, word, or deed; whether they read it in the fresh, vigorous style of a book, or listened to it in interesting, unhackneyed, pure, expressive language—they shuddered—they recoiled: danger was above their heads—peril about their steps. What was this strange Thing? Being unintelligible, it must be bad. Let it be denounced and chained up.[9]

This stunning passage forms the crux of Brontë's attack on conventional literacy and education in *Shirley*. The dangers to be feared fall into two main categories. First, "the exactly-regulated lives, feelings, manners, [and] habits" are essentially, politically, socially, and culturally "pragmatical provisions." Education and literacy coalesce in the "most solid books," such as the master narratives of history, which Brontë suggests *create* a certain truth rather than merely informing readers about an unequivocal past. From these sacred tomes, educators of Sympsonian daughters distill regulatory "principles and opinions" which they convey with a "certain young-ladies-school-room code of laws," which govern every aspect of life. This disciplining not only forestalls all deviations in their students, but also transmogrifies these daughters, examples to their sex, into relentless social and moral guardians themselves. Such a process leads to the second danger that Brontë deplores: the decimation of Originality, that "unutterable Thing" which must be policed and, if prevention is impossible, "denounced and chained up." This passage becomes even more powerfully critical when one considers how it relates to other more conspicuous attacks in *Shirley*. For instance, Shirley's hypothesis that she would be stoned to death for publishing her opinions on novel heroines intersects with the preceding passage in a number of important ways—literacy once again performs a regulative patriarchal role, one which must be upheld with violence, if necessary. Furthermore, each of the passages recalls Brontë's famous criticism about Jane Austen's "most solid books," which struck her as "a carefully fenced, highly cultivated garden."[10] The Sympson daughters are, educationally, exactly such a garden.

The most significant danger about books and book-learning, for Brontë, is their patriarchal nature, and the ways in which they limit the possibilities of their female readers. Since a good portion of the final section in this discussion of *Shirley* will examine how Brontë's characters read patriarchal institutions, one extended example must suffice at this point. In yet another scene in which Caroline finds conventional literacy less than fruitful, she has rummaged through her uncle's library, looking for solace in her time of despair:

> There she read old books, taken from her uncle's library: the Greek and Latin were of no use to her; and its collection of light literature was chiefly contained on a shelf which had belonged to her aunt Mary: some venerable Lady's Magazines, that had once performed a sea-voyage with their owner, and undergone a storm, and whose pages were stained with salt water; some Mad Methodist Magazines, full of miracles and apparitions, of preternatural warnings, ominous dreams, and frenzied fanaticism; the equally mad Letters of Mrs. Elizabeth Rowe from the Dead to the Living, a few old English Classics:—from these faded flowers Caroline had in her childhood extracted the honey,—they were tasteless to her now. [11]

Brontë, through Caroline, seems to conduct a survey of the types of literature available to young women in early nineteenth-century England, in service of demonstrating how irrelevant each text seems. From dogmatic magazines aimed at women to polemical religious directives, and from Greek and Latin classics to old English classics, these forms of textuality interconnect to form the same message for Caroline: she is to live a passive, domestic, weary life of an "old maid," rather than the life of activity reserved solely for men. She must remain unemployed professionally, and completely passive romantically, if she is to meet the standards which such texts demand for proper femininity.

Just in case we miss these connections, Brontë has Caroline subsequently contemplate such literary figures as Ovid's "Lucretia, spinning at midnight in the midst of her maidens, and Solomon's virtuous woman, [who] are often quoted as patterns of what 'the sex' (as they say) ought to be."[12] Each of these literary representations of the ideal woman is a pattern of their sex because of their submissiveness and their "ability" to remain cheerfully and virtuously passive. One waits at home, working at domestic chores at midnight in her husband's absence (a characteristic that her husband's countryman finds so compelling that he later rapes her); the other is worth more than all riches because she puts her family and those that are less fortunate above herself. Brontë's point is that books and traditional literacies are not always empowering for their readers. Certainly, in this case, the normalizing function of these texts for women creates a truth about femininity that destroys the lives they only ostensibly represent. Just as education marginalizes and contains female possibilities, these related books also erect boundaries, as "the taming of women is enacted through their acquisition of their master's language."[13] Throughout *Shirley*, we will encounter examples of each of these kinds of texts that Caroline encounters in her uncle's library: from mythological mermaids to Biblical narratives to English classics like Shakespeare. In each case, these "fictions that sustain men are precisely those that have contributed to the sickening of women."[14] Brontë, however, offers her characters an alternative visual literacy to complement book-learning and counteract the hegemonic effects of those literacies discussed above. This reading of social texts and institutions allows marginalized characters to recognize dangerous pedagogical sites, challenge them, and begin to transform them.

Caroline and Shirley turn their critical gazes toward the patriarchal society in which they live by watching men's actions, institutions such as male-created literature and educational tactics, and religious texts and practices whose dogmatic content results in real-life containment of women and their possibilities. However, this very marginalization offers the women a space of resistance by affording them a critical perspective that allows both a reading of dominant power structures at the center of patriarchal society and, consequently, the knowledge they will need to subvert such domination. Rather than being "taught in a culture of domination by those who dominate,"[15] Brontë's women read society in ways that offer lessons which allow them to refuse the hegemony of the colonizing discourse that circulates through and maintains the power of the dominant group. As bell hooks argues: "As a radical standpoint, perspective, position, 'the politics of location' necessarily calls those of us who would participate in the formation of counter-hegemonic cultural practice to identify the spaces where we begin the process of re-vision."[16] For *Shirley*'s heroines, that space proves to be the margins, from which they can read crucial social texts that allow them ways of knowing that can lead to re-vision.

By reading the men's interactions in various social situations, Shirley and Caroline learn things that they could never find in books. On the night of the school-feast, the women read in the expressions of the gentlemen that something is not quite right. Shirley proposes a course of reading that she intimates will provide answers: "We will talk of Moore, then, and we will watch him: I see him even now." How well they read the men as a text is remarkable. The way in which the men are arranged permits Shirley to translate their meeting, realizing "a war-council it is, if I am not mistaken." The demeanor of Robert and Helstone indicates that they are reconciled for a good reason, "making common cause against some common foe" (309).[17] Shirley astutely reads the summoning of Malone to the men's inner circle as a call for a strong arm. She also notices how they shake hands with emphasis, "as if they were ratifying some solemn league and covenant." All of these textual clues for Shirley build to one thesis, her exclusion from matters that deeply affect her own position in the community: "They won't trust me . . . that is always the way when it comes to the point."[18] The women, however, refuse to accept this exclusion without attempting to read their way into the heart of the matter:

> "Observe how engaged that group appear: they do not know we are watching them."
> "If we keep on the alert, Shirley, we shall perhaps find the clue to their secret."
> "There will be some unusual movements erelong—perhaps tomorrow—possibly tonight. But my eyes and ears are wide open: Mr. Moore, you shall be under surveillance. Be you vigilant also, Lina." [19]

Their reading of the war-council, of course, does keep them involved, by resulting in their attendance at the raid on the mill, another social text they read, observing yet unobserved. Along with reading the men in social situations, the women read the ways in which patriarchal literature and educational tactics legislate the kind of exclusion carried out by Moore, Helstone, and the others.

When Helstone's library no longer proves nourishing to Caroline, she turns her reading gaze to the institutions that prove so inadequate for women like Miss Ainley (and, as she augurs, herself). Analyzing the restrictive life so many women are forced to lead, she reads how patriarchal society suggests that woman's reward should be sought after in the next life, rather than in their current lives. As depictions of ideal women like Lucretia and Solomon's virtuous woman equate perfection with self-denial and sacrifice, real women suffer miserable existences.

Caroline, however, is able to read this institutional text and interpret its effects on her own life, and the lives of women around her. She realizes that "poor Miss Ainley would cling closer to life, if life had more charms for her. God surely did not create us, and cause us to live, with the sole end of wishing always to die."[20] Caroline thus is equipped to challenge standard narratives of representation through her visual literacy, even to the point of interpreting God's intentions (as she does with St Paul).

Although she struggles to make sense of things, her alternative reading will eventually permit her not only to recognize the power of patriarchal narrative, but to challenge its effects on women:

> nobody in particular is to blame, that I can see, for the state in which things are; and I cannot tell, however much I puzzle over it, how they are to be altered for the better; but I feel there is something wrong somewhere. I believe single women should have more to do—better chances of interesting and profitable occupation than they possess now. And when I speak thus, I have no impression that I displease God by my words; that I am either impious or impatient, irreligious or sacrilegious. [21]

Caroline's narrative of resistance, especially because it occurs in Brontë's novel, seeks to overturn the "logic" of Lucretia and Solomon's ideal woman. To arrive at this knowledge, she has had to circumvent books, to read from the margin, to textualize in ways that escape dominant coding. Caroline once again anticipates others trying to censor her thoughts based on narratives like St Paul, which are used to justify women's enforced silence. Furthermore, although she cannot bring herself to admit it, she does know where to lay blame: "The brothers . . . they have something to do: their sisters have no earthly employment, but household work and sewing; no earthly pleasure, but an unprofitable visiting; and no hope, in all their life to come, of anything better. . . . their minds and views shrink to wondrous narrowness."[22] Echoing the famous passage in *Jane Eyre* in which Jane argues that women must be active, Brontë insists on the re-vision of women's roles in society by exposing the conventional discourses that normalize the narrowness of existing roles. Women like Caroline must become empowered through an alternative literacy to create their own narratives, new discursive practices that, among other ends, reveal dominant ideology as a created discourse itself, rather than the natural way life is. Women will continue to suffer "until new stories are created that confer upon them the power of naming themselves and controlling their world."[23] However, much like Wollstonecraft, Brontë makes it clear that men will suffer from this constrictive environment as well: "Keep your girls' minds narrow and fettered—they will still be a plague and a care,

sometimes a disgrace to you: cultivate them—give them scope and work—
they will be your gayest companions in health; your tenderest nurses in
sickness; your most faithful prop in age."[24]

Caroline and Shirley take pleasure in their alternative literacy
throughout *Shirley*, deconstructing a number of patriarchal narratives, and
offering re-visions of their own in their stead. When Shirley proposes a
trip to the Faroe Isles with Caroline as a prophylactic for her declining
health, the women laugh over the possibility of encountering "mermaids in
Stromoe,"[25] and subsequently develop a counter-narrative of their
encounter with this male-mythologized mermaid. Shirley describes the
scene for Caroline:

> "It looks at us, but not with your eyes. I see a preternatural lure in its wily
> glance: it beckons. Were we men, we should spring at the sign, the cold
> billow would be dared for the colder enchantress; being women, we stand
> safe, though not dreadless. She comprehends our unmoved gaze; she feels
> herself powerless; anger crosses her front; she cannot charm, but she will
> appal us: she rises high, and glides all revealed, on the dark wave-ridge.
> Temptress-terror! monstrous likeness of ourselves![26]

Shirley's narrative emblematizes exactly how Brontë's visual literacy
works. The power to gaze clearly on such male myths as mermaids is the
very thing that can keep the women safe from their power. Her re-vision of
this enchantress figure subverts the latent politics of this signification by
rewriting the mermaid not as the *sign* at which all men jump, but rather as
a contrived paradigm for femininity that situates women as temptresses.
Shirley's constant excavation of such myth-making seeks to uncover the
connections among signs that construct artificial identities. By reading
how such texts as mermaids coalesce with other narratives like the Biblical
story of Eve, Shirley exposes a discursive network that *creates* truths
about dangerous femininity in order to validate the social containment that
often makes life such a weary prospect for women. Caroline, in turn,
responds to the inaccuracy of these "truths":

> "But, Shirley, she is not like us: we are neither temptresses, nor terrors, nor
> monsters."
> "Some of our kind, it is said, are all three. There are men who ascribe to
> 'woman,' in general, such attributes."[27]

Shirley's pedagogical strategy, like Brontë's, forces women to read
institutions from the margin and pass on this vigilant epistemology that
will help them resist such domination.[28]

Caroline also reads the institution of male-authored narrative and, when she and Robert read *Coriolanus*, she attempts her own re-vision of the bard. Caroline, like Brontë, realizes how much is at stake when such canonical texts are deployed. As Nancy Armstrong argues, we are not "as conscious of the politics of literary interpretation as she was."[29] Having read the pedagogical dynamic that obtains between herself and Hortense, Caroline enters her reading with Robert stipulating "I am to be the teacher then, and you my pupil."[30] While Robert reads the book, Caroline puts herself in the position to read the reader. She notices that he identifies with the haughty speech of Caius Marcius, a reading that allows her to offer a corrective: "you sympathize with that proud patrician who does not sympathize with his famished fellow-men, and insults them."[31] Caroline aggressively interprets both texts, Shakespeare and Robert, as her visual literacy complements the book. By combining the two literacies, she is empowered to enter a conversation from which she would otherwise be excluded, the debate about Robert's responsibilities to the mill workers. As her double reading continues, her hermeneutical strategy permits her to interject her own re-vision of Robert's "vicious, perverse points"[32]: "With the revenge of Caius Marcius, Moore perfectly sympathized; he was not scandalized by it; and again Caroline whispered, 'There I see another glimpse of brotherhood in error.'"[33] Caroline's reading leads her to remonstrate with Robert about his totalizing social theories, such as including "all working people under the general and insulting name of 'the mob,'"[34] or his inflexible pride. Although she does not end up under a cairn of avenging stones for her resisting reading, Robert tries to situate her reading outside of the play proper, calling her conclusions "the moral you tack to the play."[35] Nonetheless, his response, in itself, requires the admission that literary meaning is up for grabs, rather than a static, given norm. When Robert finishes his reading, she takes the position of power in their conversation by catechizing him.[36]

Along with literary and educational institutions, the women in *Shirley* read the related religious institutions in the novel. On the evening of the school-feast, Shirley persuades Caroline to remain outdoors instead of attending church, as is expected of them. Her justification seems to be that the women will then have the opportunity to read a natural text which will offer another counter-narrative to the dogmatizing that takes place indoors. Since "Nature is now at her evening prayers," she presents a devotional text that can challenge conventional religious narratives like the story of Eve. Shirley's access to universal origins becomes unmediated: "Caroline, I see her! and I will tell you what she is like: she is like what Eve was when she and Adam stood alone on earth."[37] When Caroline suggests that

Shirley's version of Eve differs from the male-created first-rate character of Eve that Milton made "truth" for so many, Shirley makes the difference emphatic:

> "Milton's Eve! Milton's Eve! I repeat. No, by the pure Mother of God, she is not! Cary, we are alone: we may speak what we think. Milton was great; but was he good? His brain was right; how was his heart? . . . Milton tried to see the first woman; but, Cary, he saw her not."
> "You are bold to say so, Shirley."
> "Not more bold than faithful."[38]

Like the mermaid narrative, Shirley presents the Biblical and Miltonic narrative of Eve as a text in need of re-vision. Hence, reading nature allows her to reconfigure this narrative, and offer one in which Eve is the mother of all Earth, in which her "first woman's breast that heaved with life on this world yielded the daring which could contend with Omnipotence."[39] She insists to Caroline that a close reading of "mother Eve, in these days called Nature," will be all that is necessary to make the requisite connection: "you will see her and feel as I do, if we are both silent."[40] Shirley's challenge of this patriarchal religious script once again maintains the efficacy of alternative literacies to resist from the margin.[41]

When Shirley and Caroline encounter Joe Scott outside of church, the crucial battle waged through literacies becomes unmistakably prominent. After Shirley and Scott argue about the propriety of women reading newspapers and talking politics, his argument turns to the scriptural narratives that men have traditionally invoked to keep women in their place:

> "Joe, do you seriously think all the wisdom in the world is lodged in male skulls?"
> "I think that women are a kittle and a froward generation; and I've a great respect for the doctrines delivered in the second chapter of St Paul's first epistle to Timothy."
> "What doctrines, Joe?"
> "Let the woman learn in silence, with all subjection. I suffer not a woman to teach, nor to usurp authority over the man; but to be in silence. For Adam was first formed, then Eve."[42]

Shirley, of course, has read the institutionalization of the Eve narrative well, and is prepared for Scott's marginalizing line of argument. Her ability to develop a counter-narrative proves valuable immediately; even by remaining outside of church, the women do not escape the reaches of patriarchal narrative. When Scott directly blames Eve's transgression for man's fallen state, Shirley questions the authenticity of such a polemic: "To confess the honest truth, Joe, I never was easy in my mind concerning that chapter: it puzzles me."[43]

Caroline's counter-narrative of St Paul parallels Shirley's translation of the Eve narrative, by exemplifying exactly how traditional literacy facilitates co-optation by the dominant group. Her version of the scripture is only possible because of her visual literacy, and the lessons she has learned by reading institutional texts:

> "I account for them in this way: he wrote that chapter for a particular congregation of Christians, under peculiar circumstances; and besides, I dare say, if I could read the original Greek, I should find that many of the words have been wrongly translated, perhaps misapprehended altogether. It would be possible, I doubt not, with a little ingenuity, to give the passage quite a contrary turn; to make it say, 'Let the woman speak out whenever she sees fit to make an objection;'—'it is permitted to a woman to teach and to exercise authority as much as may be. Man, meantime, cannot do better than hold his peace,' and so on."[44]

Caroline's skill in alternative reading results in this extremely challenging re-vision.[45] First, she questions the context of the scriptural text, avowing that a stable meaning is now inaccessible. Next, she calls attention to the inevitable fallibility of translation—another certain impediment to establishing certainty of any kind. She reminds us how patriarchal educational models exclude women from reading Greek. Finally, she maintains that, as far as reading and interpreting a text goes, objectivity is merely a fallacy—all reading is subjective and, hence, self-serving (albeit often unconsciously so). As Scott himself has just stipulated: "Human natur', taking it i' th' lump, is naught but selfishness."[46] Caroline, and Brontë, anticipate many of the arguments advanced in postmodern cultural studies, not merely situating truth as relative, but also exposing its social and political consequences for living people. For Brontë, one must read from the margins to transform the dominant center. And, just as Shirley writes her own text in the margins of Louis' books, Brontë's novel reinscribes master narratives with a counter discourse.

Works Cited

Armstrong, Nancy. *Desire and Domestic Fiction: A Political History of the Novel*. New York: Oxford University Press, 1987.

Dupras, Joseph A. "Charlotte Brontë's *Shirley* and Interpretive Engendering." *Papers on Language and Literature* 24:3 (1988): 301-316.

Gaskell, Elizabeth. *The Life of Charlotte Brontë*. New York: Penguin Books, 1975.

Gilbert, Sandra M. and Susan Gubar. *The Madwoman in the Attic: The Woman Writer and the Nineteenth-Century Literary Imagination*. New Haven: Yale University Press, 1979.

Greene, Sally. "Apocalypse When? *Shirley*'s Vision and the Politics of Reading." *Studies in the Novel* 26:4 (1994): 350-371.

hooks, bell. *Yearning: Race, Gender, and Cultural Politics*. Boston: South End Press, 1990.

Langer, Nancy Quick. "'There Is No Such Ladies Now-a-Days': Capsizing 'the Patriarch Bull' in Charlotte Brontë's *Shirley*." *Journal of Narrative Technique* 27:3 (1997): 276-296.

Lawson, Kate. "The Dissenting Voice: *Shirley*'s Vision of Women and Christianity." *Studies in English Literature: 1500-1900* 29:4 (1989): 729-743.

Shuttleworth, Sally. *Charlotte Brontë and Victorian Psychology*. Cambridge, Cambridge University Press, 1996.

Notes

[1] Bronte, *Shirley,* 95-96.

[2] Ibid, 96.

[3] Ibid, 105.

[4] Langer, "'There Is No Such Ladies Now-a-Days': Capsizing 'the Patriarch Bull' in Charlotte Brontë's *Shirley*," 278.

[5] Bronte, *Shirley*, 98.

[6] Ibid, 122.

[7] Ibid, 210.

[8] Ibid, 210.

[9] Ibid, 428-29.

[10] Gaskell, *The Life of Charlotte Brontë*, 337. Interestingly, in *Shirley*, a book may also still provide a "fresh, vigorous style" that can oppose the regulation of the "most solid books" that discipline. As she moved toward *Villette*, Brontë offered far fewer reassurances that suggest that books can remain efficacious in resisting dominant ideology.

[11] Bronte, *Shirley,* 376.

[12] Ibid, 378

[13] Shuttleworth, *Charlotte Brontë and Victorian Psychology*, 214.

[14] Gilbert and Gubar, *The Madwoman in the Attic: The Woman Writer and the Nineteenth-Century Literary Imagination*, 374.

[15] bell hooks, *Yearning: Race, Gender, and Cultural Politics,* 150.

[16] Ibid, 145.

[17] Bronte, *Shirley*, 309.

[18] Ibid, 310.

[19] Ibid, 310.

[20] Ibid, 376.

[21] Ibid, 376-77.

[22] Ibid, 377.

[23] Gilbert and Gubar, *Madwoman in the Attic*, 391.

[24] Bronte, *Shirley*, 379.

[25] Ibid, 248.

[26] Ibid, 249.

[27] Ibid, 250.

[28] See Langer for a detailed reading of the mermaid episode in terms of a patriarchal script. She writes: "When Shirley recognizes Caroline in the mermaid's face, she suggests that a conventional narrative construction of Victorian womanhood paralyzes the female subject by defining her according to an already-written script that valorizes male desire at the expense of female agency. By rewriting the script so that she and Caroline gaze upon the mermaid, Shirley is able to interrogate the system that necessarily constructs women as either 'temptresses, . . terrors, [or] monsters.' Because they are not men, Shirley and Caroline 'stand safe' from potential seduction, and instead are confronted by the 'terror' of the 'monstrous likeness' patriarchal discourse constructs for them. Shirley's revision exposes the artificiality of this 'likeness'; a woman sees herself in the mermaid's image only insofar as she participates in a discourse that defines her according to her desire for masculine validation. Recognizing the dangers of seeing herself through the male gaze, Shirley rejects identification with the mermaid: 'Are you not glad, Caroline, when at last, and with a wild shriek, [the mermaid] dives?'" (285).

[29] Nancy Armstrong, *Desire and Domestic Fiction: A Political History of the Novel*, 215. In an extended section of her chapter that deals with *Shirley* and this "scene of reading," she goes on to stipulate that "she understood the politics of encountering Shakespeare, not as public theater, but as a work of literature is immediately apparent. It is perhaps not surprising that Caroline Helstone, in one of her notably few acts of self-assertion, reads Shakespeare as a way of passing leisure hours with her cousin Robert Moore" (215). Armstrong's analysis grants too much power to book-learning, however, and underestimates Caroline's acts of self-assertion, since each act of visual literacy is an act of self-assertion. Her main thesis deals more with Caroline's ability to civilize Robert in the English mold: "Far more detailed than similar exchanges of an earlier period, this scene of reading indicates an acute awareness of the power of literacy. Brontë gives the power far more clarity than the vaguely civilizing force that women in earlier fiction could exercise over aristocratic men by way of the written word. Robert

Moore is half Belgian, half English. It is through reading English literature, according to Caroline, that he 'shall be entirely English'" (215).

[30] Bronte, *Shirley*, 115.

[31] Ibid, 116.

[32] Ibid, 115.

[33] Ibid, 116-17.

[34] Ibid, 118.

[35] Ibid, 117.

[36] See Armstrong, 219, who also makes this point about catechism.

[37] Bronte, *Shirley*, 314.

[38] Ibid, 314-315.

[39] Ibid, 315.

[40] Ibid, 316.

[41] See Shuttleworth, 213, for her treatment of Shirley's counter-narratives. She writes: "Brontë's most overt celebration of female potentiality and alternative knowledge comes in Shirley's rewriting of the triple authorities of the Bible, Milton and classical legend in her inspiring vision of Eve." Although Shuttleworth seems to grant some efficacy to Shirley's alternative knowledge, her analysis of Caroline's subsequent counter-narrative to St Paul seems to situate this knowledge as ultimately a delusionary dream: "Caroline too joins in this challenge to political and religious orthodoxy. Her deft retranscription turns St Paul's famous proscription on female speech into a proto-feminist text: woman is to be permitted to speak out and teach as much as she wishes whilst the man is enjoined to hold his peace. The dream is quickly quashed, however: Brontë underscores the unattainability of the girls' visions by interrupting them with the alternate vision of 'martial scarlet', heralding the coming bloodshed, and the religious and political chauvinism of Joe Scott. The male community of the novel band together to enforce a unified interpretation of a single text: women's subordination." As I will suggest, the visual literacy that Shirley and Caroline (and Brontë) practice provides much more than a "dream" of personal agency.

[42] Bronte, *Shirley*, 322

[43] Ibid, 323.

[44] Ibid, 323

[45] A number of critics, however, persist in reading Caroline's re-vision in ways which underestimate its efficacy. See Lawson, "The Dissenting Voice: *Shirley*'s Vision of Women and Christianity." Lawson writes: "Caroline's attempt to 're-translate' Paul here, although perhaps both brave and amusing, is hardly convincing. It will take more than 'a little ingenuity' to understand the words of scripture differently. As Joe Scott remarks: 'he that runs may read.' A successful feminist dissent must come from another direction" (731). Her view of *Shirley* as a narrative of resistance is not a hopeful one: "Closure in *Shirley* brings with it the silencing of the female voice of dissent and the reestablishment of male authority" (738). See also Dupras, "Charlotte Brontë's *Shirley* and Interpretive Engendering." Dupras misses Brontë's repeated references to looking and watching as an alternative method of reading: "Brontë illustrates here what happens when a

prejudiced 'over-looker' or someone who is merely a 'looker,' not a reader, engages a work" (310). Sandra M. Gilbert and Susan Gubar conclude that "Brontë is far more pessimistic about the results of revisionary poetics . . . she suggests that the private broodings of women writers cannot eradicate the powerful effect of public myths" (374). See also Greene, "Apocalypse When? *Shirley*'s Vision and the Politics of Reading." Greene is a bit more hopeful, writing that Brontë "was able to use the form of the romance novel as a forum for the articulation of a revisionist, feminist interpretation of the Bible. Through alternative readings of scripture proposed by both Caroline Helstone and Shirley Keeldar, Brontë looks forward to an indefinitely conceived utopian moment when women will share with men an equal opportunity for education and a career. Moreover, these unorthodox interpretations are part of a larger series of challenges to the mimetic surface of the novel that serve to thematize the process of fiction-making itself in a way that . . . shifts the burden of meaning to the reader" (355). Greene's explanation of the proliferation of criticism that underestimates the power of Brontë's challenge to patriarchal authority is also very convincing: "A substantial body of feminist criticism of *Shirley* . . . neglects to examine the novel's contexts and, accordingly, imposes on it twentieth-century ideological assumptions, with the result that Brontë is perceived as reinforcing or creating, rather than challenging, the confining roles that women still find themselves in today" (368).

[46] Bronte, *Shirley*, 320.

CHAPTER NINE

THE DANGER OF DYING IN ONE'S OWN LANGUAGE: LITERACY AND LYING IN ELIZABETH GASKELL'S *SYLVIA'S LOVERS* AND *COUSIN PHILLIS*

DOROTHY H. MCGAVRAN

In *Sylvia's Lovers*, the semi-literate Daniel Robson, Sylvia's father, reports how he preferred to cut off part of his thumb and forefinger rather than be impressed into military service for his country against Americans in their war for independence. Elizabeth Gaskell puts his reason for such self-mutilation in a linguistic metaphor when she has Robson say, "I could na stomach the thought o' being murdered i' my own language."[1] Though Robson refers to his chances of dying in a war against English-speaking Americans, Gaskell's curious metaphor highlights the importance of language and literacy, which reverberates through all her works. In Daniel Robson's case, being "murdered in [his] own language" arises from the control that impressment laws exercised over helpless sailors in the late eighteenth century. While Robson escapes the American war through his desperate act, he is hanged later in the novel for his part in the "Randyvowse" riot. Through his inability to read the letter of the law and his no longer appropriate romantic rebellion against the law, his earlier words prove prophetic. It can be said that he *is* murdered in his own language: English laws lock in his fate.

Gaskell's works demonstrate many ways of dying in one's own language. Repeatedly in her novels, the transition from the oral culture to the written culture is fraught with danger for characters who are slow to acquire the requisite literacy to read changing times. The literacy needed for survival in Gaskell's worlds is the ability not only to read texts but also to read contexts. She explores the margins and the marginalized in order to teach how to read change as it is happening. In her society, moreover, no project was more vital than the educating of the masses. As Unitarians, the Gaskells believed in universal education, and both William and Elizabeth Gaskell taught in working-class schools. Though Gaskell is precise in making clear the educational level of every one of her characters, she sets up no simple privileging of the literate over the illiterate characters or the lettered over the oral traditions. In fact, the oral culture in Gaskell's novels is vital and admirable in its energy; the written is often confining and regimented through law and prohibitions. All literacies, however, are valued because all people need to read both the texts and the contexts of their culture.

Searching for truth in untrodden ways, Gaskell offers alternative readings of circumstances and events, and she often uses the lie to gain access to new ground. Lying in Gaskell's novels has long received attention from critics but not always with understanding of her project. I believe that lying in Gaskell's novels does not represent a turning away from truth but an expansion of the grounds for truth.[2] "Ground" is context, and therefore the spatial setting on which Gaskell founds her fictional worlds. Kenneth Burke's *Grammar of Motives* explores the scenic word *ground* as it is used in philosophy for describing motives. Burke says, "'On what grounds did he do this?' is translated 'What kind of scene did he say it was, that called for such an act?'"[3] By pursuing the lie and the grounds for it, Gaskell subverts the comforting myths of middle-class complacency and aims to expand the awareness and sympathy of her readers by teaching them to read the margins. Gaskell's works warn that some people—either wittingly or unwittingly—are caught by change in unfortunate, even life-threatening, situations by a failure to read their world correctly.

Mikhail Bakhtin's analysis in *The Dialogic Imagination* offers an explanation of the novelist's role as ventriloquist, clarifying the voices of truth.[4] Bakhtin maintains that the novelist "orchestrates all . . . themes," permitting "a multiplicity of social voices and a wide variety of their links and interrelationships (always more or less dialogized)."[5] The many national and social languages gathered by the novelist, according to Bakhtin, are all "equally capable of being 'languages of truth,' but since such is the case, all . . . are equally relative, reified, and limited, as they are merely the languages of social groups, professions and other cross-sections of everyday life" (367). The world view that Gaskell wanted to introduce to her readers was decentered and shaken by industrialism. The truth, as she put it in a letter, is not "the abstract absolute truth,"[6] but the multi-vocal truths of people's lives. By using an analogy to Galileo's shift away from a geocentric universe, Bakhtin explains what makes the novelist differ from the poet in a parallel decentralization of language:

> The novel is the expression of a Galilean perception of language, one that denies the absolutism of a single and unitary language—that is, that refuses to acknowledge its own language as the sole verbal and semantic center of the ideological world. (366)

Bakhtin has said that what he calls the "living utterance" is charged with meaning taken from "a particular historical moment in a socially specific environment" (276). The object is charged with the past, its social context and the individual's private meanings. It "unfolds" in a dialogue of "social heteroglossia," resulting in "the Tower-of-Babel mixing of languages that goes on around any object" (278). It is the business of the novelist to ventriloquize these languages. Gaskell's ventriloquism allows silenced people to speak through her novels—the workers of Manchester, the women of Cranford and Hollingsford, the sailors of Whitby captured by the press gang, the railroad workers, the farmers, the dissenting ministers.

All Gaskell's novels, consequently, are novels of education, teaching the reader the many languages of truth in times of conflict and in places in transition. Two works, written in close succession, present the battle on the field of discourse through the intersection of literacies. Both *Sylvia's Lovers* and *Cousin Phillis* focus particularly on the value of literacy and learning, though their main characters approach the subject from opposite directions. Both also turn upon lies and point out the danger of being locked into illiteracy of one kind or another. Sylvia is illiterate, but her mother wishes her to acquire the skills she herself never had and so favors the evening sessions with her cousin Philip Hepburn. Sylvia resists her schooling by Hepburn as useless:

> Mother! . . . what's the use on my writing "Abednego," "Abednego," "Abednego, all down a page? If I could see t'use on 't, I'd ha' axed father to send me t' school; but I'm none wanting to have learning. (93)

Phillis Holman of *Cousin Phillis*, on the other hand, readily approaches learnedness in her study of Latin, Greek, and Italian. The cousins of the two girls—Philip Hepburn and Paul Manning—react to the literacy level demonstrated by Sylvia and Phillis. Philip spends his evenings with Sylvia, trying by candlelight to teach her reading, spelling, geography, and love for him. Paul, on the other hand, is shamed by Phillis's learning to admit the little training in—and small remembrance of—his own Latin lessons. Paul is appalled to find Phillis's name in the books on the shelf, including Virgil, Caesar, and a Greek grammar. He tries to rationalize her superior learning by calling her books "her dead-and-gone languages."[7]

But if the women are the pupils of language study in these novels, the men are also learners. In knowing Sylvia and Phillis, Philip and Paul learn the literacy of the heart. They learn how to apply the vitality of the oral tradition and carry the values of the lettered past into times of change. In *Sylvia's Lovers* the genres of oral cultures—the ballad and tall tale—prove false to reason but true to the heart, while in *Cousin Phillis*, allusions to classic tongues of Virgil, Dante, and even Wordsworth present a pastoral Eden with a lurking, well-read, glib-tongued serpent. Gaskell demonstrates that those who speak with the tongues of men and of angels need also to speak with love.

As the title suggests, Sylvia is courted by two lovers: her prosaic shopkeeper cousin, Philip Hepburn, and the seaman and teller of romantic tall tales, Charley Kinraid. Hepburn's tools of ruled tablets and dry spelling exercises do not have a chance when compared to the whaling tales told by Kinraid. Sylvia's father used similar tales to woo her mother. Gaskell parallels the tall tales with the various smuggling devices practiced without guilt by men and women, whalers and merchants, alike. In smuggling, the sailors join with the merchants to evade the import laws. Gaskell pictures Sylvia and her mother listening to Kinraid and Robson's account of the latest smuggling exploits:

> There was no question of the morality of the affair; one of the greatest signs of the real progress we have made since those times seems to be that our daily concerns of buying and selling, eating and drinking, whatsoever we do, are more tested by the real practical standard of our religion than they were in the days of our grandfathers. Neither Sylvia nor her mother was in advance of their age. Both listened with admiration to the ingenious devices, and acted as well as spoken lies, that were talked about as fine and spirited things. Yet if Sylvia had attempted one tithe of this deceit in her every-day life, it would have half broken her mother's heart. (98)

Deceit is justified not only in business practices but especially in the case of unfair government taxation. Gaskell goes on to defend the common people's resistance to the duty on salt, which was imposed in 1702 and revived in 1732, according to Andrew Sanders.[8] "Government," Gaskell warns, "did more to demoralize the popular sense of rectitude and uprightness than heaps of sermons could undo" (99). Standards of truth, Gaskell wants her readers to realize, grow out of their contexts: "It may seem curious to trace up the popular standard of truth to taxation; but I do not think the idea would be so very farfetched" (99).

The lies in *Sylvia's Lovers* present another problem of interpretation. Storytelling, a vital function in oral societies, was Gaskell's strength. But, as Donald Stone notes in *The Romantic Impulse in Victorian Fiction*, "Storytelling is the fabrication of lies and the endorsement of acts of subterfuge."[9] Stone claims that Gaskell is torn by her sympathy for the two liars: Kinraid and his romantic lies about whaling and Hepburn and his down-to-earth lie, which "presses" Sylvia to marry him. To Stone, Gaskell's "split focus . . . becomes bothersome." Kinraid's lies are judged "the stuff of romance" but Hepburn's lie has the makings of tragedy. Rather than seeing Gaskell's double attitude as a split, I prefer to see it as another instance of the opening up of grounds for truth. Gaskell's attitude toward storytelling is complex. She is a teller of stories herself and knows their power. Something almost magical is seen in Gaskell's presentation of the art of storytelling, but the magic is simply a sign of the power that language can and does assume. The magical power of storytelling is also suggested in *Cranford* by Miss Pole's study of conjuring in the encyclopedia. Her conclusion is "very clear indeed! My dear Mrs. Forrester, conjuring and witchcraft is a mere affair of the alphabet."[10] Hilary Schor has taken Miss Pole's cue to conclude that Gaskell "rewrites [the] marginality" of women's languages and by the subversion of literary traditions, "rewrite[s] the novel."[11] I agree with Schor's conclusion but would submit that truth-telling is Gaskell's larger purpose, which she achieves paradoxically by expanding the acceptable languages of truth. These languages include—but are not limited to—women's languages. By use of tale telling, Gaskell completes the context necessary to understand the characters, but at the same time, she gives their viewpoints a validity that does not come from the literal truth of the stories. It comes from the truth of emotions and is comprehended by the literacy of the heart.

Gaskell values both the oral tradition, which produced the tall tales, and the written tradition. But, in *Sylvia's Lovers*, as in *North and South*, the most "literate" people are not those who can read texts, but those who also can read contexts. Sylvia and her mother have successfully read the context of their home and understand the spirit of its law, which is to humor Daniel Robson. They think nothing of allowing him to state lies to feed his illusion that he is in control of his own hearth. Daniel, for example, while confined to the house by rheumatism, has to be managed by the women for his own good. They tolerate his "ignorant" suggestions for running the house, even though they know the true value of his housekeeping knowledge. Sylvia once suggests they try one of these suggestions and feed her father the results, but Bell Robson rejects the conspiracy. She knows Daniel cannot be taught (46). They arrange for the tailor to visit to take up his time and provide male gossip. They indulge him with just enough liquor, then put him to bed. In an early scene a short exchange illustrates how Bell allows lies to flourish for the sake of her husband's ego. Daniel speaks first as he observes Sylvia come home in the company of Philip:

> "Tak off thy pan o' milk, missus, and set on t' kettle. Milk may do for wenches, but Philip and me is for a drop o' good Hollands and watter this cold night. I'm a'most chilled to t' marrow wi' looking out for thee, lass, for t' mother was in a peck of troubles about thy none coming home i' t' dayleet, and I'd to keep hearkening out on t' browhead."
>
> This was entirely untrue, and Bell knew it to be so; but her husband did not. He had persuaded himself now, as he had done often before, that what he had in reality done for his own pleasure or satisfaction, he had done in order to gratify someone else. (37)

Daniel's lack of awareness in reading the politics of his own hearth explains his ignorance of the politics of his little world. He is caught then by the letter of the law and "murdered in his own language."

Lies connect the political and the domestic scenes in *Sylvia's Lovers*. The press-gang forms only the background for the romance and family story, which is the focus of the novel, but it is an important thematic background with political and economic implications for Gaskell's own times. The acquiescence of the gentry to the press-gang laws is based on economic jealousy, as Gaskell indicates. Magistrates uphold property rights over human rights. The romantic plot, therefore, has political implications as it moves out of sexual jealousy to center on a lie. Philip Hepburn withholds what he knows about Charley Kinraid's impressment so that he can marry Sylvia himself. Philip's lie is like that told by the fire-bell, which flushes the men out to fight a nonexistent fire. It flushes Sylvia out of her shelter in the promise of marriage to Kinraid. Moreover, it receives added backing from her father's treatment at the hands of the law so that Sylvia feels forced to provide for her mother the security of a home with Philip. Government policy provides the climate in which Philip's lie can be effective. Consequently, through his lie Philip "press-gangs" Sylvia into marriage. Terry Eagleton stresses the way legality ties the novel's family concerns with its government concerns: "The issue of legality . . . opens out, in fact, into a wide range of preoccupations with fraudulence and fidelity, honesty and deceit, truth and trickery, in the substance of both personal and social relations."[12] All of these preoccupations grow from

Gaskell's concern that her own contemporary society learn to read the contexts in its own time of change. Gaskell found in the historical situation of the impressment laws a connection to the common themes in all her novels: the injustice of the laws of man, the difficulty in knowing the absolute truth, the need for moral action, and the accountability of all before God.

The competing literary genres used by Sylvia's two suitors emphasize Gaskell's point that people at different times and in different circumstances use different languages—yielding in the novel Bakhtin's social heteroglossia. This basis for Gaskell's linguistic approach to truth appears when Philip tries in chapter ten to teach "A Refractory Pupil." Sylvia "was much more inclined to try and elicit some sympathy in her interest in the perils and adventures of the northern seas, than to bend and control her mind to the right formation of letters" (107). Letters lock in the thoughts and feelings and make possible more abstract thought, as Jack Goody and Ian Watt have described in their article, "The Consequences of Literacy." But at the same time, Goody and Watt claim that "literate culture . . . is much more easily avoided than the oral one."[13] Abstract reasoning, logic and categorizing are not as deep and permanent as direct face-to-face experience in the oral culture. Moreover, "Literate society, merely by having no system of elimination, no 'structural amnesia', prevents the individual from participating fully in the total cultural tradition to anything like the extent possible in non-literate society."[14] To Sylvia at the edge of literacy, the letters seem like fetters and the words a burden:

> It's bad enough wi' a book o' print as I've niver seen afore, for there's sure to be new-fangled words in 't. I'm sure I wish the man were farred who plagues his brains wi' striking out new words. Why can't folks just ha' a set on 'em for good and a'? (107)

Philip's response to this outburst of frustration is to point out the many sets of vocabularies and languages that exist for the different contexts and occupations of people even like herself:

> "Why you'll be after using two or three hundred yoursel' every day as you live, Sylvie; and yet I must use a great many as you never think on about t' shop; ant' folks in t' fields want their set, let alone the high English that parsons and lawyers speak. (107-8)

Jenny Uglow points out that the many vocabularies of Sylvia's Lovers make "a complex, developing and competing universe through the words of land, sea, trade, church, state and war."[15] Gaskell is equally attuned to and at home with those who speak the many languages of Monkshaven's occupations and preoccupations.

Sylvia, however, must learn to read texts to get beyond the past and its mythologies and to have more control over her future. Significantly, she does not wholeheartedly begin to learn to read words until she softens her heart to her husband's lie. Then Alice Rose teaches her from the Bible. In Gaskell's view, literacy requires the training of the heart, which cannot be imposed by law or parental decree but must be approached through suffering. Sylvia cannot forgive her husband's lie until she understands the grounds for it. Sitting beside his deathbed, she reads his heart. Her earlier self had not been educated to read beyond the level of her father's literacy.

Cousin Phillis also deals with times of change through the metaphor of reading and understanding languages. The title character has been educated to read Latin and Greek by her minister father. The problems of reading faced by Phillis and her contemporaries are those of a later world than Sylvia Robson's 1790s. Phillis's isolated Eden-like world is about to be changed by the coming of the railroad. Both the narrator, Paul Manning, and his boss, Edward Holdsworth, work on the construction of the railroad. Holdsworth is a man in motion, who, as Uglow puts it, "translates" the pastoral Phillis "to a different state."[16] As the railroad is a sign of the times, Holdsworth is a man of the times, and his stories, like Kinraid's in *Sylvia's Lovers*, carry Phillis beyond her safe world. Holdsworth, however, while keeping his integrity in all but the most exact moral analysis, lies to Phillis. Like Philip Hepburn, he breaks a promise which he never said aloud. Hepburn had promised to tell Sylvia that Kinraid was seized by the press gang and would return. Since he never utters a promise to Kinraid, he reasons, technically he is not responsible for carrying the message. Holdsworth, in later more sophisticated times, never promises his love to Phillis. Paul tries to excuse his friend from Betty's accusation of his doing harm to Phillis: "I don't believe Holdsworth ever spoke a word of—of love to her in all his life. I'm sure he didn't." Betty responds, "Aye. Aye! But there's eyes, and there's hands, as well as tongues; and a man has two of the one and but one of' t'other" (336). Phillis nearly dies as a result of her reading love in Holdsworth's nonverbal eyes and hands.

In *Cousin Phillis*, the no-fault lie committed by Holdsworth is a sign of the changing times. The consequent suffering of Phillis, whose knowledge of foreign tongues qualifies her for the role of tragic hero, educates her cousin Paul and commits him and the reader to a more learned reading of the heart. Phillis's somewhat unusual position as a woman with a classical education places her in the center of conflicting worlds: the one represented by the land-centered learning of her father, Ebenezer Holman, and the other represented by the more fluid, cosmopolitan knowledge of the railroad man Holdsworth. Her father commands the tongues of ancient Greece and Rome, while Holdsworth commands the tongues of steel. Holdsworth moves at ease between the classical languages of his education and the modern language of contemporary Italy where he lived while building the railroad.

The changing times Gaskell describes in pastoral terms in *Cousin Phillis* demand a new professional literacy, and Phillis and her father are at pains to acquire it. The degree and depth of learning of each character in the drama contribute to Gaskell's truthful portrayal of changing times. Wendy Craik emphasizes Gaskell's "delicate and unobtrusive, yet structural and thematic, use of various kinds of knowledge and learning."[17] Included is "book-learning," of course, but Craik also identifies what she calls "lore . . . that whole area of knowledge, skill and expertise that is . . . learned without books or text, but by oral transmission and practice." Conflict springs from characters who do not understand the language spoken by another. Through the metaphor of translation, Gaskell emphasizes the need for people to open their minds and hearts to understand different languages. Paul is skilled in reading the language of mechanics and is helpful to Holman in explaining the technical vocabulary in a "volume of stiff mechanics" (277). Paul's father, who was responsible for inventing "Manning's Patent Winch," opens his mind to learn farming lore when he comes to visit Hope Farm. Phillis, of course, struggles to translate Dante's *Inferno*, but she also listens attentively to Holdsworth's practical suggestions for improving drainage. The changing times require that one open up the mind to apply it to new knowledge and new languages.

Paul's story forms Gaskell's primer for reading changing times. The reader follows Paul, who enters the world of Hope Farm and becomes a man in the course of his visits there. When Paul first comes to Hope Farm to visit his cousin Holman, he does not meet her husband, the Reverend Ebenezer Holman, until late in the day. Then their daughter Phillis leads Paul to the fields where her father is finishing a day of work with his fellow farm laborers and chapel members. Before greeting Paul, Holman begins singing what he calls a psalm: "Come all harmonious tongues" (271). This hymn and the one before it in Isaac Watts' collection have as their subject "the passion and exaltation of Christ,"[18] but they share the missionary subtext of spreading the word through all nations.

Significantly, Paul's first sight of Holman is of the farmer-preacher beating time to this hymn with his spade. But Paul is silent. He does not know the words to the hymn. The harmony of tongues in the dream world of pastoral simplicity at Hope Farm is about to be disturbed by the changes brought about, not by the railroad itself, but by the clash of discourse it facilitates. The spreading of the Word to all nations parallels the laying of the steel for the expanding railroad. But in that expansion of the empire both of church and state lie inherent problems and suffering for individuals along the way.

Holman, as his name suggests, leads a self-sufficient existence as farmer and minister to an unnamed dissenting sect. Holman, therefore, integrates religion, farming, and learning. He finds the tongue of Virgil more harmonious to his way of living than the tongue of Brother Robinson, his fellow minister. Robinson criticizes Holman's learning, but the servant Betty knows that Brother Robinson would rather wrap his tongue around her victuals than try to keep up with Holman and his studies. Holman's "prodigious big appetite" (278), however, is for learning. Through her imagery Gaskell unites food, tongues, and knowledge in an echo of *Paradise Lost*. Like Milton's, Gaskell's story is about the increasing hunger for knowledge and experience. Like Milton, Gaskell explores the roots of the concept of sapience, but, unlike Milton, Gaskell finds the root of all evil to be not a failure of the mind but a failure of the heart to read the languages of others. It is this failure that leads to dying in one's own language.

Holman refers to Virgil's "enduring epithets" suggesting a subtle message, which Holman with all his learning fails to read. If Virgil's *Georgics* contains ancient agricultural methods, which describe "to a T what is now lying before us in the parish of Heathbridge," so does the plot of his *Aeneid* point out the suffering that comes to some in times of transition, especially to those caught in the founding or expansion of empires. Aeneas abandons Dido to found the Roman empire, just as Holdsworth will abandon Phillis to expand the railroad in Canada.[19] During his first visit, Paul Manning finds out, to his dismay, that Phillis is as well read as her father. Paul feels inferior to his better educated cousin, and she is disappointed that he cannot help her to translate Dante. Phillis' ambition to read Dante parallels the hunger of her imagination stirred by her learning.

Holdsworth brings a classical education but also the experience of travel in the contemporary world to the isolated farm. Uglow explains that he is an alien—wearing his hair differently and talking with his southern drawl.[20] Moreover, his stories, like Kinraid's in *Sylvia's Lovers*, cast a spell that captures even Holman in spite of his better judgment:

> Yes . . . I like him, and I think he is an upright man; there is a want of
> seriousness in his talk at times, but, at the same time, it is wonderful to
> listen to him! He makes Horace and Virgil living, instead of dead, by the
> stories he tells me of his sojourn in the very countries where they lived,
> and where to this day, he says—But it is like dram-drinking. I listen to him
> till I forget my duties, and am carried off my feet. (305)

Holdsworth, for his part, cannot understand the language spoken at Hope
Farm. In arguing for Manzoni's *I Promessi Sposi*, [*The Betrothed*], as his
choice of Italian reading material for Phillis, Holdsworth claims it is "as
pretty and innocent a tale as can be met with. You don't suppose they take
Virgil for gospel?" (304).

Paul can speak the same language as the Holmans when it comes to
"kinds of goodness," though he cannot read any foreign tongues. He is
also right about Holdsworth—his is not the kind of goodness that the
Holmans expect. They expect truth in word and deed. Holdsworth, on the
other hand, gauges words to match the effect he intends on the hearers. He
admits to Paul that he has to think when talking with the minister:

> I was on the verge of displeasing him once or twice, I fear, with random
> assertions and exaggerated expressions, such as one always uses with other
> people and thinks nothing of; but I tried to check myself when I saw how it
> shocked the good man; and really it is very wholesome exercise, this trying
> to make one's words represent one's thoughts, instead of merely looking to
> their effect on others. (303)

Holdsworth has developed skill in audience analysis, but his words are not
backed by moral integrity.

Certainly Holdsworth is a calculator of more than engineering
calibrations. He never shows any interest in Paul's trips to Hope Farm
until he catches the words "pretty mouth" from Paul's father as
Holdsworth interrupts their talk of Paul's possible marriage to Phillis.
From that time on, Holdsworth shows an active interest in meeting Phillis.
But he always freezes Phillis in an attitude of beauty. He pictures her as a
pretty mouth, then does an abortive sketch of her head, and finally refers
to her as a Sleeping Beauty whom he may awaken when he returns from
Canada in two years. Gradually, for his part, Paul begins to read
Holdsworth for what he is. Paul's first step is to see him as a coxcomb,
when Holdsworth spins his fairy-tale ending to his relationship with
Phillis: "I shall come back like a prince from Canada, and waken her to
my love. I can't help hoping that it won't be difficult, eh, Paul?" (315).
Then, after reading Holdsworth's letters and seeing the reduction of
Phillis's place in them to a postscript, which combines her with his "kind

friends at Hope Farm," Paul becomes impatient with Holdsworth's "happy egotism, his new-fangled foppery" (331). The truth is that Paul as well as Phillis must move beyond the power exerted by Holdsworth. Gaskell compares Holdsworth's "hold" on Paul to empire-building when she has Paul admit in an early evaluation: "My hero resumed all his empire over me by his bright merry laugh" (293). Of course, Holdsworth does go on to Canada, building his railroads and his empire and leaving a shattered world at Hope Farm. Gaskell's text suggests that he is an unthinking empire-builder, who resumes and extends power across oceans without the sensitivity to read the impact of change in times of transition. As well-read and cosmopolitan as he is, Holdsworth lacks the literacy of the heart.

Holdsworth's view of Phillis embodies the tendency of every man in her life to objectify her. Holdsworth isolates the parts of her in images that deny her an active life of the mind: she is a talking head, or a pretty mouth, or a Sleeping Beauty. Even her father sees her frozen in childhood. Paul is shocked to find his full-grown cousin still wearing a child's pinafore over her dress (266). But Paul too objectifies Phillis as he quotes Wordsworth's poem comparing his cousin to the Lucy whom there were none to praise and very few to love (327). Immediately, however, Paul has the sense to realize she is not like Lucy, nor is he William Wordsworth. But Phillis is not silenced as Wordsworth's Lucy was by the poet. Holdsworth moves on with the railroad to Canada where he marries another girl—appropriately named Lucy—Lucille Ventadour, to be exact. Though every man tries to objectify Phillis to suit his reading of the incidents that eventually bring her close to death, Gaskell rewrites the Lucy-script to have Phillis survive.

Though he may begin in ignorance—not able to read the dead-and-gone languages or to sing the words of "Come all harmonious tongues," not alert to his boss's engineering of his ambitions, not knowing when he has blundered in telling Phillis of Holdsworth's supposed love—Paul Manning does ultimately read the story with an understanding heart. What is more, he never cuts himself off from learning—whether his teacher is Minister Holman or the servant Betty or Half-wit Tim. In *Cousin Phillis,* Gaskell presents a democratization of learning that does not omit or devalue the least of her characters. Betty makes Paul aware of Holdsworth's "beguiling" and puts poor Paul in his place as she advises him to manage his own relationships with women better:

> Don't you be non of 'em, my lad. Not that you've got the gifts to do it, either; you're no great shakes to look at, neither for figure, nor yet for face, and it would need be a deaf adder to be taken in wi' your words, though there may be no great harm in 'em. (337)

After giving Paul this whipping with her tongue, Betty promises to keep Phillis's love secret: "I give you leave to cut out my tongue, and nail it up on th' barn door for a caution to magpies, if I let out on that poor wench" (338).

Paul also takes verbal abuse from the half-wit Timothy Cooper, but he learns from him also. When Phillis is near death, Paul escapes from the sick watch to walk down the road to Hornby. There he finds Tim sitting by the bridge. Tim had been dismissed by Minister Holman, who in his distraction lost patience with his stupidity. But Tim had been keeping the carts off the bridge all day to guard the quiet needed by the sleeping sick girl. Paul is dense when Tim tries to teach him the goal of his day-long watch over the bridge: "I reckon yo're no better nor a half-wit yourself" (353). Holdsworth had visualized Phillis as a Sleeping Beauty with himself as rescuing prince. Half-witted Tim knows she is a human being who can heal with rest. And Paul is open to what Tim can teach him.

Paul eventually proves himself better than a half-wit as he comes to read the multi-vocal truth. The crisis comes when, after Holdsworth's departure, Paul discovers Phillis's love by reading the margin of her book. Paul had been unaware of the reason for the change in Phillis, but when he visits at Christmastime, he finds out her secret. Significantly, she is reading a book when he catches her sobbing. As she runs out into the cold, Paul looks at the book and finds it is "one of those unintelligible Italian books," with Holdsworth's penciled handwriting in the margin (321-2). Paul learns to read the margin and suddenly knows the reason for the change in Phillis. He tells her of Holdsworth's spoken love for her and feels he has done right and spoken the truth. Later Holman accuses Paul of disturbing Phillis's innocence: "To put such thoughts into the child's head . . . to spoil her peaceful maidenhood with talk about another man's love; and such love too" (345).

Paul, however, has not been responsible for what has happened. He has read the margins of the experience even if he is slow and cannot translate the main text yet. He knows what has happened at Hope Farm. He recalls the pinafore Phillis wore past her childhood, and he cannot accept Holman's blame. Paul concludes, "I knew that the truth was different, though I could hardly have told it now" (345). Phillis's thirst for a wider experience has carried her beyond the harmony of Hope Farm. Her fall from innocence has broken that harmony. As Paul comments about the conversation at the dinner table, "Until now everything which I had heard spoken in that happy household were simple words of true meaning" (340). Paul has not caused the change, but he can understand and feel the impact of the changing world which brings discord to Hope Farm.

In deciding on the ending for *Cousin Phillis*, Gaskell did not allow the changes in Victorian society and the expansion of empire to bring about the death of Phillis; she rejected the script she inherited from the Romantics. Though Phillis is educated beyond her rank and station in Victorian society, this education does not protect her from the utilitarian language of the lie as Holdsworth practices it. Consequently, she suffers and draws close to death. Gaskell, however, did not permit the calculating, no-fault lie to become a sign of changing times, nor does she imply that learning is harmful to women. Women, as well as men, need to be educated to read the contexts of their world and to be able to translate their moral life into new contexts. No one can be sheltered by location, or gender, or class in changing times.

In an ending to the story which Gaskell did not publish but which she projected in a letter, Phillis was later to apply her knowledge of drainage, lore learned from Holdsworth on his visit, to modernize the village and protect it from the dangers of typhus fever. The letter also reveals that Gaskell imagined Phillis with orphaned children under her protection. This letter, which Gaskell sent to her publisher George Smith before finishing the story, also reveals Paul's position in the story, not as a bungler, but as a reader. Gaskell writes in her narrator's voice, "Phillis hearing her father's loud voice comes down, a cloak over her nightdress, & exculpates me by telling out how I had seen her fretting & *read her heart*."[21] In the ending of the novel Gaskell actually published in the *Cornhill*, readers know only that Phillis survives the attack of brain fever. Gaskell would not permit her to die, but in print she did not project such future activities as building drainage ditches and adopting orphans.

In *Cousin Phillis* as in *Sylvia's Lovers*, Gaskell has shown the interaction of multiple literacies: illiteracy, professional literacies, lore, and various degrees of classical learning. But rather than seeing the clashes of the many resulting discourses as an invitation to continuing misunderstanding, Gaskell reveals the mediating literacy of the heart, which is acquired not by reading but by suffering. In pushing her readers to question the Victorian standards of educations proper for class and gender, she promotes universal education. She argues for the reading of contexts as well as texts, but most of all she argues for the literacy of the heart.

Works Cited

Bakhtin, M. M. *The Dialogic Imagination*. Translated by Caryl Emerson and Michael Holquist, edited by Michael Holquist. Austin: University of Texas Press, 1981.

Bonaparte, Felicia. *The Gypsy-Bachelor of Manchester: The Life of Mrs. Gaskell's Demon*. Charlottesville: University Press of Virginia, 1992.

Burke, Kenneth. *A Grammar of Motives and a Rhetoric of Motives*. Cleveland: World Publishing, 1962.

Chapple, J. A. V. "Elizabeth Gaskell: Two Unpublished Letters to George Smith."*Etudes Anglaises* 23(1980): 183-87.

Chapple, J. A. V. and Arthur Pollard, eds. *The Letters of Mrs. Gaskell*. Cambridge: Harvard University Press, 1967.

Craik, Wendy. "Lore and Learning in *Cousin Phillis*, I." *Gaskell Society Journal* 3 (1989): 68-80.

D'Albertis, Deirdre. *Dissembling Fictions: Elizabeth Gaskell and the Victorian Social Text*. New York: St. Martin's Press, 1997.

Eagleton, Terry. "*Sylvia's Lovers* and Legality." *Essays in Criticism* 26 (1976): 17-27.

Furbank, P.N. "Mendacity in Mrs. Gaskell." *Encounter* 40 (1973): 51-55.

Gaskell, Elizabeth. *Cranford*. 1853. Edited by Elizabeth Porges Watson. Oxford: Oxford University Press, 1972.

—. *Cousin Phillis and Other Tales*. Edited by Angus Easson. Oxford: Oxford University Press, 1981.

—. *Sylvia's Lovers*. 1863. Edited by Andrew Sanders. Oxford: Oxford University Press, 1982.

Goody, Jack, and Ian Watt. "The Consequences of Literacy." *Comparative Studies In Society and History* 5 (1963): 304-45.

Kucich, John. *The Power of Lies: Transgression in Victorian Fiction*. Ithaca: Cornell University Press, 1994.

Lucas, John. *The Literature of Change: Studies in the Nineteenth-Century Provincial Novel*. 2nd ed. Sussex: Harvester, 1980.

Sanders, Gerald DeWitt. *Elizabeth Gaskell*. New Haven: Yale University Press, 1929.

Schor, Hilary M. *Scheherezade in the Marketplace: Elizabeth Gaskell and the Victorian Novel*. New York: Oxford University Press, 1992.

Stone, Donald D. *The Romantic Impulse in Victorian Fiction*. Cambridge: Harvard University Press, 1980.

Stone, Marjorie. "Bakhtinian Polyphony in *Mary Barton*: Class, Gender, and the Textual Voice." *Dickens Studies Annual* 20 (1991): 175-200.

Uglow, Jenny. *Elizabeth Gaskell: A Habit of Stories*. London: Faber and
Faber, 1993.
Watts, Isaac. *The Psalms of David Together with Hymns and Spiritual
Songs In Three Books*. Boston: I. Thomas and E. T. Andrews, 1791.

Notes

[1] Gaskell, *Sylvia's Lovers*, 38. Following references to *Sylvia's Lovers* are to this
edition and inserted in the text.

[2] Lying in Gaskell's novels was noted as early as 1929 by Gerald DeWitt Sanders
who listed instances of lying in three novels—*Ruth, North and South*, and *Sylvia's
Lovers*. "It appears that Mrs. Gaskell had more than a cursory interest in lying and
its effects" he noted in *Elizabeth Gaskell, 72*. Writing about narrative stance in
North and South led P.N. Furbank in 1973 to write an article published in
Encounter on "Mendacity in Mrs. Gaskell." Furbank concludes, "Mrs. Gaskell is
the poet of deceit; she knows the country of shams better than anyone" (55).
Postmodern criticism has found Gaskell split or even two-faced. John Lucas splits
her into her "official side . . . liberal, pious, incuriously middle class" and "the
unofficial side [which] keeps pushing this pattern [of reconciliation] awry,
revealing different patterns of inevitability, or antagonism, misunderstandings,
hatred" (*The Literature of Change: Studies in the Nineteenth-Century Provincial
Novel,*. 13). What Lucas calls the "marvelously anarchic force" in Gaskell's works
is not, in my view, the result of an unconscious split in the thrust of her novels, but
rather a conscious project to expand the truth. Nor do I believe it is a split in her
personality as Felicia Bonaparte has maintained in *The Gypsy-Bachelor of
Manchester: The Life of Mrs. Gaskell's Demon*. Bonaparte claims it was "only
through images that she could tell the world those truths she wanted not to know
herself" (11). According to Bonaparte, lying is one of Gaskell's "central images"
(170). Lies bother the official "Mrs. Gaskell" but express the secret self that she
has hidden even from herself. Two other works in the 1990s have given Gaskell
the benefit of a conscious project in her attention to lying. John Kucich in *The
Power of Lies: Transgression in Victorian Fiction* devotes a chapter to Gaskell in
which females are associated with lying and males with impulsiveness, but through
inversion many of these gender roles are reversed. Kucich recognizes the energies
released by these "transgressions" but locates Gaskell's project only within the
"logic of middle class power" (128) or for the purpose of preserving "existing
social boundaries" (141). On the other hand, I argue that lying opens up the
grounds for finding truth in the discourse of the working class, women, and other
marginalized voices. Deirdre D'Albertis in her *Dissembling Fictions: Elizabeth
Gaskell and the Victorian Social Text*, focuses on Gaskell's plots, finding three
forms of dissembling: 1) disguising, or doubling characters; 2) withholding or
misrepresenting the truth, and 3) resisting or subverting political or social
authority. I agree with D'Albertis and her recognition of Gaskell's subversive

plots, but my emphasis is on language. Both Kucich and D'Albertis recognize the energy and power Gaskell's lies call up and the resulting interrogation of her culture, but neither argues that her project expands the language of truth.

[3] Burke, *A Grammar of Motives and A Rhetoric of Motives*, 12.

[4] Marjorie Stone has made an excellent case for applying Bakhtin to Gaskell's conscious use of "varieties of middle-class, working-class, and women's discourse in *Mary Barton*." "Bakhtinian Polyphony in *Mary Barton*: Class, Gender, and the Textual Voice." 177. Stone's analysis deals well with the key concepts of duty and improvidence in that novel, but I believe that Bakhtin speaks to Gaskell's project to expand the grounds of truth in all of her novels.

[5] Bakhtin, *The Dialogic Imagination*, 263. Further citations to this work are given in the text.

[6] Chapple and Pollard, eds. *The Letters of Mrs. Gaskell*, 67.

[7] Gaskell, *Cousin Phillis and other Tales*, 275. Following references to *Cousin Phillis* are to this edition and are inserted in the text.

[8] Sanders, ed. Note. *Sylvia's Lovers*, 521.

[9] Stone, *The Romantic Impulse in Victorian Fiction*, 164.

[10] Gaskell, *Cranford*, edited by Elizabeth Porges Watson, 84.

[11] Schor, *Scheherezade in the Marketplace: Elizabeth Gaskell and the Victorian Novel*, 84.

[12] Eagleton, "*Sylvia's Lovers* and Legality," 22.

[13] Goody and Watt, "The Consequences of Literacy," 337.

[14] Ibid., 334.

[15] Uglow, *Elizabeth Gaskell: A Habit of Stories*, 515.

[16] Ibid., 546.

[17] Craik, "Lore and Learning in *Cousin Phillis*, I," 68.

[18] Watts, *The Psalms of David Together with Hymns and Spiritual Songs in These Books*, 184.

[19] Gaskell, *Cousin Phillis*, 363.

[20] Uglow, *Elizabeth Gaskell: A Habit of Stories,* 546.

[21] Chapple, "Elizabeth Gaskell: Two Unpublished Letters to George Smith," 184. Italics are mine.

CHAPTER TEN

IDENTITY, IDEOLOGY, AND INSCRIPTION: NARRATIVE ACTS AS THE SITE OF RESISTANCE IN *THE WOMAN IN WHITE*

ARIA CHERNIK

Wilkie Collins' *The Woman in White* is a novel that emphasizes text and textuality to a remarkable degree. The book is presented as a compilation of diary entries and personal narratives, and while Walter Hartright plays a significant role as an actor within the plot, he arguably serves a more critical role as the editor who weaves disparate tales into a coherent story about the social, narrative, and ideological construction of identity formation. Although Walter opens the tale by exclaiming that *The Woman in White* is "the story of what a Woman's patience can endure, and what a Man's resolution can achieve," I posit that *The Woman in White* is more accurately a story about the narrative element of ideology; namely, about the intersection of identity, ideology, and inscription. What is particularly fascinating about this intersection as enacted in *The Woman in White* is that the narrative element of ideology is most powerfully revealed not in the novel's densely textual or even metatextual moments, but in moments of blank space. These blank spaces bring moments of resistance to and reformation of the dominant patriarchal and class order to the fore. That is, gender and social identity in *The Woman in White* are most sharply defined vis-à-vis blank textual spaces because it is during these moments in which the illusory nature of ideology is made clear, a counter ideology is reinscribed back into ideological discourse, and resistance to a dominant order is made possible. Marxist philosopher Louis Althusser reveals the essential connection between identity and ideology, and it is Althusser's theory of identity formation that serves as the methodological paradigm of my analysis of how narrative acts enact ideological fracture and gender and class reformation in *The Woman in White*.

According to Althusser, identity is inexorably tied to interpellation, which is the process through which an individual is transformed into a subject. When an individual recognizes that he or she is being hailed as a specific someone and acknowledges the connection between the one hailing and himself or herself, if he or she answers the hailing he or she is transformed from an individual into a subject. Althusser suggests that

> "ideology 'acts' or 'functions' in such a way that it 'recruits' subjects among the individuals . . . or 'transforms' the individuals into subjects . . . by that very precise operation which I have called *interpellation* or hailing, and which can be imagined along the lines of the most commonplace everyday police (or other) hailing: 'Hey, you there!'"[1]

It is with the turning of the "you," what Althusser calls the "mere one-hundred-and-eighty-degree physical conversion,"[2] that the "you" becomes a subject by the very action of recognizing that the hail was addressed to him or her and that it was really he or she who was hailed. Under such a theory of subject formation, one cannot separate identity from ideological or narrative elements, as all are embedded in human interaction, and particularly within the discourse through which we navigate such interaction.[3] Discussing the narrative element of ideology, as well as the way in which ideology is deeply embedded within everyday thoughts and practices, Catherine Belsey has reasoned that "we cannot simply step outside [ideology]. To do so would be to refuse to act or speak, and even to make such a refusal, to say 'I refuse', is to accept the condition of subjectivity"[4] that results from the interpellative process. I suggest that while it may not be possible to step "outside" ideology, it may be possible to reinscribe a counter ideology back into the discourse and engage in one's own form of narrative radicalism, practices which are enacted in *The Woman in White*.

One of the most compelling scenes in *The Woman in White* occurs when Sir Percival Glyde orders Lady Laura Glyde (née Fairlie) to mark her signature on a legal document, which would provide Percival control over some of his wife's income. Laura assents under the condition that she be allowed the opportunity to read the deed first:

> "I ought surely to know what I am signing, Sir Percival, before I write my name?"
> "Nonsense! What have women to do with business? I tell you again, you can't understand it."
> "At any rate, let me try to understand it. Whenever Mr. Gilmore had any business for me, he always explained it, first; and I always understood him."

"I dare say he did. He was your servant, and was obliged to explain. I am your husband, and am *not* obliged."[5]

When Laura continues to express her reasonable request to read the document before she becomes legally bound to it, Percival raises the deed and angrily strikes it back on the table, after which his mentor, Count Fosco, counsels him, "Control your unfortunate temper, Percival."[6] As an astute reader of human nature, Fosco understands that Percival's rising temper will not effect the desired result; rather, it only instills in Laura a more resolute stance to be mistress of her own inscription, signature, and self. Indeed, up until this scene Laura had been docile, marrying Percival even though she was in love with Walter and agreeing thus far to all of the terms of their marriage.

Upon Percival's threatening stance, and subsequent insult that Laura had lost all scruples upon marrying him, even Laura's sister Marian is stunned at Laura's fierce resistance to providing her signature, to preserving the blank space on the legal deed. In a gesture of marking and demarcating herself that is opposite from the one that Percival had attempted to force, Laura throws down the pen and, as Marian describes, "looked at him with an expression in her eyes, which throughout all my experience of her, I had never seen in them before—and turned her back on him in dead silence."[7] Laura, the previously malleable and submissive wife, boldly retorts to Percival, "I refuse my signature until I have read every line in that parchment from the first word to the last. Come away, Marian, we have remained here long enough."[8]

Having remained contained—both literally within the bounds of the room and within the bounds of the dominant ideology of patriarchal oppression—Laura makes commands about her body and her own signature and identity for the first time. Notably, her refusal to be prescribed to inscribe mirrors her growing resistance to having ideological prescriptions inscribed on her identity. In "'Conscience Doth Make Subjects of Us All,'" Judith Butler comments on the criminalizing, or at least self-implicating, aspect of Althusser's theory of interpellation. Butler explains that the hail always carries within it a charge, that the "Hey, you there!" is "a demand to align oneself with the law . . . and an entrance into the language of self-ascription—'Here I am'—through the appropriation of guilt."[9] It is through ideological recognition, and its attendant material practices—shaking hands, inviting one in—that subjects are interpellated. Butler goes on to ponder, "What is the significance in turning to face the voice of the law? This turning toward the voice of the law is a sign of a certain desire to be beheld by and perhaps also to behold the face of authority."[10]

When Laura responds with written and verbal silence to Percival's demand that she inscribe her mark, when she preserves the blank space awaiting her signature, she refuses Percival's hail. Indeed, rather than engaging in Althusser's ideological recognition, Laura turns *away* from her husband's call. Percival's attempt to prescribe Laura to inscribe is ultimately impotent, and rather than a mark being left in the form of Laura's signature, the two marks that remain after this scene are merely Percival's insult, which "had left the mark of its profanation so plainly on [Laura's] face that even a stranger might have seen it,"[11] and Laura's mark of narrative resistance to Percival's dominant ideology that a husband, unlike a servant, is not obliged to explain matters of import to his wife, particularly when the topic is a monetary one. Percival's prescription ("'Come back and sign!'") is futile, and serves only to reinforce the material, blank space of the *pre*-scription, what is there *before* the mark, before the writing, and *after* Laura's tracing out boundaries, after Laura's breaking the Law by withholding her signature and thereby marking herself.

In a second scene in which Laura and Marian are once again confronted with Percival's brute force, Marian understands that, as the exploited gender, resistance in kind is futile.[12] In fact, it is the corporeal embodiment of Percival's repression (in the form of a bruise mark that Percival inflicts on Laura's arm) that Marian makes her most direct and explicit statement about the necessity to resist the dominant order of feminine submission. Marian tells her sister Laura that "our endurance must end, and our resistance must begin, to-day. That mark is a weapon to strike him with."[13] The "strike," however, is not a physical blow, but rather is leveled via Marian's own written narrative. In "The Madwoman Outside the Attic: Eavesdropping and Narrative Agency in *The Woman in White*," Ann Gaylin notes that in this scene, Marian "refuses the role of feminine passivity in favor of linguistic . . . action" and explains that the mark on Laura's body "is translated into a mark on the page, as the battlefield becomes an explicitly textual one."[14]

The subversive ability of a woman to resist the command of her husband—i.e. resist the command of the State and the state of the patriarchal order—via narrative acts in *The Woman in White* is emphasized by the existence of the character Anne Catherick, who may be viewed as Laura's doppelgänger. Anne resists answering the narrative and ideological hail of the Law when we first meet her. Having escaped from a psychiatric asylum, Anne flees the hail of the police, the ultimate embodiment of the physical repression of the dominant Law and State, and the asylum attendants, who are paid by Percival to keep Anne contained.

When Anne meets Walter in the street, she does operate within the framework of ideological recognition by implicating herself as a suspect answering the hail so as to individuate herself. She questions Walter, "You don't suspect me of doing anything wrong, do you? I have done nothing wrong. I have met with an accident – I am very unfortunate in being here alone so late. Why do you suspect me of doing wrong?"[15] This narrative echoes Judith Butler's explanation of how interpellation, including submission to the dominant ideology, makes suspects out of individuals:

> The "submission" to the rules of dominant ideology might [] be understood as a submission to the necessity to prove innocence in the face of accusation, a submission to the demand for proof, an execution of that proof, and the acquisition of the status of the subject in and through a compliance with the terms of the interrogative law. To become a "subject" is, thus, to have been presumed guilty, then tried and declared innocent.[16]

However, while Anne wishes to declare herself a subject, what Butler characterizes as an "emblem of lawfulness" and a "citizen in good standing,"[17] upon meeting Walter, she resists this declaration, this hail, this "Stop!", when it is asserted by the State.

Considering Laura and Anne's refusal of the hail as a refusal of the Law underscores the legal aspect of the interpellative process and identity formation. Indeed, in *The Woman in White* identity is cast not just as narrative and ideological issues, but as a legal one as well.[18] The intersection of these issues, and the way in which blank space paradoxically highlights rather than effaces the connection between these issues in the novel, culminates in the manner in which Walter discovers the truth about Percival's identity. Although Sir Percival represents the dominant gender and class order, this representation is complicated by the fact that Percival has obtained his title and class status in an illegitimate way. The secret that Sir Percival desperately attempts to contain is that he is the product of a union between his unmarried parents, and that to conceal his illegitimate title he has forged an entry with his parents' names into the original, though not into the copy, of the marriage register of his parish church. It is by discovering this blank space on the register copy that Walter learns that Percival has wrongfully appropriated both his inheritance and his title. Dispersing Percival's identity with the astonishing revelation that Percival's parents' "marriage was not there," Walter notes the blank space on the deed and exclaims, "That space told the whole story!"[19]

Walter's emphasis on the significance of blank space is particularly noteworthy given the import he places on his self-assigned "editorial authority"[20] to assemble written narratives as the way to reveal the truth. That it is through exposing a space of noninscription that actually authenticates Walter's authority as editor, and, ultimately, as a member of the upper class through his marriage to Laura, demonstrates the power that such a space holds in the novel's theory of containment and subject formation, in which one's identity is tied to inscription of title or prescription into a lower class. Once Sir Percival's body is stripped of "Sir," he is cast out of the aristocracy and, even further, his very corporeality ends as he is killed just as his secret is revealed. Unlike Percival, who attempts to illegitimately assert his identity into a class to which he does not by birth belong, Walter locates the site of his resistance to strict class separation via narrative with successful results. While Percival increasingly loses power and comes to look, according to Marian, more "like a prisoner at the bar than a gentleman in his own house,"[21] Walter's ability to leave the middle, working class and inscribe himself into the upper class relates directly to his ability to control the narrative of *The Woman in White*.

Walter introduces himself at the opening of the novel by confiding that, "For my own poor part, the fading summer left me out of health, out of spirits, and, if the truth must be told, out of money as well."[22] When the Fairlies employ Walter as a drawing instructor at their home, it is not by his working hard that Walter ultimately ascends the ranks of the Fairlie family, but rather by his seizing narrative control. In Walter Hartright's preamble to his edited collection of first-person narratives that compose *The Woman in White*, he signifies himself as "Walter Hartright, of Clement's Inn, Teacher of Drawing." Walter also promises that "the story here presented" has the object "to present the truth always in its most direct and most intelligible aspect; and to trace the course of one complete series of events, by making two persons who have been most closely connected with them, at each successive stage, relate their own experience, word for word."[23] Walter is neither of Clement's Inn nor a teacher of drawing at the time he writes his narrative; in fact, he is securely installed as head of Limmeridge House and a member of the non-working, upper class. Further, *The Woman in White* is not presented in the most direct way, but rather is driven in its very narrative style by circumlocution, concealment, and selective editing. It is many more than two persons who write the text, but only one, Walter himself—who, as self-proclaimed editor admittedly defaces certain words from Marian's diary as he deems appropriate—who controls the text. Indeed, it is because of Walter's narrative proof that the body which the townspeople are viewing is indeed Laura Fairlie and not her doppelgänger Anne Catherick that Laura is legitimately accepted back into her original social class and, in turn, that she inscribes Walter as her husband into this upper class.[24]

In her discussion of Althusser's paradigm of subject formation, Judith Butler uses the phrase "place-holder" to explain how the Althusserian term "individual" provisionally satisfies the grammatical need for a word to signify the entity that is pre-subject, i.e., has initiated or been initiated by but has not completed the process of interpellation.[25] "Place-holder" is extraordinarily apt as a description of this Althusserian moment, as a "place-holder" is used to *mark* one's place in a text, and the *Oxford English Dictionary* states that "mark" denotes "to leave an indicator of the point up to which one has read in a book," "to put a person's initials or other identifying mark on," "to affirm," "to show or manifest (displeasure) by some significant action," "to characterize a person," "to trace out boundaries for," "to demarcate," "to inscribe," and "to set down in writing." The intersection of the existence of distinguishing and identifying characteristics with the processes of separation, classification, staking out ground, avowal, disavowal, and writing manifests the way in which narrative acts in *The Woman in White* provide a space of resistance to reinscribe a counter ideology about the re-formation—and indeed the reformation—of dominant gender and class order.

The import of ideological reinscription and identity reformation in the novel is materially realized in blank textual spaces. These spaces may be better understood in light of Butler's explication of a "place-holder," and in light of the fact that the title character of the novel, Anne Catherick/Laura Fairlie, the woman in white, is a corporeal representation of these blank textual spaces. Frequently described in the novel in terms suggestive of blank pages—dressed in all white or light colors and easily impressed upon—the bodies of Anne and Laura are used to mark a space until Walter's whole narrative text, the "true" story, is ready for public consumption and judgment, until Laura can resist physical containment by the State via narrative acts. Indeed, as Walter notes, because "the Law is still . . . the pre-engaged servant of the long purse,"[26] Walter, Laura, and Marian must find a different venue for their project of resisting both the violent repression and the dominant ideology asserted by that very Law. Thus, although she does not contribute a formal narrative to *The Woman in White*, Anne Catherick is an essential formal feature of the novel. Indeed, the woman in white is not an embodiment of passivity and the bareness of a blank space, of the ghostly illusion to which she is so frequently alluded throughout the novel; rather, she is Butler's "place-holder," the pre-interpellative subject, the possibility for resistance and reform, the possibility of being written into an existence that provides the richness of a blank space to reinscribe a counter ideology in the form of radical narrativism.

Works Cited

Althusser, Louis. "Ideology and Ideological State Apparatuses (Notes Towards an Investigation)." *Lenin and Philosophy and Other Essays*. Trans. Ben Brewster. New York: Monthly Review Press, 1971. 127-186.

Belsey, Catherine. *Critical Practice*. 2ed. London: Routledge, 2002.

Bernstein, Stephen. "Reading Blackwater Park: Gothicism, Narrative, and Ideology in *The Woman in White*." *Studies in the Novel* 25 (1993): 291-305.

Butler, Judith. "'Conscience Doth Make Subjects of Us All.'" *Yale French Studies* 88 (1995): 6-26.

Collins, Wilkie. *The Woman in White*, edited by Matthew Sweet. London: Penguin, 1999.

Gaylin, Ann. "The Madwoman Outside the Attic: Eavesdropping and Narrative Agency in *The Woman in White*." *Texas Studies in Language and Literature* 43 (2001): 303-333.

Loesberg, Jonathan. "The Ideology of Narrative Form in Sensation Fiction." *Representations* 13 (1986): 115-138.

Perkins, Pamela and Mary Donaghy. "A Man's Resolution: Narrative Strategies in Wilkie Collins' *The Woman in White*." *Studies in the Novel* 22 (1990): 392-402.

Thomas, Ronald R. "Detection in the Victorian Novel." *The Cambridge Companion to the Victorian Novel*, edited by Deirdre David. Cambridge: Cambridge U P, 2001. 169-191.

Notes

[1] Althusser, "Ideology and Ideological State Apparatuses," 174.

[2] Ibid.

[3] Althusser explains that it does not behoove the dominant order, or Repressive State Apparatus (RSA), to make explicit the necessary relationship between identity, ideological, and narrative elements. Indeed, Althusser notes that dominant ideology functions as a veil of sorts, as it masks the reality of the conditions of existence of individuals, and perpetuates "the reproduction of the relations of production," Althusser, "Ideology and Ideological State Apparatuses," (154). Notably, because they represent an imaginary existence, ideologies constitute an

illusion; however, despite their illusory nature, ideologies do make an allusion to reality, even if the allusion is what forms the basis of distortion, or illusion. Thus, ideologies, once interpreted, can actually lead individuals to reality, as that reality represents "the reality of the world behind their imaginary representation of that world," (162). Expressed another way, ideologies are both the vehicles for distorting the reality of one's position and signature in the world, and for revealing the truth behind that distortion, for providing a site of interpretation and resistance to the illusion. Significantly, Marxist ideological theory holds that because of the difficulty of an exploited class to resist the brute force attendant to the RSA, it is through the Ideological State Apparatuses (ISAs)—such as narrative acts—that resistance to and clarity about the dominant order can be realized.

[4] Belsey, *Critical Practice*, 58.

[5] Collins, *The Woman in White*, 244.

[6] Ibid.

[7] Ibid., 247.

[8] Ibid.

[9] Butler, "'Conscience Doth Make Subjects of Us All,'" 6.

[10] Ibid., 11.

[11] Collins, *The Woman in White*, 247.

[12] Althusser contends that resistance to the State Apparatus is most effectively realized at the ideological—as opposed to repressive—level because ISAs function predominantly by ideology while the RSA functions predominantly by physical force.

[13] Collins, *The Woman in White*, 299.

[14] Gaylin, "The Madwoman Outside the Attic," 316.

[15] Collins, *The Woman in White*, 25.

[16] Butler, "'Conscience Doth Make Subjects of Us All,'" 16.

[17] Ibid.

[18] The narrative and criminal elements underlying the interpellative process are particularly interesting when considered in the context of the nineteenth-century novel generally and the sensation novel *The Woman in White* specifically, as it was during this historical period that saw the emergence of the modern police force and the Foucaultian panopticon, Thomas, "Detection in the Victorian Novel," (170, 176). In "Reading Blackwater Park: Gothicism, Narrative, and Ideology in *The Woman in White*," Stephen Bernstein considers Percival's gothic residence as enacting "the growth of Foucault's panoptical model of society, that modern system whereby all can be known, transcribed, and regulated by central modes of control," Bernstein, "Reading Blackwater Park," (293). Bernstein notes how within the confines of Blackwater Park, Percival and Fosco uphold the aristocratic and patriarchal order, and that the estate "takes on the characteristics of the marriages which it houses and begins to appear as a socio-economic, as well as literal, carceral," (295). One scholar notes that the essential difference between nineteenth-century sensation fiction and other novels' forms is that the sensation novel envisions the problem of identity "in its legal and class aspects rather than in

its psychological aspect," Loesberg, "The Ideology of Narrative Form in Sensation Fiction," 117.

[19] Collins, *The Woman in White*, 509.

[20] Perkins and Donaghy, "A Man's Resolution," 397.

[21] Collins, *The Woman in White*, 244.

[22] Ibid., 10.

[23] Ibid., 9.

[24] Thomas, "Detection in the Victorian Novel," 180-81.

[25] Butler, "'Conscience Doth Make Subjects of Us All,'" 15.

[26] Collins, *The Woman in White*, 9.

PART IV

EXPANDED PERSPECTIVES

CHAPTER ELEVEN

REFORMING BEAUTY IN BRONTË'S *SHIRLEY*

MARGARET E. MITCHELL

As an industrial novel, Charlotte Brontë's *Shirley* explicitly confronts the Victorian problem of the relationship between capital and labor, or mill owners and their workers. In this sense, the novel overtly claims a place in the discourse of nineteenth-century social reform, a claim strengthened by the unusual fact that many chapters go by before the novel introduces us to our heroine, her domestic surroundings, or the merest hint of anyone's marriage prospects.[1] Ultimately, *Shirley* promotes the familiar Victorian notion that increased sympathy between masters and workers will generate improved class relations and mutual prosperity. The novel is clearly interested in social justice, in other words, but its explicit recommendations, however movingly dramatized, might have strayed in from any of a number of other novels.

The belated introduction of the novel's heroine, however, introduces a more provocative register of ethical possibility, inviting us to consider beauty—particularly feminine beauty—as an alternative site for the exploration of social conflict. Caroline Helstone is a rare exception to Brontë's tendency to reject the convention that the heroines of novels ought to be beautiful. In fact, Brontë does not so much embrace this convention, in *Shirley*, as insist that we pay attention to it. If, as Lori Lefkovitz argues in *The Character of Beauty in the Victorian Novel*, "we have actually been trained to ignore descriptions of beauty,"[2] Brontë challenges us to ignore our literary lessons. She refuses to let us see Caroline's beauty as a mere matter of course, but presents it instead a phenomenon worthy of evaluation, one crucial to understanding Caroline's character and her choices. Ultimately, Caroline's recognition and studied negotiation of her own beauty provide a model for social relations on a larger scale.

The curiously negative syntax of the sentences with which Brontë introduces Caroline Helstone's aesthetic charms immediately alerts our attention to the significance of her appearance: "To her had not been denied the gift of beauty,"[3] Brontë writes, suggesting that Caroline is at once anomalous and perhaps simply lucky. A later description echoes this pattern, informing us that "her cheek had a colour, her eyes a light, her countenance an expression [. . .] which would have made even plain features striking; *but there was not the grievous defect of plainness to pardon in her case*" (Emphasis added).[4] The narrator's presentation of Caroline's charms is slightly ironic, even rather grudging; this holds true later for the title's Shirley, too, when we are assured that "Shirley Keeldar was no ugly heiress."[5] Such constructions, forcing us to acknowledge the possibility of plainness before negating it, invite us to conjure up grievously defective heroines and ugly heiresses before rejecting them in favor of the painstakingly described and aesthetically agreeable Caroline and Shirley, and, crucially, to assume that their beauty will have narrative significance.

Having thus engaged the reader's own aesthetic prejudices, these descriptions also immediately claim for beauty an explicitly social dimension: "[I]t was not absolutely necessary to know her in order to like her," the narrator remarks of Caroline, adding that "her eyes [...] were gifted at times with a winning beam that stole into the heart, with a language that spoke softly to the affection."[6] Embedded in a long catalogue of Caroline's physical charms, observations like these seem designed to beguile us into assigning to her corresponding moral traits, those conventional virtues belonging to pretty, modestly dressed Victorian heroines—virtues that might reasonably elicit approval and admiration. But the narrator, as if anticipating our impulse, interrupts: "So much for Caroline Helstone's appearance; as to her character or intellect, if she had any, they must speak for themselves in due time."[7] This rather severe narrator, carefully unwilling to give beauty more than its due, also establishes an unsettlingly fragmented conception of Caroline: if her character and intellect speak for themselves, while her pretty eyes possess a "language" that speaks to the "affections," then by implication she is less a coherent subject than an assemblage of speaking parts, parts which might have conflicting, even contradictory things to say. Shirley's features also speak, though rather more enigmatically than Caroline's: "their changes were not to be understood, nor their language interpreted all at once."[8] Endowing beauty with language, the novel produces not only an interpretive impulse but an evaluative one: beauty must not only be read and interpreted as a text, but its veracity questioned, its effects examined.

Such passages—which are numerous and often lengthy—position the reader as an impartial observer, bringing an eye as critical and perceptive as the narrator's to these figures. But the novel complicates its examination of female beauty by assigning Caroline herself an even more intimate perspective. Ignoring the conventions which dictate that properly modest and virtuous heroines must be tactfully oblivious to their own physical attractions, Brontë insists that Caroline, like anyone else in the Yorkshire village, is bound to read her own face and draw conclusions from what she finds there. In the scene in which she combs her hair before her mirror, we are told that "she saw her own face and form in the glass. Such reflections," the narrator remarks,

> are sobering to plain people: their own eyes are not enchanted with the image; they are confident then that the eyes of others can see in it no fascination; but the fair must naturally draw other conclusions: the picture is charming, and must charm. Caroline saw a shape, a head, that, daguerreotyped in that attitude and with that expression, would have been lovely: she could not choose but derive from the spectacle confirmation to her hopes.[9]

Experiencing her own beauty as a "spectacle," imagining her features not just reflected but represented in a "daguerreotype" and thereby recognizing her own "loveliness," Caroline establishes a conscious and critical relationship with her beauty.[10] For her, the narrator points out, there is only one way to read this pleasing image: it can only confirm her hopes—hopes that revolve, specifically, around her cousin, mill owner Robert Moore, with whom she has been enjoying the early stages of a mutual attraction. In her pretty face, then, she confidently reads her destiny—her narrative trajectory. At the same time, she stands curiously outside of herself: as she gazes upon her reflection, "[h]er thoughts," we are told, "were speaking with her; speaking pleasantly, as it seemed, for she smiled as she listened."[11] Once again, the novel presents Caroline as divided: her thoughts converse with her as with another person; she studies and reads her face as if it were someone else's. Her experience of her beauty is pleasurable, because of the impending happy marriage it implies, but it also demands a profoundly fractured form of consciousness: an observing self and an observed self; a judging self and a self that is judged; a listening self and a speaking self. Such divisions present no difficulties in this scene, because the divided elements of Caroline's self are in agreement,; but such a model of the self also clearly presents the potential for conflict.

Specifically, it is Caroline's ability to identify and correctly interpret her beauty that becomes a site of discord. Elaine Scarry offers a way of thinking about this in *On Beauty and Being Just* when she proposes that a kind of propensity for what she calls "error" is intrinsic to beauty. After cataloguing the possibilities for error generated by the perception—or misperception—of beauty, she observes that "the experience of 'being in error' so inevitably accompanies the perception of beauty that it begins to seem one of its abiding structural features," arguing that while beauty "fills the perceiver with a sense of conviction about that beauty," at the same time, "the act of perceiving that seemingly self-evident beauty has a built-in liability to self-adjustment and self-correction, so much so that it appears to be a key element in whatever beauty is."[12] In other words, not only are we capable of failing to recognize beauty when we see it, or to thinking something (or someone) is beautiful when it is not, but such a capacity for mistakes is built into our very perception of beauty. To see beauty is to doubt it. For Caroline, as both the beautiful thing and the perceiver of that beauty, this intrinsic conflict is necessarily dramatized at the level of her very selfhood. Despite the confidence evident in the scene just described, in which Caroline rests secure in the belief that both her perception and her interpretation of that perception are accurate, ensuing events force her to reevaluate both.

Her error, though, is not precisely accounted for by Scarry's categories, which distinguish the failure to recognize beauty when it exists from the mistaken attribution of beauty to things that do not, in fact, possess it .[13] In other words, it is not that Caroline—at this point—suddenly ceases to see herself as beautiful. Instead, Moore's failure to follow through on the trajectory Caroline has imagined forces her to consider that her *interpretation* of her beauty might have been flawed, that her beauty might not, in fact, mean what she assumed it did. Sitting again in her bedroom, reflecting on Moore's altered behavior and deliberate avoidance of her company, Caroline acknowledges the likelihood that she has erred and revises her reading accordingly, thereby engaging in a version of the process of self-correction Scarry describes: "I shall not be married, it appears…Probably I shall be an old maid."[14] Caroline's recognition of her error forces her to consider alternative narrative trajectories for her life; significantly, it leads her to imagine that the scope of her life might extend beyond a narrow private sphere to a wider social one.

Formulated explicitly in response to Caroline's revised reading of her beauty, this reorientation is a significant shift. Earlier in the novel, Caroline expresses a desire to be a boy so that she might apprentice herself to Robert, work in his counting house, and help him—as she states quite baldly—to get "rich." Later, when the possibility emerges that she might unite herself with him in a more conventionally feminine way, her imagination presents her with a slightly different picture: she might venture to "tell him of his faults," but primarily she would "study his

comfort, and cherish him, and do [her] best to make him happy."[15] Both
fantasies posit a subordinate position within a closed world, an acceptance
of Robert's desires as her own, an exchange of her beauty and labor for
Robert's company; moreover, they bear little trace of the Caroline Robert
has once teased as a "little democrat."

Although Caroline has frequently voiced a passionate if rather vague
interest in social justice, lecturing Moore on his harsh treatment of his
workers and his tendency to, as she says, "include all poor working people
under the general and insulting name of 'the mob,'"[16] she has never
considered that her own life might offer a social role beyond that of
Robert's helpmate. Scarry's articulation of the effect of beauty offers a
way of understanding Caroline's social and ethical development.
According to Scarry, "[s]omething beautiful fills the mind yet invites the
search for something beyond itself, something larger or something of the
same scale with which it needs to be brought into relation."[17] Now that
Caroline has relinquished the idea of bringing herself into "relation" with
Robert Moore, she must search for something else, a different kind of
meaning in her life, a process which leads her mind along unfamiliar
paths. Rejecting the notion that beauty "causes us to gape and suspend all
thought," Scarry argues that, on the contrary, "the beautiful person or thing
incites in us the longing for truth"; that beauty is, in fact, "the starting
point for education."[18]

For Caroline, as both the beautiful person and the perceiver of that
beauty, the form that education takes is caught up in the construction of
her very identity. Moore's apparent rejection provokes in her, not tears or
despair, but a meditation on virtue and selfhood: "Does virtue," she asks
herself, "lie in abnegation of self? I do not believe it."[19] If beauty may
incite a search for truth, and if Caroline's recognition of her beauty is an
essential component of herself, then her rejection of "self-abnegation"
implicitly proposes a relationship, rather than a conflict, between self and
virtue, beauty and truth. Caroline, at this point, still questions the validity
of her untested reflections: "Queer thoughts, these, that surge in my mind:
are they right thoughts? I am not certain."[20] Her lack of certainty echoes
the new sense of fallibility introduced by her initial misreading of her
beauty, and her musings on virtue lead her away from beauty to an
investigation of its opposite: her pilgrimage-like venture into the world of
the "goblin-grimness" of "old maids" Miss Mann and Miss Ainley, two
local women as notorious for their ugliness as they are admired for their
altruism. This curious education encourages Caroline to embark upon
various altruistic projects of her own, and inspires weekly visits to the old
women; it brings her into contact with poverty and misfortune, and permits

her to begin shaping an active role in the community, fashioning an ethical and social function for her labor as well as her beauty.

By this point in the novel, however, Caroline's beauty has in fact been fading for some time, in a characteristically Victorian response to Robert's apparent loss of interest in her. Her physical decline, which culminates in a serious illness, generates or reveals a proliferation of "errors" on the part of various onlookers, serving not only to emphasize the extent to which Caroline's narrative trajectory is (and has been) caught up in her beauty, but to set up turning points for the plot of the novel itself. Caroline's altered appearance provokes the entire community, for instance, to revise its own reading of her countenance: "Everyone noticed the change in Miss Helstone's appearance," the narrator informs us, "and most people said she was going to die."[21] For them, too, her beauty implied a destiny; deprived of it, her life is unimaginable. Robert Moore himself observes the change in her, but falls into a different kind of error, failing—or refusing—to acknowledge his own role in her physical decline. Meanwhile, he is intent upon compounding his error, adopting the goal of marrying Shirley, his business partner and, of course, an heiress capable of repairing his finances. Finally, Caroline's health crisis prompts Caroline's unknown mother to identify herself and to offer an explanation for her early abandonment of her daughter that hinges, significantly, on the little girl's beauty. "I let you go as a babe," Mrs. Pryor plains, "because you were pretty, and I feared your loveliness, deeming it the stamp of perversity."[22] Interpreting her daughter's beauty as a mark of heredity and a link to her profligate father, Mrs. Pryor's error regarding Caroline's beauty becomes the key determining factor in her early life, leaving her motherless and in the care of her chilly uncle.

Ultimately, then, the resolution of the novel depends to a considerable extent upon the correction of these errors. Mrs. Pryor comes to see that beauty is not the sign of "a mind warped and cruel," as she had feared; that it can in fact be a concomitant" of "truth, modesty, [and] good principle."[23] Robert Moore must confess that only his "judgment" pronounces Shirley beautiful, but she does not "make him better."[24] And, although my emphasis has been on Caroline, it is worth noting that Louis Moore makes a similar discovery about Shirley's beauty and its effect upon him: "Once I only *saw* her beauty;" he observes; "now I feel it." [25] In both cases, beauty is revealed, not as a static, observable quality, but as a relation, a kind of force, and it is precisely this force that ultimately unites the novel's domestic plots with its overarching political claims. According to Scarry, beauty is "a contract between the beautiful being...and the perceiver," a contract which not only bestows upon each "the gift of life," but exerts what she calls a "pressure toward distribution,"[26] which she associates with justice.

It is no coincidence, surely, that Caroline's earlier self-oriented meditation on altruism and human rights appears in a chapter that opens with gloomy reflections on the political and economic state of England. Ultimately, Caroline's experience of her own beauty leads her not *away* from the political and economic realm but into it, while her influence on Robert Moore—despite his resistance—leads him way from self interest and toward a newfound commitment to social justice. When at last he proposes marriage to Caroline, their conversation moves swiftly from practical domestic arrangements to the social function of their union: "If you get rich," Caroline asks, "you will do good with your money, Robert?" He reassures her: "I will do good; you shall tell me how: indeed, I have some schemes of my own, which you and I will talk about on our hearth one day. I have seen the necessity of doing good: I have learned the downright folly of being selfish."[27] Thus the effect of Caroline's beauty finds expression in a "distributive" impulse concretized in their mutual vision for the district as a whole.

Brontë does not substitute domestic peace for political strife, but constructs an ending that makes domestic happiness contingent upon social change, and infuses domesticity with social purpose. Robert's impending prosperity is not, after all, a vague novelistic reward for personal virtue, nor a chance endowment of inheritance: it is a direct result of legislation, namely the 1812 repeal of the Orders in Council, that frees up Moore's trading prospects and enables him to marry for non-mercenary motives. Robert and Caroline's romantic vision of discussing future schemes for social "projects" by their hearth, the very place from which such concerns are supposed to be most thoroughly banished, fuses the domestic and the political elements of the novel. Brontë's conclusion emphasizes the ethical and social dimension of marriage in this novel, and insists that beauty may foment reform.

Works Cited

Brontë, Charlotte. *Shirley.* New York: Penguin Classics, 1985.
Langland, Elizabeth. *Telling Tales: Gender and Narrative Form in Victorian Literature and Culture.* Columbus: The Ohio State University Press, 2002.
Lefkovitz, Lori Hope. *The Character of Beauty in the Victorian Novel.* Ann Arbor, MI: UMI Research Press, 1987.

Michie, Helena. *The Flesh Made Word: Female Figures and Women's Bodies.* New York: Oxford University Press, 1987.

Scarry, Elaine. *On Beauty and Being Just.* Princeton: Princeton University Press, 1987.

Notes

[1] "One sixth of the novel," in fact, as Elizabeth Langland points out. She argues that this delay implicitly asks "What meaningful role can women have in men's lives in a patriarchal culture?"—a question with important implications for narrative possibility. Langland, *Telling Tales,* 26.

[2] Lefkovitz, *The Character of Beauty in the Victorian Novel,* 1.

[3] Brontë, *Shirley,* 119.

[4] Ibid., 119.

[5] Ibid., 212.

[6] Ibid., 102.

[7] Ibid., 102.

[8] Ibid., 212.

[9] Ibid., 123.

[10] Helena Michie offers a rather different reading of this passage, and of Caroline's beauty itself: for her, Caroline is a mere "outline" or "sketch" compared to Shirley, and not quite vivid enough to be a "picture" in her own right (*The Flesh Made Word,* 115). In this context, though, I am more interested in Caroline's relationship to her own beauty than in the novel's positioning of her in relation to Shirley.

[11] Ibid., 123.

[12] Scarry, *On Beauty and Being Just,* 28-9.

[13] Scarry offers a number of examples to illustrate these versions of error. In the first category, she simply recounts her longstanding inability to see anything aesthetically pleasing in a palm tree, a view she eventually came to see as completely mistaken. In the second category, she presents a few lines from Gerard Manley Hopkins describing a boy who experiences "sceptic disappointment and loss" when a poet he has loved "becomes less and less sweet to him"—that is, ceases to be beautiful (13).

[14] Brontë, *Shirley,* 190.

[15] Ibid., 123.

[16] Ibid., 118.

[17] Scarry, *On Beauty and Being Just,* 29.

[18] Ibid., 31.

[19] Brontë, *Shirley,* 190.

[20] Ibid., 190.

[21] Ibid., 207.

[22] Ibid., 413.

[23] Ibid., 414.

[24] Ibid., 502.
[25] Ibid., 568.
[26] Scarry, *On Beauty and Being Just,* 90-1.
[27] Brontë, *Shirley,* 597.

CHAPTER TWELVE

"WE, WHO HAPPIER, LIVE / UNDER THE HOLIEST DISPENSATION": GENDER, REFORM, AND THE NEXUS OF EAST AND WEST IN TORU DUTT

CHRISTOFER FOSS

Toru Dutt was born in Calcutta on March 4, 1856 and raised within a converted Christian family that moved to Europe when she was 13 so that she and her sister Aru might be exposed to Western culture. According to Chandani Lokugé, they were the first Bengali women to travel to England,[1] and when she was 15 the family moved to Cambridge, where she attended the Higher Lectures for Women. They returned to India when she was 17; the next year, Aru died from consumption (as had their only brother, Abju, when Toru when 9).

In 1876 Toru published *A Sheaf Gleaned from French Fields*, a volume of French poems she had translated into English, with Saptahiksambad Press of Bhowanipore, India. (Aru had translated a small handful of poems for this project before her death, so Toru included these as well.) This volume came to the attention of Edmund Gosse in 1877, who reviewed it quite favorably in the *Examiner* that year. *Sheaf* would see a second Indian edition in 1878 and a third edition by Kegan Paul of London in 1880, but Dutt lived to see neither of these triumphs. On August 30, 1877, she died of consumption at the age of 21, leaving behind two unpublished novels—*Le Journal de Mademoiselle d'Arvers* (thought to be the first novel in French by an Indian writer) and *Bianca, or the Young Spanish Maiden* (thought to be the first novel in English by an Indian woman writer)—in addition to an unfinished volume of original poems in English, *Ancient Ballads and Legends of Hindustan*. Her father, Govin Chunder Dutt, ensured that these works would be published posthumously. Through his efforts, *Bianca* was published in Calcutta's *Bengal Magazine* (1878), *Le*

Journal by Didier of Paris (1879), and *Ancient Ballads* with Kegan Paul (1882).

Dutt's contemporaries seem to have been more aware of her rightful place in literary history than we are today. As Sir Edmund Gosse (her British "discoverer") observes in his Introductory Memoir to *Ancient Ballads*, "Her name . . . is no longer unfamiliar in the ear of any well-read man or woman."[2] Indeed, according to Gosse,

> It is difficult to exaggerate when we try to estimate what we have lost in the premature death of Toru Dutt. Literature has no honours which need have been beyond the grasp of a girl who at the age of twenty-one, and in languages separated from her own by so deep a chasm, had produced so much of lasting worth.[3]

Gosse thus concludes the Introductory Memoir by insisting, "When the history of the literature of our country comes to be written, there is sure to be a page in it dedicated to this fragile exotic blossom of song."[4]

Unfortunately, that page has yet to be written. Dutt's work has remained largely unread by students and scholars of British Victorian literature, and critical work by Western academics on this fascinating Indo-Anglian poet is still virtually nonexistent.[5] Yet Dutt is a writer who has a crucial role to play in extending our understanding of both British and Indian literary history. The question of how exactly to position her as a writer is an extremely complicated one, to say the least. She was Indian—but she was Christian rather than Hindu, she was educated in Europe rather than in Calcutta, and she wrote in English rather than Bengali. Her Christian faith complemented her interest in beneficial social change for women; indeed, these two combine to form the impetus behind her critique of Hindu orthodoxy. At the same time, her clear affinities with Hindu culture (particularly its literary traditions) served as the primary basis for a parallel critique of British imperialism. One thus must examine the nexus of East and West in her life and work if one is to arrive at a more complex understanding of her views on gender and reform—and, in turn, if one is to begin to theorize how one might (or, might not) position this Indo-Anglian writer as more properly an Anglo and/or an Indian voice. In the final analysis, a consideration of Toru Dutt is absolutely essential to any thorough plumbing of the complex intersections of class, gender, and race in the Victorian era, particularly within the contexts of imperialism and colonialism (and, by extension, within the contexts of post-colonialism and transnationalism).

Ancient Ballads, composed primarily of new renditions of classic Hindu tales in English, is divided into two sections. The first part contains nine poems that together comprise over 90 percent of its total lines. All of these texts foreground the Indian experience for Dutt's British readers, presenting them with an Indian mythography (as well as a whole new set of intertexts) and with catalogues of Indian flora and fauna. The choice of ballads and legends is interesting in itself—Dutt primarily selects those with a focus on women, children, and the lower castes. Their content is quite thought-provoking as well, particularly where gender and reform are concerned: protagonists are both true to their traditional representations and at the same time subtly inflected by contemporary circumstances (see, for example, "Savitri"), just as Dutt's obvious pride in and love for her heritage is qualified by some explicit Christian/Western revisionings (see, for example, "The Royal Ascetic and the Hind").[6]

The second part of the volume consists of seven short miscellaneous poems, only one of which is not either about or in part in dialogue with Europe, thus further allowing one to tease out Dutt's complex positioning via-à-vis India and England. These poems also serve to corroborate the anglophilia and francophilia of the translated French poems in *A Sheaf Gleaned from French Fields*, as do many of her letters. The bulk of these letters are to her British friend Mary Martin, and in them she continually reiterates her desire to return to England and to settle there for good. She was not particularly happy with her life in Calcutta after the family's return from Europe, and much of this unhappiness seems to have stemmed from the fact that she was a young woman. On 20 September 1874 she writes to Martin, "The free air of Europe, and the free life there, are things not to be had here. We cannot stir from our own Garden without being stared at . . . ."[7] A few years later she will express her broader frustration with such lack of mobility in "Savitri," the substantial piece with which she leads off *Ancient Ballads*. There, her poetic speaker takes a swipe at women's current claustrophobia in India by foregrounding their now largely former freedoms:

> In those far-off primeval days
> Fair India's daughters were not pent
> In closed zenanas. On her ways
> Savitri at her pleasure went
> Whither she chose. . . .[8]

Dutt lived at a time when there most certainly were calls for social change on numerous women's issues (such as child marriage, female education, polygamy, sati, and zenanas), but conservative attitudes prevailed, even in the most privileged families. Dutt herself, however, was progressive on this front.

In a letter dated 13 January 1876, she tells Martin of the controversy surrounding the decision by a notable Bengali gentleman to open his zenana to the visiting Prince of Wales. Her own opinion concurs with one particularly "sensibly and fairly put" article from *The Indian Daily News*, which she summarizes as suggesting that

> If the Babu means to bring out his family . . . and let his friends visit and mingle with his family, as behaves civilized men and manners, he is a very well-meaning man, and his aims are laudable; but if he has only made an exception for the Prince, and his suite, and means to 'lock up' his wife and family, as all Hindus do, his allowing the Prince to visit his family is a bit of flunkeyism, quite unpardonable, and worthy of the highest disapprobation.[9]

That Dutt remained unmarried into her twenties was in and of itself highly unusual and, for many, highly suspicious—a fact she jokes about in her letters on multiple occasions. As a 16-year-old she had attended the Higher Lectures for Women at Cambridge, and she consistently alludes to supporters of female education favorably in her letters. At one point she calls attention to a report that two young Indian women had passed the Entrance Examination "very creditably," and concludes, "I do hope Indian girls will be in the future better educated, and obtain more freedom and liberty than they now enjoy."[10]

Yet Dutt's isolation and her relative lack of freedom is not exclusively an effect of her gender; it also is an effect of her Christianity, and not simply because a typical rhetorical strategy of missionaries (and women missionaries in particular) was to contrast an idealized version of Western domestic partnership with the oppressiveness of the zenana. For example, Dutt relates to Martin why she had not attended the marriage ceremony of her mother's cousin: "She is a Hindu and so is her family, so of course we were not invited."[11] Certainly this is a major part of the reason she later tells Martin, "you are quite mistaken to think that we should be greatly missed by [friends and relatives], if we leave Calcutta."[12] Dutt believes that "Hindus are getting more liberal in their views" on social interactions with Europeans and with those Indians associated with them, noting, "indeed, Hindus, liberal ones, will dine at a European's table without much demur, but it is done *en cachette*."[13] At the same time, she also insists that, even if such families are becoming rarer all the time, "there are some orthodox families who will not mix with friends and relations who have been to England, unless these make the necessary purifications ordained in the Hindu shastras and by pundits."[14]

Dutt's Christianity does not simply serve as an obstacle to more lively social relations, however; it equally leads her to separate herself intellectually from Hindu society. For instance, while on some occasions she seems to thoroughly enjoy the music and processions of the Hindu holidays, at other times she is less than appreciative, with the noise and crowds mentioned as more of a bother than anything. Particularly suggestive is her comment on the festivities of the *Kali-Poojah*:

> one feels sometimes so sad when one looks on all these processions following a graven image, offering goats, and other sacrifices to it, and bowing themselves before it. Oh, that all India should turn to the true and loving God, who is alone able to save us and cleanse us from our sins![15]

Her expressed interest in such Christian conversion is not merely an abstract concept, but rather it also extends to such dear and favorite individuals as her maternal grandmother, of whom she writes, "she is, I am sad to say, still a Hindu,"[16] and, "I wish she would become a Christian."[17]

Not surprisingly, then, one may find expressions of Dutt's Christian faith in her poetry as well. There are Christian allusions in some of the miscellaneous poems (see, for example, "Near Hastings," "France, 1870," and "The Tree of Life"), and there even are a few explicit moments of Christian proselytizing in her renditions of the Sanskrit legends. One of these is found in "Prehlad," a tale from the *Mahabharata* about an ancient king who bans all religious thought and practice, decreeing everyone must worship him and him alone. One of his sons, Prehlad, rebels by worshipping Vishnu instead, so the king has him put in prison. In Dutt's version, Prehlad's account of the effect of his imprisonment for his beliefs (which also includes an echo of Ecclesiastes) allows her British readers to suspect he actually is speaking as a devotee of Dutt's Christian God rather than of Vishnu:

> For I have in my dungeon dark
> Learnt more of truth than e'er I knew
> There is one God—One only—mark!
> To Him is all our service due[18]

and,

> In Him I trust,
> He can protect me if He will,
> And if this body turn to dust,
> He can new life again instill.[19]

Eventually, the deity appears as a colossal lion-headed warrior who vindicates Prehlad by killing the king.

Dutt's most overt challenge to Hinduism comes in the aforementioned "The Royal Ascetic and the Hind." In this tale from the *Vishnu Purana*, Dutt faithfully renders the details of a great king who abdicates to pursue the ascetic rites and privations of a hermit. His proper devotion is undermined when he allows himself to care too deeply for a fawn that he saves from drowning. After narrating the royal ascetic's death, Dutt's poetic speaker takes a decidedly editorializing turn and offers a brazen rebuttal of the traditional Hindu interpretation of the tale. It is long, but worth quoting in full:

> Thus far the pious chronicle, writ of old
> By Brahman sage; but we, who happier, live
> Under the holiest dispensation, know
> That God is Love, and not to be adored
> By a devotion born of stoic pride,
> Or with ascetic rites, or penance hard,
> But with a love, in character akin
> To His unselfish, all-including love.
> And therefore little can we sympathize
>   With what the Brahman sage would fain imply
> As the concluding moral of his tale,
> That for the hermit-king it was a sin
>   To love his nursling. What! A sin to love!
>   A sin to pity! Rather should we deem
>   Whatever Brahmans wise, or monks may hold,
>   That he had sinned in *casting off* all love
>   By his retirement to the forest-shades;
>   For that was to abandon duties high,
>   And, like a recreant soldier, leave the post
>   Where God had placed him as a sentinel.
>
> This little hind brought strangely on his path,
> This love engendered in his withered heart,
> This hinderance to his rituals,—might these not
> Have been ordained to teach him? Call him back
> To ways marked out for him by Love divine?
> And with a mind less self-willed to adore?
>
> Not in seclusion, not apart from all,
> Not in a place elected for its peace,
> But in the heat and bustle of the world,
> 'Mid sorrow, sickness, suffering and sin,
> Must he still labour with a loving soul

Who strives to enter through the narrow gate.[20]

Given such a strident Christian agenda, Gosse's insistence upon orientalizing his "fragile exotic blossom of song" may perhaps seem a bit of a stretch. According to Gosse, Dutt "was pure Hindu, full of the typical qualities of her race and blood, . . . preserving to the last her appreciation of the poetic side of her ancient religion, though faith itself in Vishnu and Siva had been cast aside with childish things and been replaced by a purer faith."[21] In *Ancient Ballads*, then, he writes,

> No modern Oriental has given us so strange an insight into the conscience of the Asiatic . . . . The poetess seems in these verses to be chanting to herself those songs of her mother's race to which she always turned with tears of pleasure. They breathe a Vedic solemnity and simplicity of temper, and are singularly devoid of that littleness and frivolity which seem, if we may judge by a slight experience, to be the bane of modern India.[22]

Gosse's whole posture, however well-intentioned, is offensive. Yet, if his orientalist assessment seems to suggest a dimension to Dutt's relationship to Hinduism thoroughly absent in "The Royal Ascetic and the Hind," that is because in many of the other ballads and legends there is in fact a very different relationship, an undeniable affection for and pride in her Hindu heritage.

Take, for example, "Sîta," the last poem in the ballads and legends section of the volume. Not a retelling of a ballad or legend at all, this short poem evokes with profound nostalgia the scene of a mother singing the "old, old story"[23] of Sîta at bed-time to "Three happy children . . . / . . . with wide-open eyes."[24] Her song is so powerfully rendered that all three children are moved to tears, and we are told that they shall "dream of it until the day."[25] The elegiac, if not anguished, note of the poem's final question ("When shall those children by their mother's side / Gather, ah me! as erst at eventide?"[26]) grows not merely out of a yearning for childhood innocence or for the simplicity of yesterday. Surely one also may read these lines as an implicit lament for the fate of the ancient ballads and legends of Hindustan and their tradition of storytelling in the modern era of British imperialism. Indeed, we find a similar sentiment in the conclusion to "Jogadhya Uma," a story (not from a puranic source but from Bengali folklore) of how the goddess Uma appeared to a pedlar of shell-bangles. The poem concludes,

> Absurd may be the tale I tell,
> Ill-suited to the marching times,

I loved the lips from which it fell,
  So let it stand among my rhymes.[27]

For an even more intriguing ending in support of this other dimension
to Dutt's relationship to Hinduism, one need only turn to "Sindhu," a tale
from the *Ramayana*. The plot revolves around a king who, while hunting,
mistakenly kills a boy, the only son of two ascetic sages who in turn die
upon learning of Sindhu's fate. After noting that the king fulfilled "with
royal pomp / Their funeral obsequies,"[28] Dutt's poetic speaker concludes
the poem with the following stanza:

What is the sequel of the tale?
  How died the king?—oh man,
  A prophet's words can never fail—
  Go, read the Ramayan.[29]

At this point, fresh upon the success of her first book of poems with the
British press, Dutt is consciously writing for a British audience as well as
to the Indo-Anglian community, so the fact that she directs the reader to
the original Hindu source material itself (or, does she actually challenge,
or even command, the reader to look there?) for the final word on the tale
and its moral is quite provocative—certainly a very different approach
from that of the poetic speaker in "The Royal Ascetic and the Hind."
    What all this should suggest is that delineating the nexus of East and
West in Dutt is a much more complex and complicated matter than at first
it may have appeared to be. For, if Dutt is (as, first and foremost, a
Christian) only antagonistic towards Hinduism, then why does she decide
to glean a poetic sheaf from Sanskrit fields in the first place, when her first
sheaf was exclusively European in its origins? Why does she develop such
an interest in learning Sanskrit and work so hard at it even as her health is
failing? Why is she so pleased that Mary Martin takes up reading the
Ramayana: "I am so glad you like the Ramayana and that my country's
heroine [Sîta] has won your heart"?[30] Why does this Indo-Anglian poet
even enjoy giving her friend little lessons in Bengali, at one point telling
her, "I think our Bengali language is very rich in words"?[31]
    Surely it is Dutt's profound affinities with Bengali culture, in
conjunction with a more properly Christian form of righteous anger, that
leads her increasingly to offer personal critiques of British imperialism in
the letters to Martin. So she relates a police case in which a hunting party
dispute left nine Bengalis dead and seven more wounded, with one British
soldier severely beaten on the other side. The magistrate fined all of the
villagers and acquitted the soldiers, she reports, in order that "natives

should know how precious is the life of one British soldier in the eyes of the British government."[32] So also she caustically proclaims, "We have no real English gentlemen or ladies in India, except a very few. People generally come out to India to make their fortunes, you see, and real gentlemen and ladies very rarely leave home and friends for the 'yellow gold.'"[33]

In her letter to Martin dated 7 August 1876, the very same letter in which she effuses about Sîta and the *Ramayana*, Dutt reports another egregious miscarriage of justice in which an Englishman in effect beat one of his servants to death, only to be 'punished' with a fine of 2 pounds! She bitterly observes, "You see how cheap the life of an Indian is, in the eyes of an English judge . . . ."[34] She then goes on to laud the efforts of Lord Lytton, the Viceroy, for swiftly and strongly condemning this injustice, removing the ruling magistrate, and initiating a review of the appropriate section of the Indian Penal Code. It is obvious that to Dutt, while its religion and its intellectual foundations have much to offer her country, British imperialist rule in India urgently needs to be reformed.

Once again, Dutt's poetry in *Ancient Ballads* contains reformist sentiments similar to those found in the letters. In "The Legend of Dhruva," from the *Vishnu Purana*, Dutt only narrates the story as far as Dhruva's departure into the forest after his slight by his father (the king) in favor of his half-brother. By doing so—and by not including Dhruva's subsequent ascetic devotions, his eventual return to rule, and his eternal reward from Vishnu—she maintains her readers' focus squarely on the motivating injustice that impels Dhruva to (re)act. In "Buttoo," a retelling of the story of Ekalavya the archer from the *Mahabharata*, the poem's questioning of rank and caste—particularly when taken together with its portrayal of the imperious Dronacharjya—allows for a parallel questioning of British assumptions of imperial privilege and racial superiority.

To more clearly establish Dutt's poetic engagement with the excesses of Empire, one need only return to "Prehlad." "Prehlad" is a poem with a clear message about one's higher duty to God (for Dutt, her Christian God), but it also is a poem with a politically charged final message. After the king's demise at the hands of the lion-headed representation of the deity, Dutt's poetic speaker tells her readers that "A sovereign people's wild acclaim"[35] is, "Kings rule for us and in our name."[36] With this in mind, the speaker turns to address "Tyrants of every age and clime"[37] and assures them they all have their own awful lion-headed shape that will just as surely bring them down "when comes the time."[38] The poem concludes with this warning:

As human, peoples suffer pain,

But oh, the lion strength is theirs,
Woe to the king when galls the chain!
Woe, woe, their fury when he dares![39]

This poem thus effectively positions its subversive, even overtly threatening political challenge to all forms of earthly Power that are not ultimately answerable to the people whom they rule as a type of the higher duty endorsed by God.

Indeed, Dutt's very project in *Ancient Ballads* on the one hand would seem to set her up as a classic female tradition-bearer (in line with a nationalist project). As Alpana Sharma Knippling has observed, one may see Dutt's decision to work on these ancient Sanskrit texts as reflecting a need to (re)connect with her country and its heritage in response to her time in Europe.[40] There had long existed a perceived need (certainly heightened after the Revolt of 1857) for a more properly Indian voice in the face of British imperialism, and Dutt would have been well aware of the nascent nationalist sentiments current in her day—particularly after her return to Calcutta in 1873. In fact, the ballads and legends she decides to work on are set in a variety of regions, the rough modern-day equivalents of which range from Kolkata (Calcutta) to Bhopal and Chennai (Madras) to Delhi. She would have had personal examples of nationalist sentiment to draw upon as well. Her father quit his job with the British administration because Indian workers could not look forward to the opportunity for equal advancement and her cousin, Romesh Chunder Dutt, was a prominent nationalist figure who would serve as President of the Indian National Congress at the turn of the century.

Dutt's anglophilia, however, should at the very least qualify any simplistic positioning of her as an Indian voice in a more properly nationalist space. In fact, when Meenakshi Mukherjee makes a token reference to Dutt in setting up her version of Indian literary history in her very early work on Indian fiction (from 1971), she insists Dutt is so "highly Westernized" that she cannot qualify as an authentic Indian voice.[41] For Mukherjee, as Dutt was not a product of the general Indian culture and as Indo-Anglian literature itself ultimately is "written in Victorian idioms" and "fashioned by English sensibility," Dutt's work should be understood as "a colonial venture vaguely aspiring to continue the great English tradition."[42]

Historically, most Indian scholars have responded to Dutt's westernization less pejoratively, instead using it to paint her as an international writer who nevertheless retains enough identity as an Indian writer to win their pride and admiration. According to Padmini Sen Gupta, "There are some writers who belong to the world in general . . . . They may be born in any country, the stamp of which they will always bear, but they are universal in their creative output."[43] Such a one, he says, is Dutt. For A. N. Dwivedi, Dutt is "a citizen of the world, and not of any particular race or country."[44] K R. Ramachandran Nair even goes so far as to claim Dutt, "unhindered by national, linguistic, or religious inhibitions," is the first Indo-Anglian writer to effect a "rapprochement" between East and West.[45]

In Mukherjee's more recent work (1999), she rightfully acknowledges more fully Dutt's significance within Indian literary history, and in the process of reassessing Dutt's place suggests yet another plausible option for positioning Dutt's multi-dimensional reformist poetics. Dutt still does not qualify as a representative Indian writer in Mukherjee's eyes in that, far from championing "Indian tradition," she instead offers a "running critique" of its caste and gender hierarchies.[46] Yet, if Dutt's project is not an Indian (or, a nationalist) one, according to Mukherjee, neither is it an Anglo or international one. Dutt's Indian vocabulary, she suggests, is "stubbornly regional."[47] Her ethos, for Mukherjee, is distinctly Bengali, despite her use of English. In fact, "writing in Bengali . . . might not have automatically guaranteed an unproblematic continuation of an anterior precolonial poetic tradition" in that all of the major male poets writing in Bengali at the time were "swept off their feet by . . . British Romantic poetry" and thus were prone to their own form of imitativeness.[48] In any case, Mukherjee finds Dutt's verse much more preferable than that of the women who were writing in Bengali, since their poetry was highly stylized, formulaic, and conservative in its endorsement of approved feminine codes.[49]

At the same time, as Mukherjee reminds us, voice and authenticity are not innocent qualities but rather are "imbricated . . . with possibilities of insidious complicity with, or co-option by, the prevailing literary culture."[50] According to Shu-mei Shih, "non-Western Others who . . . *affect* Western-centric values . . . join in the essentialization of the non-West."[51] This may in part explain why the typical British reaction to Dutt—represented most (in)famously in the response of Gosse—seems to completely elide the political dimensions of *Ancient Ballads* in favor of an orientalizing aestheticism, despite the fact that from our own contemporary vantage point Dutt's project appears to be engaging in at the very least a covert critique of British imperialism. What does it mean that her subversiveness (at least as far as British imperialism was concerned) does not seem to have been acknowledged by British readers, or to have affected their ability to appropriate or co-opt it for orientalist or other imperialist purposes?

A pair of 2003 *PMLA* articles by Paul Giles and John Carlos Rowe on transnationalism and nineteenth-century American literature suggest yet another possibility when it comes to positioning Dutt and *Ancient Ballads*. Rowe argues for a comparative transnationalism for nineteenth-century American studies that would "extend [ ] transnationality [back] to the heyday of United States nationalism."[52] For Rowe, "if we identify transnationalism only with postmodern forces of globalization or with resistances to them, such as creolization and hybridization, then we are likely to forget the roots of these postmodern economic and cultural practices in modernization."[53] His elaboration on his comparative transnationalism that follows not only involves re-thinking and re-presenting works by canonical figures such as Nathaniel Hawthorne, Harriet Jacobs, and Harriet Beecher Stowe, but also involves expanding our conceptions of the American canon to include lesser-known writers such as Native American John Rollin Ridge and Asian-American Lee Yan Phou. For Giles, American literature is "interwoven systematically with transversals between national territory and intercontinental space."[54] "To problematize the geographical integrity of America"[55] is thus to "challenge circular, self-fulfilling definitions of American literature" by "seek[ing] various points of intersection . . . where cultural conflict is lived out experientially."[56]

Works by the likes of Antoinette Burton, Iderpal Grewal, and Billie Melman have been effecting similar paradigm shifts in our understanding, where India is concerned, of nineteenth-century British literature for some time, though it seems that most teaching syllabi (at least at the undergraduate level) have yet to reflect this. If we are at all interested in re-visioning the field along these lines, then Dutt's *Ancient Ballads* surely is one of the texts to which we must turn. Indeed, Knippling's article already contains the seeds of such a re-visioning when she argues for Dutt's poetry as the sort of "site . . . of re-invention and improvisation" that Homi Bhabha has characterized as an "interstitial passage between fixed identifications."[57]

According to Debjani Banerjee's dissertation on Indian women's fiction, a writer like Dutt "offers powerful perspectives on women writers and their contrapuntal negotiations of the ambivalence of colonialism as well as the empowerment and the circumscription of nationalist identities."[58] Dutt's work does seem, like much writing coming out of the post-colonial Indian diaspora, "vulnerable to neo-colonial forces of co-optation, but precisely because of this vulnerability "it also serves as an important nodal point [from which] to strategize resistance and generate counter-discursive practices"[59]—for women writers in particular, whose identity resembles "an ensemble of plotted positions which is simultaneously involved in relations of domination and subordination, producing ambivalent power relations and resisting oppression."[60]

In discussing Li Xiaojiang's articulation of "an ethics of transnational encounter," Shih suggests that "the key to transnational communication is the ability and willingness to situate oneself in both one's own position and the Other's position, whether on the plane of gender, historical contexts, or discursive paradigms,"[61] and that transvaluation "is the result of such transpositionality, since to position oneself in the history of the Other is to be given the opportunity to see how a given system of value production works and thus to be exposed to the mechanisms of value-coding and knowledge production as political, material, and affective acts."[62] *Ancient Ballads* is potentially the result of a similar sort of transpositionality. I would thus suggest that one may posit Dutt as a writer who, to some extent, already has fulfilled Shih's concluding charge to "border-crossing intellectuals and scholars," that they "must use their radically multiple positions to destabilize the production and circulation of value from any one given locational standpoint as preparation for transpositional dialogues in transnational encounters."[63] That is, Dutt's "ability and willingness" to speak from the multi-locational spaces present in *Ancient Ballads* allows one to explore how Indian and European "value-coding and knowledge production" work (separately, as well as in conflict or in dialogue with one another), which in turn allows one to read her poetics as effecting the sort of transpositional dialogue that seems one of the more hopeful possibilities transnationalism contains.

D. N. Rodowick's discussion of a *new cosmopolitanism* sees the mobility associated with transnationalism as "by no means qualitatively positive" owing to the all-too-evident negative effects of dis-location and exclusion, but he also feels it "opens possibilities for contestation and critique."[64] For Rodowick, "The mobility of deterritorialized transnationals must be characterized across several levels"—including "the transformation of identity as a set of complex cultural and political allegiances that unite as well as divide local communities subnationally, nationally, and transnationally."[65] One arguably may find such a transformation of identity, again, in *Ancient Ballads*. This is not to claim, with Nair, that Dutt effects a rapprochement between East and West; instead, it is to suggest that her poetry fosters an awareness of regional (subnational), national, and global (international and/or transnational) spaces—and to suggest that this awareness, in containing possibilities for both new unity and the same old (and/or further) division, above all productively foregrounds rather than forecloses the question of space(s) in both nineteenth-century Indian and nineteenth-century British literatures.

Nineteenth-century British colonial administrator James Thomason hoped for an Indian Sir Walter Scott, whom he felt was needed to "make [literature] the vehicle of historic and other instruction" by creating "not Christian books, but books written in a Christian spirit"[66]—the sort of book that, in Henry Schwarz's words, "must reach under the skin and inject [Christian] morality via its lessons."[67] Over a century later, contemporary Indian scholar K. R. Ramachandran Nair proclaims Dutt as a very different sort of Indian Scott, one whose work "gave a habitation and a name to the hoary past of [her] ancient land" through "essentially Hindu stories, steeped in the age-old values of Hindu culture," of which she "was a product."[68] It is by exploring the nexus of East and West in the life and work of Toru Dutt that one may plumb more fully her complex position as a writer with a reformist agenda, and by doing so that one may begin to grasp how one actually might simultaneously cast her as either one of these diametrically opposed versions of an Indian Scott. It is to begin to grasp, as well, how one might simultaneously cast her both as Gosse's thoroughly co-opted Orientalized "fragile exotic blossom of song" and as Makarand Paranjape's creator (in a tradition extending from Rammohun Roy to Gandhi) of "not so much a counter-modernity as an alternative modernity that was distinctly Indian . . . . not a hybrid, not some kind of mongrel in-betweeness, but a third world, without the pejorative associations of that term."[69]

Works Cited

Banerjee, Debjani. "Nationalist and Feminist Identities: Moments of Confrontation and Complicity in Post-Colonial Fiction and Film." Ph.D. diss., State University of New York-Stony Brook, 1995.

Dutt, Toru. *Ancient Ballads and Legends of Hindustan*. London: Kegan Paul, 1882.

—. *Toru Dutt: Collected Prose and Poetry*, edited by Chandani Lokugé. New Delhi: Oxford University Press, 2006.

Dwivedi, A. N. *Toru Dutt: A Literary Profile*. Delhi: BRPC, 1998.

Giles, Paul. "Transnationalism and Classic American Literature." *PMLA* 118, no. 1 (2003): 62-77.

Gupta, Padmini Sen. *Toru Dutt*. New Delhi: Sahitya Akademi, 1968.

Knippling, Alpana Sharma. "'Sharp Contrasts of All Colours': The Legacy of Toru Dutt." In *Going Global: The Transnational Reception of Third*

World Women Writers, edited by Amal Amireh and Lisa Suhair Majaj. New York: Garland, 2000. 209-228.

Mukherjee, Meenakshi. "Hearing Her Own Voice: Defective Acoustics in Colonial India." In *Women's Poetry, Late Romantic to Late Victorian: Gender and Genre, 1830-1900*, edited by Isobel Armstrong and Virginia Blain. New York: Macmillan, 1999. 207-229.

—. *The Twice Born Fiction: Themes and Techniques of the Indian Novel in English*. New Delhi: Heinemann, 1971.

Nair, K. R. Ramachandran. *Three Indo-Anglian Poets: Henry Derozio, Toru Dutt and Sarojini Naidu*. New Delhi: Sterling, 1987.

Paranjape, Makarand. "'Home and Away': Colonialism and AlterNativity in India." *New Literatures Review* 40 (2003): 116-30.

Rodowick, D. N. Introduction to Special Topic: Mobile Citizens, Media States. *PMLA* 117, no. 1 (2002): 13-23.

Rowe, John Carlos. "Nineteenth-Century United States Literary Culture and Transnationality." *PMLA* 118, no. 1 (2003): 78-89.

Schwarz, Henry. "Aesthetic Imperialism: Literature and the Conquest of India." *Modern Language Quarterly* 61, no. 4 (2000): 563-86.

Shih, Shu-mei. "Towards an Ethics of Transnational Encounter; or, 'When' Does a 'Chinese' Woman Become a 'Feminist'?" *Differences* 13, no. 2 (2002): 90-126.

Notes

[1] Lokugé in Dutt, *Toru Dutt: Collected Prose and Poetry*, xvii.

[2] Gosse in Dutt, *Ancient Ballads and Legends of Hindustan*, vii.

[3] Ibid., xxvi.

[4] Ibid., xxvii.

[5] To date, there are only 7 articles on Dutt listed in the *Modern Language Association International Bibliography*, all published since 1999. Tricia Lootens and Alpana Sharma have been leading the way so far, with two articles apiece. For a sample of Dutt's poetry, see my editorial contribution to the short anthology of colonial poetry in the 2004 special issue of *Victorians Institute Journal*, Poetry and the Colonies—or, see my annotated electronic edition of *Ancient Ballads* at http://foss.elsweb.org/toru_dutt.

[6] The story of Savitri comes from the *Mahabharata*, one of the two great Sanskrit epics. Dutt has her readers follows Savitri as she wins her husband Satyavan's life back from Death. Due to her devotion to her husband, Savitri traditionally has served as a type for the ideal Hindu wife, and certainly one may see Dutt's version as reinforcing this legacy, yet at the same time the independence and strength of her hero just as certainly allows one to detect in her rendering a more modern, if not Western, type. "Royal Ascetic," originally published in *The Calcutta Review* in

January 1877, tells the tale of Bharat (Bharata, the royal ascetic), a king who gave up his kingdom to live a solitary life of devotion in the forest. He was diverted from his devotions by his love for the hind (deer). This legend is, as Dutt indicates below its title, from the *Vishnu Purana*, a set of religious texts that promote the worship of Vishnu, the Preserver (one of the gods of the Hindu trinity). Dutt's poetic speaker, however, after narrating the royal ascetic's death, takes a decidedly editorializing turn and offers a brazen rebuttal of the traditional Hindu interpretation of the tale.

[7] Dutt, *Toru Dutt: Collected Poetry and Prose*, 231.
[8] Ibid., "Savitri," lines 25-9.
[9] Ibid., 259.
[10] Ibid., 334.
[11] Ibid., 261.
[12] Ibid., 321.
[13] Ibid., 325.
[14] Ibid., 325.
[15] Ibid., 313.
[16] Ibid., 228.
[17] Ibid., 274.
[18] Ibid., "Prehlad," l. 293-96.
[19] Ibid., l. 301-04.
[20] Ibid., "The Royal Ascetic and the Hind," lines 101-132.
[21] Gosse in Dutt, *Ancient Ballads and Legends of Hindustan*, xi-xii.
[22] Ibid., xxiv.
[23] Dutt, *Toru Dutt: Collected Poetry and Prose*, "Sîta," line 16.
[24] Ibid., l. 1-2.
[25] Ibid., l. 20.
[26] Ibid., l. 21-2.
[27] Ibid., "Jogadhya Uma," l. 237-240.
[28] Ibid., "Sindhu," l. 317-18.
[29] Ibid., l. 321-24.
[30] Ibid., 295.
[31] Ibid., 330.
[32] Ibid., 283.
[33] Ibid., 302.
[34] Ibid., 295.
[35] Ibid., "Prehlad," l. 342.
[36] Ibid., l. 344.
[37] Ibid., l. 345.
[38] Ibid., l. 347.
[39] Ibid., l. 349-352.
[40] Knippling, "'Sharp Contrasts of All Colours': The Legacy of Toru Dutt," 219.
[41] Muhkerjee, *The Twice Born Fiction: Themes and Techniques of the Indian Novel in English*, 17.
[42] Ibid.

[43] Gupta, *Toru Dutt*, 7.

[44] Dwivedi, *Toru Dutt: A Literary Profile*, 5.

[45] Nair, *Three Indo-Anglian Poets: Henry Derozio, Toru Dutt and Sarojini Naidu*, 55.

[46] Mukherjee, "Hearing Her Own Voice: Defective Acoustics in Colonial India," 222.

[47] Ibid., 220.

[48] Ibid., 224.

[49] Ibid.

[50] Ibid., 207.

[51] Shih, "Towards an Ethics of Transnational Encounter; or, 'When' Does a 'Chinese' Woman Become a 'Feminist'?", 115.

[52] Rowe, "Nineteenth-Century United States Literary Culture and Transnationality," 88.

[53] Ibid., 79.

[54] Giles, "Transnationalism and Classic American Literature," 63.

[55] Ibid., 64.

[56] Ibid., 65.

[57] Knippling 217.

[58] Banerjee, "Nationalist and Feminist Identities: Moments of Confrontation and Complicity in Post-Colonial Fiction and Film," 84.

[59] Ibid., 4.

[60] Ibid., 29.

[61] Shih, "Towards an Ethics of Transnational Encounter," 118.

[62] Ibid., 119.

[63] Ibid.

[64] Rodowick, Introduction to "Special Topic: Mobile Citizens, Media States," 15.

[65] Ibid.

[66] Thomason in Schwarz, "Aesthetic Imperialism: Literature and the Conquest of India," 582.

[67] Schwarz, "Aesthetic Imperialism," 582.

[68] Nair, *Three Indo-Anglian Poets,* 78.

[69] Paranjape, "'Home and Away': Colonialism and AlterNativity in India," 128-29.

CHAPTER THIRTEEN

BECOMING MODERN: REFORMING WOMEN'S DRESS IN VICTORIAN ENGLAND AND AMERICA

LORETTA CLAYTON

Throughout the nineteenth century, a passionate and public debate over contemporary dress took place in both large and small forums: from the popular press to radical journals and pamphlets to great lecture halls to private meetings of devoted "dress reformers." This essay focuses on a circle of women in London in the 1880s, many of whom can be described as socialites-turned-artists/activists (including Alice Comyns Carr, Constance Wilde, and Lady Archibald "Janey" Campbell), who were involved in the aesthetic dress reform movement. These women were also connected to the late Victorian writer Oscar Wilde—an important advocate of dress reform and a kind of aesthetic spokesperson in the 1880s before he became a successful playwright in the 1890s—not in the least because they wrote for the women's magazine Wilde edited in the late 1880s, *The Woman's World* (1887-1890). Considering both the discourse of aesthetic dress and its unconventional costume, I will tease out the radical and elitist elements of aesthetic dress reform and explain how these coexisted to explore the all-important question: were these prominent aesthetic dress reformers in meaningful dialogue with Victorian women of social classes outside their own? In the matter of "liberating" dress, were they able to make a difference to Victorian women? To begin to answer these questions, I will offer a brief background on dress reform through the nineteenth century, both in England and America. I will situate the aesthetic dress reformers of the late nineteenth within that background and describe their particular costume, which will be revealed as a radical statement in contrast to conventional Victorian female dress. It will also be shown that the appeal to self-stylization inherent in the discourse of dress reform is part of its radical content. I will conclude by focusing on the

Woman's World as an example of an alternate commercial venture: a progressive fashion magazine that advocated the unconventional designs of aesthetic dress. Ultimately, it cannot be said that aesthetic dress reformers influenced their contemporaries to any great extent, but their efforts undoubtedly served as inspiration for later generations of women seeking a new and modern costume. Perhaps most importantly, the writings and ventures of aesthetic dress reformers demonstrates a particularly Wildean idea: radical discourse is not limited by social class and might be found in surprising venues.

Dress Reform in the Nineteenth Century: A Transatlantic Story

Many early feminists equated political and social oppression with the restricted, ultra-gendered Victorian traditional style of dress. Dress reform began in America as part of the health reform movement (in particular as part of the "water cure" movement), but beginning in the 1850s, American feminists located dress reform at the center of the women's rights movement.[1] The discourse of dress reform had an interesting transatlantic movement throughout the nineteenth century, a narrative that eventually included Oscar Wilde. The first important generation of feminist dress reformers were a group of American women of the mid-nineteenth century who seem to have drawn their inspiration from the English actress Fanny Kemble. Kemble began a celebrated tour of America in 1832 and eventually took residence in the country, having married—and then having famously divorced—an American husband. In addition to exhibiting other kinds of "masculine" public behaviors, Kemble sometimes wore an athletic outfit of pants, mainly for mountain climbing. Her practical if bold outfit predated the most famous garment of dress reform and symbol of feminist affiliation—the "bloomer" costume, a short dress worn over loosely fitting pants—which was popular in women's rights circles in the 1850s.[2] A kind of spontaneous, communal act of self-fashioning—the result of good ideas passed among women of similar interests and agendas— produced the famous Bloomer, but it was named for a single woman, social reformer Amelia Jenks Bloomer. Bloomer emulated a costume that was said to look like "Turkish trousers" conceived by Elizabeth Smith Miller, cousin to suffragist Elizabeth Cady Stanton, good friend, neighbor and political ally of Bloomer. Miller herself admitted to being influenced by Fanny Kemble's earlier self-made costume. When Miller paid a visit to Seneca Falls to see her cousin, she was dressed in her own self-made short dress and comfortable pantaloons; soon after Cady

Stanton and Bloomer made their own versions of the costume, and Amelia Bloomer promoted the costume in her journal *The Lily* as "the Turkish trousers."[3] As people came to associate her with the specific look, it came to be known as "the Bloomer."

In *The Lily*, in other journals, and in public speeches, mid-Victorian American feminists wrote and spoke eloquently on the association between fashion and politics, using themselves as models for a new feminist costume. Women wrote to Bloomer at *The Lily* asking for dress patterns and other advice so they could retire their hoops and crinolines, but the mainstream press fiercely ridiculed the Bloomer. American feminists ultimately abandoned the bloomer costume and the message of dress reform because they felt it garnered too much unflattering public attention and distracted from their main message of women's suffrage. They were often accused of acting "unmanly," and this was an accusation that stung women who were themselves inculcated in Victorian gender ideology. (The National Dress Reform Association in America was founded in 1855, but by 1865 had expired mainly because women's rights advocates dissociated themselves from the subject of dress reform. American dress reform efforts were continued by other reform-minded groups, like the communist living experiment of Oneida, New York in the 1860s, but, again, was largely abandoned by feminists.)

Dress reform resurfaced in the 1880s both in America and in England as a part of the larger "aesthetic revival." Throughout the 1880s, Oscar Wilde wrote and lectured on the twin aesthetic projects of reforming the style of the traditional English family home and reforming traditional Western dress—mainly women's dress. During those years of lecturing, both in England and America, Wilde would have often looked across the podium to find that his audience, seated in auditoriums, or perhaps standing at an outdoor venue, was often mainly—and enthusiastically—made up of women. It is only in the most recent scholarship that Wilde's relationship to a female audience has been taken seriously. In fact, according to historian Mary Warner Blanchard, several of the women who went to see Oscar Wilde on his famous lecture tour of America in 1882 wore an aesthetic costume to the event, so, like Wilde himself—who wore a rather idiosyncratic male "aesthetic" costume when he first arrived in America—they were living symbols of the movement.[4] So, it might be possible to say that some fifty years after Fanny Kemble's first tour of America, an idea about modern dressing was again brought to America from England that resonated with American women.

In *fin-de-siècle* England and America, the association between fashion and women's rights dovetailed again: the New Woman of the late nineteenth century needed a new costume. Unlike feminists of their mothers' or grandmothers' generations, however, progressive women of the 1880s and 1890s did not see their experiments in dress as obstacles to success of other goals like women's suffrage. Dress reform had a new way to appeal to women at the end of the century; as in the earlier part of the century, it appealed in the terms of health and in the terms of women's liberation, but it also appealed to women—and men—in the very language of fashion that it set itself against. Amelia Bloomer and her associates expressed pride in their self-made garments, but they did not emphasize their "beauty" or fashionability. If mid-Victorian feminists spoke of "beauty" of dress, it was the beauty of the natural body freed from the pressure of corsets and stays, not of the clothes themselves.

Dress reform movements later in the century on both sides of the Atlantic took an aesthetic interest, an artistic interest, and a fashionable interest, in the problem of dress. Several garments were conceived as alternatives to Victorian fashion: a "divided skirt," more streamlined than the earlier Bloomer; the aesthetic wrapper, smock dresses, and other elegant column dresses—or dresses whose proponents described them as elegant or "graceful," one of Oscar Wilde's favorite words in association with dress—that did not rely on hoops, "dress improvers," or corsets to shape the body. (In America especially "Hubbard" dresses were marketed as the "Bloomer" never had been, as attractive modern dresses.) In his lectures on dress, Oscar Wilde suggested an edited Bloomer costume that did away with a belt at the waist of its over-tunic and instead "[fell] from the shoulder to the knee, or below it, in fine curves and vertical lines, giving more freedom and consequently more grace."[5] These are garments consistent with an emerging modern aesthetic that elevated the concept of form and a particular style of "clean" lines—androgynous in style. The late Victorian aesthetes, including Oscar Wilde, are to be thanked for the insertion of fashionability into dress reform, as a discourse and a practice.

The Rhetoric of Dress Reform at the *Fin de Siècle*

"Aesthetic," "rational," "artistic," and "healthy" dress are some of the terms that were used in the rhetoric of *fin-de-siècle* dress reform in England to distinguish among specific styles and advocacy groups. Several organizations existed which held lectures and published newsletters; they often shared common members. Besides the Rational Dress Society, there was the Anti-Crinoline Society, the Anti Low-Dress League, several pro-woolens groups (including one following Dr. Jaeger, and which counted as one of its members George Bernard Shaw), some with nationalistic overtones (which endorsed British woolens exclusively), to name a few. As many people involved in the aesthetic movement were also subscribers to "rational" dress, the Rational Dress Society in particular was a locus for socialites and artists, including the painter Sir Frederick Watts. "Aesthetic dress" was not as popular a formal term as "rational dress," though it would have been clearly understood to English readers of the popular press and to theater-goers who had seen the Gilbert and Sullivan opera *Patience*, a satire of aestheticism, or any of its many imitators, what was meant by "aesthetic dress," or the nearly synonymous term "artistic dress." The basic aesthetic garment for women—referred to by costume historians as the "aesthetic dress," "aesthetic gown," or "aesthetic wrapper"—was a version of a Victorian garment called a wrapper, a loosely fitted garment worn as a housedress, in other words, a garment worn strictly indoors. There was no corset, no kind of dress improver, no stays to shape the garment. I will return to the silhouette of aesthetic dress, but first I would like to say a few words about this unique milieu of aesthetic artists and socialites.

A famous group of women prominent in the arts in London of the 1880s and 1890s, the so-called "aesthetic socialites," were champions for and models of aesthetic dress. They chose clothing in accord with the principles of aestheticism in lieu of conventional Victorian costumes. Their teas and soirées were also fashion events, where self-styled aesthetic fashions were worn by the women, and the benefits and artistic points of their costumes discussed by all.[6] They also organized and sponsored other events like lectures and readings, private art showings, and free productions of plays (otherwise known as "aesthetic philanthropy"). In addition to their patronage of artists, these women were often writers and artists themselves. Perhaps the most important and influential of these women was Lady Archibald "Janey" Campbell, a close friend to all three of the famed aesthetes in London of the 1880s, Whistler, Wilde and E. W. Godwin. Wilde enlisted Campbell to write the first article for the inaugural issue of *The Woman's World*. Alice Comyns Carr, wife of Joseph Comyns Carr, the director of the Grosvenor Gallery (and later the New Gallery) was another central member of this milieu. The Carrs' home was a nexus in London for powerful and talented people in the arts. Their elaborate soirées gathered the most prominent English artists, but also those up-and-coming ones; these "must be seen at" events were a favorite target in the pages of *Punch*. Her husband's gallery showed avant-garde art; her ideas about dress were similarly avant-garde. A vocal advocate of aesthetic dress, Alice Comyns Carr often modeled her own designs, and made costumes for the actress Ellen Terry. Oscar Wilde's wife, Constance Lloyd

Wilde, was also among this circle. When Oscar Wilde was beginning his work at *The Woman's World*, Constance Wilde was editing the *Rational Dress Society's Gazette*.[7] These influential women, costumed in aesthetic garments, and their homes, decorated in the aesthetic style, were kinds of advertisements for aestheticism.

Obviously, the problem in arguing that aesthetic dress was an important reform movement lies mainly in the fact that aesthetic dress, like most of aestheticism, lived in a rarefied sphere. Aesthetic dress, no matter how unconventional, was worn by fashion-conscious socialites of the *fin de siècle* at elegant affairs. But the designs and the discourse of aesthetic dress might well be considered radical, and perhaps relevant to the culture at large. First and foremost, the silhouette of aesthetic dress is a significant departure from the silhouette of conventional Victorian dress, although not every fashion critic takes this view. For instance, in a recent book, the authors comment, "aesthetic dress for women did not challenge in any real way the conventions of femininity, but merely the structured artificiality of high fashion."[8] They overlook, however, what was sometimes a radically streamlined silhouette in certain examples of aesthetic dress. No matter who was doing the wearing, wearing aesthetic dress would have been a bold statement for a woman to make. Because most aesthetic dresses resembled the Victorian wrapper, to those unfamiliar with aesthetic dress—or, those familiar with it but opposed to it—a woman's choice of aesthetic costume might have looked as if she were indecently exposed, wearing only her underwear in public.[9] Aesthetic dress on women, then, might register female independence and signify an act of defiance against social codes. Conventionally minded middle-class Victorians would have visually read aesthetic dress as ugly—ugly in its silliness to some, in its offensiveness to others. The aesthetic costume seemed precisely the opposite of how a middle-class Victorian woman would want to appear to others in public. The silhouette of aesthetic dress is "unwomanly" juxtaposed to Victorian mainstream middle-class clothing, which exaggerated gender difference by emphasizing, indeed exaggerating, the bust and hips of the female wearer, and cinched the waist tightly. The "divided skirt" lauded by many dress reformers and taken up by some aesthetes—nearly a version of pants for women—in particular came under attack as an attempt to duplicate the dress of men in women's attire.[10] The lines of the basic aesthetic wrapper are not nearly as masculine as the divided skirt, but they do make an almost androgynous figure by loosely draping the wearer's body. In further contrast to the Victorian ideal of female beauty and presentation, the eccentric colors and shapes preferred by aesthetes simply made women "stand out" in a culture suspicious (or worse) of female individual expression. To appear ugly, assertive, too girlish—or, absolutely the greatest offense, to appear unfeminine or mannish—would be affronts to the Victorian ideal of female presentation in dress.

What can also be interpreted as progressive and feminist about aesthetic dress is its appeal to the wearer to self-stylization, which is not only a potentially feminist statement in Victorian culture, but also an anti-consumerist gesture. Further, there is a feminist history of dress reform as outlined above that is "embedded" in the dress reform designs of late Victorian dress reformers including Wilde who were well aware of the feminist forerunners. The late Victorian aesthetic dress reformers—and particularly Oscar Wilde—reminded people of that association by reminding readers and lecture attendees about the earlier dress reform costumes, especially the Bloomer and Turkish trousers, even as they stressed beauty over ideology. Echoes of the "Bloomer" would signify a kind of feminist history even to lay people. Aesthetic dress in particular of all the dress reform styles and communities, posited an alternate female modern subject. Aesthetic dress reform created small communities of progressive thinkers, as did progressive magazines—and often the two overlapped as in *The Woman's World*. These writers and artists interrogated social norms by suggesting changes in the national costume.

Beyond the garments themselves, the discourse of aesthetic dress must be considered as part of its radical content. Not only by wearing the garments of dress reform, but by speaking and writing about dress reform, women of the late nineteenth century found new modes of liberation. Further, in certain ways, the discourse of aesthetic dress was a democratized one, particularly as Oscar Wilde practiced it. As has often been noted, aestheticism in general was both a kind of avant-garde movement in the arts and a popular cultural formation. In his lectures and writings, Wilde attempted a meaningful dialogue with people of different social classes. Wilde wrote for the popular press, including a regular column for *The Pall Mall Gazette*. He consistently answered letter writers to newspapers seriously, participating in a public and often passionate debate over the modern costume. Finally, Wilde attempted to lower the price of *The Woman's World*—an important site of aesthetic dress reform content despite its being a "high fashion" magazine—wanting very much to extend its readership beyond the upper-class reader of the earlier *Lady's World*, the conservative woman's magazine Wilde was asked to transform by the publishers at the House of Cassell. I will conclude with a reading of *The Woman's World* because I truly think it has been underestimated as a more "conservative" and/or a banal project rather than assessed as what it is at its best—a novel, perhaps nearly an alternative commercial venture within the fashion market, "alternative" largely because the discourse of aestheticism and aesthetic dress reform pervades the magazine.

Publicizing Dress Reform: Oscar Wilde and *The Woman's World*

In his editorials for *The Woman's World*, Oscar Wilde made several unexpected and radical statements about dress, applauding the dress of the working classes as a model for the middle and upper classes to follow, and constructing the working-class girl as a paragon of modernity right next to her modern "sisters," the socialite and proto-New Women who wrote for the magazine.[11] Perhaps most importantly, Wilde suggested the concept of self-fashioning to his female readers, a stark contrast to conventional editorials in other fashionable women's magazines that would brutally police any woman who would make her own clothes, an affront to the experts: the fashion houses, the dressmakers, and the editors who knew better. In response to criticism that his new magazine ought not to contain conventional fashion pages, Wilde argued that the periodical reader might be taken a little more seriously as an agent of her own style, suggesting that "it is quite easy for the children of light to adapt almost any fashionable form of dress to the requirements of utility and the demands of good taste."[12] If women were to alter the styles of fashion according to personal taste, they would be participating in a different level in the system of fashion, as did the aesthetic socialites who wrote for the magazine. Further, throughout the pages of *The Woman's World*, the aesthetic writer, reader, and consumer is telegraphed and constructed as a modern and sophisticated ideal of womanhood, a figure of expertise, discernment, creativity, and social prowess. Aesthetic women are shown in the magazine as occupying multiple positions within aesthetic discourse, as artists, directors and writers, as patrons, as invaluable and engaged consumers or readers *and* as the unconventional though beautiful models of aesthetic design. They are dynamic, potentially inspiring examples to any reader or audience.

Wilde's work at *The Woman's World* shows a utopian, perhaps, impulse: the hope that the discourse of aestheticism would inspire several different types of women across different social classes to become modern, even if they sometimes had to look to the past or to other cultures, including working-class culture, to do so, adapting foreign or old-fashioned designs for a new "costume of the future" and fashioning a modern female subjectivity largely against a prevailing bourgeois ideal of femininity. We can at least recognize the bold statements of aesthetic dress reformers, particularly the group of women socialites and activists I have discussed, as well as Wilde's appeal to and publicity of them in *The Woman's World* as a kind of feminist gesture. Perhaps if *The Woman's World* had had a longer run, and/or if Wilde had been able to secure a lower price for the magazine, the influence of these unique women would have been felt more widely in the culture. Whatever the level of success he achieved, it does seem that Wilde and several of his writers were attempting to forge an alternative commercial venture through their participation in *The Woman's World*. The late Victorian discourse of aesthetic dress was limited in scope, but the statement made by those who chose aesthetic dress was radical and would serve as inspiration for the New Women and flappers on the other side of the century who adopted a similar streamlined, uncorsetted, and glamorous silhouette as an expression of aesthetic and political liberation. In this sense, *The Woman's World* was years ahead of the marketplace.

Works Cited

Anonymous. Interview with Mrs. Fawcett. *Women's Penny Paper* (Nov. 3, 1888): 4.
—. "The Divided Skirt." *The Artist* (Sept. 1881): 281.
—. "The Rational Dress Society." *The Artist* (March 1883): 85-86.
Banner, Lois W. *American Beauty*. New York: Knopf, 1983.
Blanchard, Mary Warner. *Oscar Wilde's America: Counterculture in the Gilded Age*. New Haven: Yale University Press, 1998.
Bloomer, Amelia. "Female attire." *The Lily* 3 (Feb. 1851): 13.
—. "Mrs. Kemble and Her New Costume." *The Lily* 1 (Dec. 1849): 94.
Buckley, Cheryl and Hillary Fawcett. *Fashioning The Feminine: Representation and Women's Fashion from the* Fin de Siècle *to the Present*. London: I. B. Tauris, 2002.
Cayleff, Susan E. *Wash and Be Healed: The Water Cure Movement and Women's Health*. Philadelphia: Temple University Press, 1987.
Comyns, Alice Vansittart Strettel. *J. Comyns Carr: Stray Memories*. London: Macmillan, 1920.
Donegan, Jane B. *Hydropathic Pathway to Health: Women and Water-cure in Antebellum America*. New York: Greenwood Press, 1986.
Mullenix, Elizabeth Reitz. "So unfemininely masculine": Discourse, true/false womanhood, and the American career of Fanny Kemble." *Theatre Survey* (Nov. 1999): 27-42.

Torrens, Kathleen M. "Fashion as Argument: Nineteenth-century Dress Reform." *Argumentation and Advocacy* (fall 1999): xxx.

Wilde, Oscar. "Literary and Other Notes," *The Woman's World* 1 (Nov. 1887): 40.

—. "More Radical Ideas Upon Dress Reform." *Complete Writings of Oscar Wilde*, vol. 6, Miscellanies. New York: The Nottingham Society, 1907, 60.

Notes

[1] See Cayleff, *Wash and Be Healed: The Water Cure Movement and Women's Health* and Donegan, *Hydropathic Pathway to Health: Women and Water-cure in Antebellum America.*

[2] Mullenix, "So unfemininely masculine": Discourse, true/false womanhood, and the American career of Fanny Kemble," According to Mullenix, "Kemble's adoption of pantalettes … in effect began the Dress Reform Movement" in America when, against expressions (mostly male) of disapprobation over Kemble's clothing in the popular press, Amanda Bloomer championed Kemble's "gentlemanly dress" in her temperance journal, *The Lily*. Also see Bloomer, "Mrs. Kemble and Her New Costume," *The Lily* 1: 94 and "Female attire," *The Lily* 3: 13.

[3] Torrens, "Fashion as Argument: Nineteenth-century Dress Reform." Also see Banner, *American Beauty.*

[4] Blanchard, *Oscar Wilde's America: Counterculture in the Gilded Age*, 153. Blanchard's book is less a discussion of Wilde than of a talented group of women artists in *fin-de-siècle* America like the painter Candace Wheeler.

[5] Wilde, "More Radical Ideas Upon Dress Reform," *Complete Writings of Oscar Wilde*, vol. 6, Miscellanies, 60. The essay was originally published in the *Pall Mall Gazette*, October 14, 1884.

[6] For a description of this milieu, see Comyns, *J. Comyns Carr: Stray Memories.*

[7] Both Alice Comyns Carr and Constance Wilde wrote for *The Woman's World*; Constance Wilde contributed an article on children's dress reform.

[8] Buckley and Fawcett, *Fashioning The Feminine: Representation and Women's Fashion from the* Fin de Siècle *to the Present*, 28.

[9] See Blanchard, 144,138.

[10] Lady Harberton, director of the Rational Dress Society, was a vocal advocate of the divided skirt for women. *The Artist* reported on a meeting of the Rational Dress Society in March of 1883 in which it fell to Harberton to defend the divided skirt against detractors. Harberton bristles at the notion that a garment can be considered "feminine" or "masculine," although clearly this is a charge made against the skirt by its detractors: "Lady Harberton . . . asked 'what was the objection to having a divided skirt? It was said to be wearing men's clothes. A man walked by putting one leg forward and then bringing the other up past it, and she was not aware that

any other mode of progression had been found for women: what was entirely right for men could not logically be called inconvenient, unsuitable, and frightful for women. Which was feminine—the dress or the wearer? If a dress was to be called masculine or feminine, they should be having their furniture described by sex next."' See "The Rational Dress Society," *The Artist* (March 1883): 85-86. Lady Harberton also wrote for *The Woman's World*. In an earlier issue of *The Artist*, it is reported that the conservative "Dress Defense League" took issue with the divided skirt as being eccentric. Isabel Armstrong, the Association's secretary explains, "the association is as opposed to the 'divided skirt' as to the 'extended skirt,' or indeed to any exaggerated eccentricity in dress." Armstrong goes on to protest any hint of immorality in dress, linking gendered presentation and morality. See "The Divided Skirt," *The Artist*, (Sept. 1881): 281. In the late 1880s, even the feminist Millicent Garrett Fawcett expressed reservations about the divided skirt as "too masculine" a garment. See an interview with Fawcett in the *Women's Penny Paper*, (Nov. 3, 1888): 4. Fawcett's views were in apparent opposition to the editors at *The Women's Penny Paper*, which ran advertisements for dress shops that specialized in making the divided skirt, targeting a pro-suffragist, feminist reader.

[11] In his first editorial for *The Woman's World*, Wilde boldly claimed, "And yet how sensible is the dress of the London milkwoman, of the Irish or Scotch fishwife, of the North-country factory-girl! An attempt was made recently to prevent the pit-women from working, on the ground that their costume was unsuited to their sex, but it is really only the idle classes who dress badly." Oscar Wilde, "Literary and Other Notes,": 40.

[12] Ibid. Wilde writes, "I must, however, protest against the idea that to chronicle the development of Fashion implies any approval of the particular forms that Fashion may adopt. Besides it is quite easy for the children of light to adapt almost any fashionable form of dress to the requirements of utility and the demands of good taste."

CHAPTER FOURTEEN

TRINKETS AND TRANSFORMATIONS: CONSOLIDATION IN LATE-NINETEENTH-CENTURY BRITAIN

MAGGIE ATKINSON

Jeweler and author James Evans offered an informative presentation at a Universities Art Association of Canada conference in which he traced the life history of several examples of contemporary jewelry. Drawing on Roland Barthes's analysis of how meaning is encoded in both literary works and, by extension, objects, Evans argued that meaning is constructed not in the object's origin but in its destination and, as such, is socially constructed. Evans employed an effective biographical reading of the life history of some of his own creations, conducted over a period of time, in an effort to understand how interpretations, coupled with intercessions of time, place and ownership, contribute to multiple, sometimes diverse readings that become embedded within the object itself.[1] This complements Igor Kopytoff's model of the cultural biography of things and provides a framework in which to examine ornamental objects as re-conceptualized products of social transformation which involve a succession of phases and changes in status over time.[2]

In addition to providing a framework for the analysis of contemporary objects, Evan's approach might be used to discuss jewelry produced in late-nineteenth-and early-twentieth-century Britain. Jewelry of that period could be conceptualized as a means to both beautify and objectify women as potential commodities for the marriage market. Paradoxically, jewelry, some of which was designed and made by artists associated with the Arts and Crafts Movement, was also exploited by Suffragettes in an effort to consolidate and to promote their own social and political agenda of the emancipation of women.[3]

An historically based social and cultural biography of any object necessarily involves significant areas of contestation with regard to the polysemy of meaning; the problematics of assigned meaning; the ways that meaning is constituted and framed within various discursive practices; the interpretation of context and its reception; as well as issues with regard to class, religious affiliation, sexuality and race. A social and cultural reading, complicated by the particular political characteristics evident in specific styles of jewelry in late-nineteenth- and early-twentieth-century Britain, provides a framework in which to analyze complex, culturally produced interpretations of personal ornamental objects. Informed by Barthes' and Kopytoff's assertion that meaning is encoded into objects, I also draw on Mieke Bal and Norman Bryson's theoretical approach whose grounding in semiotics provides the methodology for an intertextual analysis.[4]

Before the nineteenth century British jewelry had acquired specific cultural interpretation through legislative means. Sumptuary Laws recorded as early as the fourteenth century in England and re-drafted during the reign of Henry VIII, sought to maintain long established customary boundaries between the newly affluent merchant class and the long established aristocracy. These laws focused on the dress and personal adornment of both men and women and codes of fashion were class specific. Personal ornamentation for the lower middle class for example, was restricted to simple designs which consisted predominantly of glass or flat-cut semi-precious stones set in brass or pewter. Pins and ornate buttons were the most common type of jewelry for the lower middle-class, while ornament classified as non-functional and therefore solely for appearance's sake was restricted to the upper classes. Penalties for violation of Sumptuary Laws could be severe and included fines, loss of property, imprisonment and even death. After the seventeenth century, however, the amount of jewelry worn by all classes increased steadily and began to include a variety of chains, earrings, brooches, and finger rings.[5]

From the end of the seventeenth and throughout the eighteenth century marriage for women also meant loss of property as any holdings automatically passed into the control of the husband. Consequently, women's access to power and liberty were severely curtailed as it was believed that to own property was to enjoy self-determination. One way women sustained a sense of agency after marriage was through the retention of personal possessions such as jewelry. Personal ornament was socially acknowledged as a visible sign of success and women used jewelry as decorative but also made, exhibited, bought and sold it.[6]

Women produced meaning and gained agency through the control and deliberate manipulation of personal ornaments. The acquisition of jewelry, as an important component for the formation of social and cultural structures, continued well into the eighteenth and early nineteenth centuries.[7] The purchase, giving and receiving of jewels marked important moments of transition in individual life experience a practice that survives today in the form of gold watches for retirement or school rings for graduation.[8] In mid-eighteenth-century England, jewelry was used as a tool of adornment for young women's bodies marking them as marriageable and simultaneously provided valuable capital, both material and symbolic.[9] Women gained control over what adorned their bodies and determined how their property would be used, exchanged or disposed of.

Jewelry functioned as a locus for self-determinative acts for women but also paradoxically as a device with which to objectify women as both commodity and display. French art critic and color theorist Charles Blanc (1813-82) wrote that "far from being a frivolous subject...ornaments are for the philosopher an indication of morals and a sign of the reigning ideas of the period."[10] His book provides some insight into late-eighteenth and early nineteenth century perspectives on personal ornament whose codes were informed by androcentric imperialist attitudes that were inevitably inscribed onto the bodies of women. Blanc delineated social and cultural mandates which prescribed the fashion for European women and girls of the early and mid nineteenth century:

> In Europe...brilliants are not allowed to be worn by young girls...They are scarcely permitted to wear pearls and turquoises, the emblems of poetry and purity. Diamonds are not worn until after marriage....[and] a widow can only wear mourning jewels, in jet, black enamel, or black onyx.[11]

Despite his recital of the litany of regulations that policed the use of jewelry, Blanc also wrote that it was important that the "designer of jewellery...think much less of displaying his talents than of enhancing the beauty of his work, in order to render the woman who is to wear it more attractive."[12]

By the nineteenth century two schools of thought with regard to personal enhancement including fashion, accessories and cosmetics had emerged. One promoted their use as a positive practice, in that they served to correct perceived physical deficiencies. The second regarded the use of personal adornments as "immoral instruments of sin and deception."[13] Artist, illustrator and critic of artistic and decorative practice, Mary Eliza Haweis wrote magazine articles and published several books that focused on domestic art and dress. One such book adhered to the first school of thought and promoted the cultivation of physical beauty for women. Haweis advanced the philosophy that female beauty should be cultivated and she delineated specific ways that women could make themselves presentable to men as potential marriage partners. She advocated then current tenets that decreed that women were expected to be attractive and also visible in order that they fulfill their "most important obligation and station in life that of wife and mother," writing that "most girls look forward to getting married [and] [t]hey are right. It is a woman's instinct…[m]ost mothers hold out marriage as the chief aim of a girl's existence."[14] One way Haweis suggested that young women improve their overall appearance was through the appropriate use of personal ornament writing that "the plain girl is the most promising" because she can "by the aid of dress make [herself] ornamental."[15] Haweis supplied information on appropriate and inappropriate styles of jewelry and also focused on how each piece was to be worn.

Between 1850 and 1920 social and cultural unrest in Britain intensified and women increased their struggle to acquire rights. The implementation of the Matrimonial Causes Act (1857), the Married Women's Property Acts, (1870, 1874, 1882), and the Sex Disqualification Removal Act (1919) extended the grounds for divorce, increased the right to control personal property, and prohibited women from being disqualified from positions within the civil professional sector on the grounds of either gender or marital status. Consequently, despite books such as Blanc's and Haweis's, transformation in the lives of women by the latter part of the nineteenth century heralded marked changes in jewelry design and display. Fashion accessories began to develop from delicate, unassuming gold and silver filigree to bolder, larger, much more colorful pieces. In her discussion of Victorian jewelry, Margaret Flower argued that "this new more flamboyant jewellery coincided with a new more confident, more self-sufficient woman."[16] Women spent their earnings on earrings, brooches, bracelets and necklaces and displayed these as boldly as possible.

Jewels created by artists such as Ernestine Mills and Charles Robert Ashbee associated with the Arts and Crafts Movement featured semi-precious, often misshapen stones set in beaten silver, rather than precious metals and stones such as gold and diamonds worn by affluent society, and were designed to be affordable to the middle classes. Craft Revival jewelers experimented with unusually juxtaposed color combinations and used heavily flawed or semi-precious cabochon stones such as amethysts couched in hammered silver and embellished enamel.[17] By the late nineteenth century, ornamental design based on natural forms and informed by medieval, Renaissance and Gothic art offered inspiration for Arts and Crafts jewelers. German-born jeweler and silversmith Charles

Wagner, whose jewelry motifs were based on neo-Gothic architectural designs, provided further material for Craft Revival artists. Wagner's influence also served to accelerate the revival of interest in jewelry designs of the Italian Renaissance which remained popular in England. In addition, ornament of Eastern origin particularly South Asia and Japan in the form of print-design, metalwork, enamel, porcelain and ivory, provided further sources of inspiration for arts and crafts designers.[18]

Artists associated with the decorative and applied arts such as May Morris, Jessie King, Charles Rennie Mackintosh, Margaret Macdonald and Frances Macdonald designed jewelry during the latter part of the nineteenth century.[19] Two black and white photographs taken in 1888 and 1898 respectively show Jane Morris wearing what is characterized as a large arts and crafts necklace and May Morris adorned with a rope of large beads.[20] In addition, designers from the Glasgow School evolved an integrated vocabulary of decorative forms inspired by William Morris, Aubrey Beardsley and Dutch symbolist painter Jan Toorop.[21] Artists experimented with innovative jewelry design and metal work and one example of this jewelry is the heart shaped brooch given to Jane Morris by Rossetti and worn by Fanny Cornforth in Rossetti's *The Blue Bower* of 1865. The brooch's vibrantly colored cabochon paste stones embedded in beaten silver are characteristic of Craft Revival jewelry production. Similarly, Rossetti's *The Beloved* dated 1865-66 is replete with minutely detailed depictions of jewelry espoused as art works in their own right by artists associated with the Arts and Crafts Movement.[22]

These developments in fashion and jewelry design corresponded with social, cultural and political transformations specific to women's increasing emancipation. Women's suffrage had existed in Britain since the 1860s but had not won the vote for women by the end of the nineteenth century.[23] Consequently, the Women's Social and Political Union (WSPU) was established in Manchester in 1903. Founded by the Pankhurst family, this new militant organization advocated an active rather than passive approach and by 1906 women involved with the organization had become infamous for rupturing what had been considered a male dominated political public space. The WSPU agenda included manipulated interventions that disturbed public meetings and directly challenged male politicians.[24] In addition, women organized massive protest marches, some of which were conducted in front of the House of Commons.[25] Several such protests earned the women criminal convictions often resulting in imprisonment. These women were not deterred; quite the opposite, such authoritarianism only encouraged them to continue to pursue their goal. Early twentieth-century women's aggressive transgression into perceived boundaries between male/female, public/private and political/apolitical succeeded in garnering national attention and helped mark the emergence of a new more determined woman.[26]

Jewelry, considered an object of artistic value, served as a site across which important social and political agendas could be negotiated and was designed for and worn by members of the WSPU to engender awareness of serious political intent.[27] Suffragettes provided a principal key to the success of their new militant campaign by adopting, marketing and wearing many different types of decorative articles including jewelry.[28] Suffragettes also employed a specific and easily recognized color combination of purple, white and green that readily identified their jewelry. Moreover, Suffragettes attached important symbolic meaning to both the stones used in jewelry designs and the colors adopted by the WSPU. The color purple, for instance, represented dignity, white denoted purity and hope was signified by a shade of emerald green.[29] Mystical meanings considered "singularly important" were also assigned to the amethyst, emerald and pearl stones used to create some of the jewelry worn by Suffragettes. Pearls, for example, represented the "tears of angels" which would "crystallize" once women had gained the right to vote while emeralds bestowed the gift of "imperviousness to derision and an eloquent tongue". Moreover, amethysts and emeralds held both magical and historical significance as they were considered to be "two of the twelve foundations of the wall of the Holy City," a quality which suggested their power to help create the new foundations on which women could build.[30]

Suffragette jewelry was often created in the Revival Craft style producing a link between Suffragettes and the Arts and Crafts Movement. Many artists were active supporters of women's suffrage and the founding of the Artist's Suffrage League in 1907 encouraged collective organization in the production of jewelry and the contribution of specialist skills to the campaign.[31] In 1914 *Studio* illustrated a gold pendant set with opals and made in an arts and crafts style and molded into an abstracted female form with arms outstretched evoking Suffragettes as victorious. This pendant was presented to Mrs. Pethick Lawrence, one of the leading figures of the WSPU, by her mother and her four sisters and the relationship between this ornament and Suffragette campaign is confirmed by the caption.[32]

In addition, Elizabeth Goring describes a portrait photograph of militant Suffragette leader Christabel Pankhurst wearing a large enameled pendant and spiraling gem-set brooch. Both pieces of jewelry are significant because they are created in an arts and crafts style and the brooch set with cabochon emerald, amethyst and pearl reveals a color combination that corresponds with the WSPU's signature color code.[33] A similar brooch attributed to C.R. Ashbee, set with a cabochon emerald, amethysts and eight small pearls that are indicative of the WSPU's colors, has led scholars Charlotte Gere and Elizabeth Goring to conclude that it is the same jewel worn by Christabel Pankhurst in a watercolor portrait.[34] Pankhurst's enameled, heart-shaped pendant also depicted in the photograph closely resembles another enameled pendant created by Suffragette arts and crafts artist Ernestine Mills. [35] The ornament designed by Mills, and presented to Louise Mary Eates on her return from Holloway prison, was made of silver and enamel and was intended to represent the "winged figure of hope singing outside the prison bars." The pendant combines stones of purple, green and white, colors symbolic of the WSPU.[36]

Tri-colored jewelry engendered a serious and progressive political agenda. Christabel Pankhurst wrote that the signature colors of the WSPU should be displayed at every opportunity to aggressively publicize the "regimental colours."[37] Jewelry, using this powerful symbolic combination, offered the revolutionary means for women to publicly advertise their identity as Suffragettes. Color integrated into jewelry and re-conceptualized as sign, instantly conveyed a complex political agenda. Furthermore, this purple, white and green combination elicited immediate, and sometimes virulent, response from early-twentieth-century British society.

The WSPU's motto "Deeds not Words" exemplified women's intention to implement a far more aggressive politicized campaign in order to ensure the procurement of the right to vote. Suffrage campaigns were efficiently organized and one way women disseminated information that clearly articulated their desire to pursue and maintain a consolidated, ongoing serious political campaign was through the vigorous commodification of jewelry. Examples of jewelry worn by those associated with the Suffragette movement ranged from highly decorative work to purely propagandizing badges, and from the highest quality ornaments created by artists affiliated with the Arts and Crafts Movement to the cheapest mass-produced brass buttons.[38] Despite the difference in ornamental design and commercial value, it was the identical color-combination that served to unite the women and that confirmed the wearer's allegiance to the cause.[39]

Black and white photographs often depict fashionably dressed upper- and middle-class women as active members of the organization when in fact women of the lower-classes were also committed to the cause. Women of all ages and backgrounds worked jointly towards the achievement of the vote for women and research suggests that thousands of examples of suffragette jewelry pieces were made, advertised, sold and worn between 1908 and 1914.[40] Moreover, these ornaments, both hand-made and mass-produced, were marketed at a range of prices which permitted women of all classes to obtain objects that signaled their affiliation to the WSPU. Jewelry and ornaments produced and marketed for and by women associated with the WSPU included affordable objects such as colored pins made from tin, medals often used for official honors, and more expensive original pieces made specifically for presentations or other special occasions.[41]

Specifically crafted jewelry designs were awarded to Suffragettes who took an aggressive stance against government policies that both excluded and subjugated women.

When fourteen Suffragettes confessed that they had deliberately broken the windows of government offices, Christabel Pankhurst defended their militant methods and stated that such actions forced men to take women's objectives seriously. Pankhurst described the rocks the women had used to cause the damage as "precious stones, jewels in the Suffragettes' crown."[42] Subsequently, the fourteen "stone-throwers" were each rewarded for their militant actions with a gold safety-pin brooch set with flint stone. These specially designed jewels demonstrated the Suffragettes' unapologetic determination to show by "deeds not words" their commitment to the fight for political freedom.[43]

Suffragettes who had been imprisoned for their activities were awarded the *Holloway Brooch* which was named after the women's prison in London. Designed by Sylvia Pankhurst, and enameled in purple, white and green, the silver brooch was formed into the shape of a portcullis and superimposed with a convict's arrow.[44] Many prominent Suffragettes, including Emmeline Pankhurst, were photographed wearing this mark of honor. Pankhurst was also presented with a chain and pendant made from amethyst, pearls and emeralds, "wrought in gold by a special expert in artistic jewellery." commemorate her release from prison. The presentation was accompanied by the following address: "We present, on the occasion of her release from Holloway prison...this chain of amethysts, pearls, and emeralds, we ask her to wear for our sake, as a symbol of...dignity, purity, and hope."[45]

In addition, Suffragettes developed another innovative and powerful tactic when, in June 1909, Scottish sculptor Marjorie Wallace Dunlop went on a hunger strike while in prison to protest the sometimes brutal treatment of imprisoned Suffragettes. In September of the same year prison authorities introduced a painful and dangerous method of force-feeding by inserting tubes up the nose and down the back of the throat. Women who had undergone this abhorrent process were awarded the highly regarded Hunger Strike Medal during ceremonies organized by WSPU members. Additional bars were added for each period of force-feeding endured by the women.[46]

Suffragettes took advantage of every opportunity to incorporate the colors into their daily lives and the marketing potential of the signal combination was exploited rapidly by retailers and manufacturers in anticipation of the thousands of women who had begun to search for the three-color combination in clothing and accessories.[47] Firms such as Mappin and Webb, who placed advertisements in *Votes for Women* marketed gold brooches and pendants set with emeralds, pearls and amethysts. In so doing, they helped to promote the Suffragette political agenda. Advertisements offered readers silver and enameled jewelry as well as other more affordable items such as hatpins and tin badges, some of which incorporated images of leading Suffragettes and painted slogans.[48] The WSPU manufactured, promoted and sold Suffragette jewelry and by the end of 1911 thirty-six branches and ten shops had opened in London. Soon after another eighty-six branches and seventeen shops located throughout the rest of the country followed. Women designed and created the jewelry, which included battery-operated brooches that flashed the slogan "Votes For Women". Pieces could be purchased from these outlets as well as from the many bazaars that were organized to facilitate further promotion of Suffragette politics.[49]

Although much of the jewelry designed between 1908 and the onset of WWI that served to encapsulate the ideological political views of Suffragette women survives today, its original significance has only recently been rediscovered. Women's innovative symbolic color design, disseminated through the design, commodification and display of this jewelry attracted national, if not international, recognition for their political crusade. Goring wrote that "better awareness and understanding of this subject will bring many more examples to light together with their associated stories, to bear witness to the women who wore this jewelery with courage and conviction, and risked their lives in the cause of equality and justice."[50] The social, political and cultural context in which these objects were made combined with stories associated with individual items of suffragette jewelery present a compelling area for further examination. Kopytoff's and Barthes' theoretical proposal of the cultural biography of things resonates with Goring's assertion that "every jewel will have had a unique personal story attached to it, with the capacity to bear witness to one of the most remarkable and sustained movements for social and political change in the twentieth century."[51]

Power ascribed to the symbolic influence of jewelery is not a recent development. Henry VIII controlled the use of jewelry through legislative process and successfully enforced class division in Britain. Similarly, in the late nineteenth century the aristocracy demonstrated power, wealth and class distinction through the display of opulent jewelry while young middle-class women were encouraged to adorn their bodies with jewels in an effort to fulfill obligatory requirements to become wives and mothers. Suffragettes utilized jewelry not as merely decorative, but as a vehicle with which to communicate their political objectives.

Works Cited

Atkinson, Diane. *Suffragettes in the Purple White & Green: London 1906-14*. London: Museum of London, 1992.

Bal, Mieke and Norman Bryson. "Semiotics and Art History." *The Art Bulletin* 73, no. 2 (1991): 174-298.

Betterton, Rosemary. " 'A Perfect Woman' The Political Body of Suffrage." In *An Intimate Distance: Women, Artists and the Body*. 46-78. London: Routledge, 1996.

Blanc, Charles. Art in Ornament and Dress. London: Chapman and Hall, 1877.

Burkhauser, Jude, ed. "By Women's Hands: the Metalworkers." In *Glasgow Girls: Women in Art and Design 1880-1920,* 178-182. Edinburgh: Canongate, 1990.

Callen, Anthea. Women Artists of the Arts and Crafts Movement 1870-1914. New York: Pantheon Books, 1979.

Carruthers, Annette and Mary Greensted., eds. "Artistically Attired: Arts and Crafts dress and jewellery." In *Simplicity or Splendour: Arts and Crafts Living – Objects from the Cheltenham Collection*, 42-47. Cheltenham: Cheltenham Art Gallery and Museums in association with Lund Humphries, London, 1999.

Cockroft, Irene. "The Alchemy of Enamelling for Equality." *Gem Jewellery News* (2002): 32-43.

Cooper, Suzanne Fagence. *Pre-Raphaelite Art in the Victoria and Albert Museum*. London: Harry N. Abrams, 2003.

Evans, James. *La Mort du Joaillier: Tales from Beyond the Grave.* Queen's University Kingston Ontario, 2003.

Flower, Margaret. "Mid-Victorian or Grand Period (1860-1885)." In *Victorian Jewellery Design*, 27-35. London: Cassell and Co., 1951.

Gere, Charlotte. "Knowledge, Money and Time: Anne Hull Grundy as
Collector of Victorian Jewellery." *Journal of the Decorative Arts
Society 1850 to the Present* 24, (2002): 80-97.

Gere, Charlotte and Geoffrey Munn. *Artist's Jewellery: Pre-Raphaelite to
Arts and Crafts*. Woodbridge: Suffolk, 1989.

Goring, Elizabeth. "Suffragette Jewellery in Britain." *The Decorative Arts
Society 1850 to Present* 26 (2003): 85.

Haweis, Mary Eliza Joy. *The Art of Beauty*. New York: Harper &
Brothers, 1878.

Hughes, Graham. *The Art of Jewellery: A survey of Craft and Creation*.
London: Studio Vista Publishers, 1972.

Kopytoff, Igor. "The Cultural Biography of Things: Commoditization as
Process." In *The Social Life of Things: Commodities in Cultural
Perspective,* Arjun Appadurai, ed., 64-91. Cambridge: Cambridge
University Press, 1986.

Lochnan, Katherine A. "Jewellery." In *The Earthly Paradise: Arts and
Crafts by William Morris and his Circle from Canadian Collections*,
Katharine A. Lochnan, Douglas E. Schoenherr and Carole Silver, eds.,
217-227. Ontario: Art Gallery of Ontario, 1993.

Pankhurst, Christabel. "The Political Importance of Colours." *Votes for
Women*. II, no. 61 (1909): 632.

Pankhurst, Sylvia. *The History of Women's Militant Suffrage Movement
1905-1910*. Boston: The Woman's Art Journal, 1911.

Pethick Lawrence, Emmeline. "Precious Stones." *Votes for Women* II, no.
73 (1909): 1005.

Pointon, Marcia J. *Strategies for Showing: Women, and Representation in
English Visual Culture, 1665-1800*. Oxford: Oxford University Press,
1997.

Sharpe Evelyn. "Painting Kensington Purple, White, and Green." *Votes
for Women* II, no. 53 (1909): 422.

Silver, Carole. *The Earthly Paradise: Arts and Crafts by William Morris
and his Circle from Canadian Collections*. Ontario: Art Gallery of
Ontario, 1993.

Studio. 60 (1913/1914): 269.

Tickner, Lisa. *The Spectacle of Women: Imagery of the Suffrage
Campaign 1907-1914*. Chicago: University of Chicago, 1988.

"The Woman Suffrage Demonstration in Hyde Park." (1908): 5.

Times. "Women Suffrage: Meeting at Queen's Hall." (1909): 10.

—. "Woman Suffrage Demonstration in London." (1910): 10.

Towards the Millenium. "Women: Mothers, Workers and Politicians 1910-1920." Birmingham: Birmingham Museums & Art Gallery Exhibition, 1992.

Vallance, Aymer. "Modern British Jewellery & Fans." In *Modern Design in Jewellery and Fans*, Charles Holme, ed., 1-10. London: Offices of the Studio, 1902.

Votes for Women. "Constitution." (1907): ii.

—. "The Hyde Park Demonstration." (1908): 158.

—. "The Procession." 16, (1908): 260.

—. "The Militant Demonstrations." II, no. 17 (1908): 282.

—. "Christabel Pankhurst's Day." 11, no. 43 (1908): 230.

—. "Popularising the Colours." II, no. 15 (1908): 260.

—. "Scene in the Streets." II, no. 17 (1908): 282.

—. "Christmas Present." II, no. 40 (1908): 178.

—. "Novelties in the Union Colours." II, no. 21(1908): 338.

—. "Concerning Dress." II, no. 30 (1 October, 1908): 7.

—. "At the Queen's Hall Presentation to Mrs. Pankhurst and Mrs. Leigh." II, no. 48 (1909): 276.

—. "The Artist's Suffrage League." II, no. 65 (1909): 752.

—. "Portrait of Christabel Pankhurst." II, no. 53 (1909): 53.

—. "Two Great Meetings: Miss Christabel Pankhurst on Mutiny." II, no. 72 (1909): 981.

—. "Badges and Colours." II, no. 51 (1909): 303.

—. "The Hunger-Strikes at St. James Hall." II, no. 74 (1909): 1043.

—. "A Lie Nailed to the Counter-Biting Charge against Miss Garnett Dismissed." II, no. 74 (1909): 1037-38.

—. "Mappin & Webb Suffragette Jewellery." III, no. 93 (1909): 183.

—. "Presentation to Mrs. Pankhurst." II, no. 42 (24 Dec 1909): 210.

—. "The 'Hunger Strike' all W.S.P.U. Prisoners Liberated." II, no. 75 (1909): 1061.

—. "Forcible Feeding: Opinions of Medical Experts Grave Danger to Life Involved." III, no. 82 (1909): 2.

—. "The Treatment of Political Prisoners: Forced Feeding, Handcuffs, Canvas Clothes, and Insults." III, no. 100 (1910): 298.

Notes

[1] Evans, *La Mort du Joaillier: Tales from Beyond the Grave* (Universities Art Association of Canada Annual Conference, Queen's University, Kingston, Ontario, 7 November 2003).

[2] Igor Kopytoff, "The Cultural Biography of Things: Commoditization as Process," in *The Social Life of Things: Commodities in Cultural Perspective,* edited by Arjun Appadurai, 64-91.

[3] The term Suffragist was used to describe members of the National Union of Women's Suffrage Societies (NUWSS) which developed in England in 1887. The Union advocated social and political reform aimed at extending the right to vote to include women. The term Suffragette was specific to members of the Women's Social and Political Union (WSPU) formed in England in 1903. Suffragettes carried out a far more militant campaign for the rights of women to vote than did the Suffragist. Suffragettes advocated direct action which included smashing windows and organizing massive, often disruptive demonstrations, as opposed to the more passive activities carried out by the Suffragists such as writing letters.

[4] Bal and Bryson, "Semiotics and Art History," 174-298.

[5] Pointon, *Strategies for Showing: Women, and Representation in English Visual Culture, 1665-1800*, 31-37.

[6] Ibid., 31-37.

[7] Ibid., 41-45.

[8] Ibid., 32.

[9] Ibid., 33.

[10] Blanc, *Art in Ornament and Dress*, 267.

[11] Ibid., 266.

[12] Ibid., 250.

[13] Ibid., 267.

[14] Haweis, *The Art of Beauty*, 261.

[15] Ibid., 273.

[16] Flower, "Mid-Victorian or Grand Period (1860-1885),", 27-35.

[17] Ibid., 39-46.

[18] Carruthers and Greensted, eds., "Artistically Attired: Arts and Crafts dress and jewellery," 42-47, Lochnan, "Jewellery," 217-227; Vallance, "Modern British Jewellery & Fans," 1-10; Hughes, *The Art of Jewellery: A survey of Craft and Creation*, 99-104; Burkhauser, "By Women's Hands: the Metalworkers," 178-182; Callen, *Women Artists of the Arts and Crafts Movement 1870-1914*, 178-9; Gere, "Knowledge, Money and Time: Anne Hull Grundy as Collector of Victorian Jewellery," 80-97.

[19] Burkhauser, "By Women's Hands," 178-182.

[20] Carruthers and Greensted, "Artistically Attired," 45.

[21] Burkhauser, "By Women's Hands," 178-9.

[22] Gere and Munn, *Artist's Jewellery: Pre-Raphaelite to Arts and Crafts*, 109; Suzanne Fagence Cooper, *Pre-Raphaelite Art in the Victoria and Albert Museum*, 134-5. The subject of the *The Beloved* is the bride from the Song of Solomon and Rossetti made ample use of textiles and jewels gleaned from his own collection

[23] *Towards the Millenium*, "Women: Mothers, Workers and Politicians 1910-1920, Birmingham: Birmingham Museums & Art Gallery Exhibition, 1992. The NUWSS (Suffragists) was formed in 1897 by Mrs. Millicent Garrett-Fawcett and by 1914 had over 100,000 members. They campaigned peacefully for the vote. (Tickner, *The Spectacle of Women: Imagery of the Suffrage Campaign 1907-1914.*

[24] Emmeline Pankhurst, and her daughters Christabel, Sylvia and Adela founded the Women's Social and Political Union (WSPU) (Suffragettes) in 1903 and their constitution made clear their intent. Their objectives included action in opposition to whatever government was in power and "vigorous agitation" against government policy that refused women the right to vote. The constitution also stated that the WSPU would educate the public through public meetings, demonstrations, debates, distribution of literature and newspaper articles. "Constitution," *Votes for Women* (October 1907): ii . Also see "Women: Mothers, Workers and Politicians," *Towards the Millennium.* Processions and demonstrations included: June 1908 – 'Women's Sunday.' A huge precession and rally ending in Hyde Park, London, organised by the WSPU. Over 500,000 people attended; November 1910 – 'Black Friday.' 400 women demonstrated outside the House of Commons. Over 100 women were arrested; June 11 – "Women's Coronation Procession.' Over 60,000 women from all organizations took part in the procession which stretched for seven miles; June/July 1913 – NUWSS 'Women's Pilgrimage.' A number of marches from all over Britain which culminated in London. In "Women: Mothers, Workers and Politicians," *Towards the Millennium.*"

[25] See for example, "The Hyde Park Demonstration," *Votes for Women* (14 May 1908): 158; "The Procession," *Votes for Women, n*o. 16 (25 June 1908): 260; "The Militant Demonstrations," *Votes for Women* II, no. 17 (2 July 1908): 282; "Two Great Meetings: Miss Christabel Pankhurst on Mutiny," *Votes for Women* II, no. 72 (23 July 1909): 981; "The Woman Suffrage Demonstration in Hyde Park," *The Times* (20 January 1908): 5; "Woman Suffrage Demonstration in London," *The Times* (20 June 1910): 10.

[26] Elizabeth Goring, "Suffragette Jewellery in Britain," *The Decorative Arts Society 1850 to Present*, 26, (2003): 85; Sylvia Pankhurst, *The History of Women's Militant Suffrage Movement 1905-1910* (Boston: The Woman's Art Journal, 1911); Tickner, *The Spectacle of Women*, (1988); Diane Atkinson, *Suffragettes in the Purple White & Green: London 1906-14* (London: Museum of London, 1992), 6-13; Rosemary Betterton, " 'A Perfect Woman' The Political Body of Suffrage," *An Intimate Distance: Women, Artists and the Body* (London: Routledge, 1996), 46-78.

[27] The National Women's Social and Political Union were specific in their objectives. The constitution stipulated that the union would secure for women the parliamentary vote, to establish equality of rights and opportunities between the

sexes, and to promote the social and industrial well-being of the community. "Constitution," *Votes for Women* (October 1907): ii.

[28] In 1906, the Daily Mail Newspaper labelled the members of the WSPU "Suffragettes" in order to distinguish them from law-abiding Suffragists. The term Suffragette continues to be used to refer to women who used militant tactics. "Women: Mothers, Workers and Politicians 1910-1920," (1992): n.p.

[29] "Christabel Pankhurt's Day," *Votes for Women* 11, no. 43 (31 December 1908): 230.

[30] "At the Queen's Hall Presentation to Mrs. Pankhurst and Mrs. Leigh," *Votes for Women,* Vol. II, No. 48 (21 January, 1909): 276.

[31] "The Artist's Suffrage League," *Votes for Women* II, no. 65 (4 June, 1909): 752; Goring, *Suffragette Jewellery*, 95.

[32] *The Studio*, Vol. 60 (1913/1914): 269; the caption reads that the pendant was presented to Mrs. Pethick Lawrence.

[33] The black and white photograph does not reveal the colours but the silver brooch was exhibited in the 1989 Wartski exhibition "'Artists' Jewellery: Pre-Raphaelite to Arts and Crafts" and was made with emerald, amethysts and pearls. Goring writes that Gere and Munn convincingly attribute this brooch to C.R. Ashbee. Goring, *Suffragette Jewellery*, 93.

[34] Goring, *Suffragette Jewellery*, 94; Gere and Munn, *Artist's Jewellery*, 188. The watercolor portrait, at the Museum of London, is attributed to Sylvia Pankhurst, although an issue of *Votes for Women* reveals that "well known" artist Ethel Wright was in the process of painting a portrait of Christabel Pankhurst in March of 1909. "Portrait of Christabel Pankhurst," *Votes for Women* II, no. 53 (12 March 1909): 422.

[35] Goring, *Suffragette Jewellery*, 94-5. Goring writes that the pendant was willed to the Museum of London by Louise Eates's daughter and the pendant is specifically described as an "enamelled silver pendant set with semi-precious stones made by Ernestine Mills to commemorate the imprisonment of my mother the late Louise Mary Eates during the struggle for votes for women" in her will.

[36] Ibid. 95.

[37] Pankhurst, "The Political Importance of Colours," *Votes for Women* II, no. 61, 632.

[38] Cockroft, "The Alchemy of Enamelling for Equality," *Gem Jewellery News*, 32-43 Goring, *Suffragette Jewellery*, 85, Atkinson, *Purple, White and Green,* 55.

[39] Emmeline Pethick Lawrence impressed women with the importance of popularising the colours in every way possible in order that they become the "reigning fashion" writing that "strange as it may seem, nothing would so help to popularise the Women's Social and Political Union," "Popularising the Colours," *Votes for Women* II, no. 15, 260.

[40] One writer noted that "a marked feature of the thousands now pouring on the scene was the large proportion of respectable women and girls, of all strata of society, and all ages." "Scene in the Streets," *Votes for Women* Vol. II, No. 17, 282; also see "Women: Mothers, Workers and Politicians," *Towards the Millennium.*

[41] The colors were advertised as Union colors and ribbons and pins in the tri-color combination could be obtained from the Women's Union Press as well as from literature stalls that were set up in different communities. *Votes for Women* Vol. II, no. 12, 199; Women were encouraged to purchase ties, belt buckles, scarves, pins and hat pins as well as Boadicea brooches all in white, green and purple as Christmas presents. The women were assured that prices suited all purses and could be purchased from the Woman's Press. "Christmas Present," *Votes for Women* Vol. II, no. 40, 178; also see, "Badges and Colours," *Votes for Women* II, no. 51, 303; Evelyn Sharpe, "Painting Kensington Purple, White, and Green," *Votes for Women* II, no. 53, 422. Sharp writes that the WSPU shop windows were filled with scarves, hatpins, badges, belts, "and anything else we can show in the fighting colours of the union…the real effect of our shop is its moral effect. There it is, a tri-colour evidence to the hundreds of people who pass every day that the 'Votes for Women' movement is in their midst, whether they like it or not."

[42] Pankhurst, "Two Great Meetings, Miss Christabel Pankhurst on Mutiny," *Votes for Women* II, no. 72, 981.

[43] Lawrence, "Precious Stones," *Votes for Women* II, no. 73, 1005.

[44] "The Hunger-Strikes at St. James Hall," *Votes for Women* II, no. 74, 1043; "A Lie Nailed to the Counter-Biting Charge against Miss Garnett Dismissed," *Votes for Women* II, no. 74, 1037-38. "Mrs. Pethick Lawrence…announced that a commemorative medal had been struck, and would be presented to each of the hunger-strikers in recognition of what they had suffered for the cause."

[45] "Presentation to Mrs. Pankhurst," *Votes for Women* II, no. 42, 210; "Women Suffrage: Meeting at Queen's Hall," *The Times*, 10. It was noted that the presentation, "took the form of an illuminated address and a jeweled chain and pendant, wrought from an original design, and introducing the purple, white, and green of the union by use of amethysts, pearls, and emeralds.

[46] "The Treatment of Political Prisoners: Forced Feeding, Handcuffs, Canvas Clothes, and Insults," *Votes for Women* III, no. 100, 298; "The 'Hunger Strike' all W.S.P.U. Prisoners Liberated," *Votes for Women* II, no. 75, 1061; "Forcible Feeding: Opinions of Medical Experts Grave Danger to Life Involved," *Votes for Women* III, no. 82, 2; Goring, *Suffragette Jewellery*, 89; Atkinson, *Purple, White & Green*, 37-8; Betterton, *A Perfect Woman*, 58-63; Tickner, *The Spectacle of Women*, 104-7

[47] "Novelties in the Union Colours," *Votes for Women* II, no. 21, 338; "Concerning Dress," *Votes for Women* II, no. 30, 7; Atkinson, *Purple, White & Green*, 25; Goring, *Suffragette Jewellery*, 86.

[48] "Mappin & Webb Suffragette Jewellery," *Votes for Women* III, No. 93, 183.

[49] Atkinson, *Purple, White & Green*, 49-54, 25; Goring, *Suffragette Jewellery*, 87.

[50] Goring, *Suffragette Jewellery*, 98.

[51] Ibid., 85.

AFTERWORD

SPECTERS OF REFORM

MARY ELLIS GIBSON

A story, not wholly apocryphal, can set the stage for reconsidering nineteenth-century reform—that nexus of evangelical and Utilitarian ideologies, of activism, self-interest and unintended consequences. I begin around the turn of the nineteenth century.

Imagine a chilly grey morning in Clapham, in the south of London. Various earnest men and women and their even more hard working servants have been up for hours. They are assembled along with a number of children at the breakfast table of William Wilberforce, already famous for leading the long effort in Parliament for the abolition of slavery. The meal is what we might call a business breakfast, a power breakfast in fact. Gathered round pots of Lapsang and plates of cooling toast are various sober men, including Zacharay Macaulay, recently returned from his efforts to resettle American slaves and their children on the malarial coast of Sierra Leone. The boys he has brought from Sierra Leone to London for schooling as future divines are too young or too ill to attend. But others have gathered, and no meal at Wilberforce's table begins without extended prayers, led by the master of the house himself. This morning as on many occasions heretofore, Wilberforce brings to the Lord's attention a long list of persons and perished souls whom he believes especially in need. Among them he recites names representing a cause almost as dear to his heart as the abolition of slavery. He prays for the souls of women who have died in India as satis, burning on the pyres of their deceased husbands.

In the years after this breakfast Wilberforce's coadjutors and many MPs acting on various interests achieved what Wilberforce surely saw as two great victories—the abolition of the slave trade in 1807 and the opening to missionaries of land controlled by the Honorable East India Company in 1813. These victories were followed in ensuing decades by the abolition of sati in Bengal in 1829 and the Slavery Abolition Act of

1833, which applied to British possessions excepting St. Helena and lands belonging to the East India Company. These "reforms" looked outward from the metropole though they had metropolitan consequences. They came in tandem with the domestic measures we commonly take as the beginning of Victorian reform: the Reform Bill of 1832, the Anatomy Act of 1832, and the Poor Law Amendment Act of 1834.

In the specters of Wilberforce's breakfast table—the small boys of Sierra Leone, the satis of north India—we can measure the ends of what Charles Dickens called telescopic philanthropy. In the specters of Dickens's own novels we can measure the ends of domestic reform—Betty Higden, who in *Our Mutual Friend* only just misses a workhouse death and an afterlife as an anatomized corpse, and Jo, who in *Bleak House* dies a worse death to prove the mutual humanity of rich and poor. But though we could marshal the ghosts of reform—its intended and unintended consequences—and line them up under headings foreign and domestic, they function in another and equally important binary, the difference between reform on one's own behalf and reform on behalf of others. Outlawing sati in Bengal had no direct relationship to Wilberforce's daily existence in Clapham; his experience differed markedly from that of his contemporary, the Indian reformer Rammohun Roy, who had witnessed the sati of his sister-in-law. Though telescopic philanthropy like Wilberforce's prayer for satis seems to be a clear case for reform on behalf of others, sometimes, perhaps even most of the time, philanthropic activities on behalf of another and self-actualizing activities are not easily distinguishable.

If we start from this binary—reform on one's own behalf, reform on behalf of others—the essays in the volume come into a curious order. The premise of the volume, and the conference from which it arose, was to trace the links between gender and reform. The writers of the essays collected here examine activities entailed in reforming gendered relations themselves. I want to reframe their concerns by arguing that the specters of reform arise in multiple contradictions of which gendered contradictions is only one. As we see in these essays, philanthropic claims, claims on behalf others, coexist uneasily with claims for variously positioned selves.

It is not novel to assert that Victorian middle class or upper class women achieved their own ends—a kind of autonomy, a version of reform on their own behalf—by advocating reform on behalf of others. Florence Nightingale is perhaps the consummate example. Nightingale's invalidism can be read as the uneasy conjunction of self and selflessness. I hypothesize that the more acute the contradictions between self-help and philanthropy—as in Nightingale's case—the more likely it is that philanthropic activities create specters, ghostly doubles of the virtues claimed in philanthropic activity. In this sense, Nightingale-the-invalid is the specter of Nightingale the self-advocate. No wonder that her tract, written on behalf of middle class women, was titled *Cassandra*. The reformer cast herself as the prophet whom no one believed. Cassandra walks on the stage as the specter of Florence, a living ghost. What I call the specters of reform are, like Cassandra, illegible alter egos of selves who claimed to act, or who indeed historically did act, philanthropically.

We could begin the genealogy of these specters with Dickens's *Bleak House*. Andre DeCuir's essay on Dickens here examines the varieties of Victorian philanthropy: Mrs. Jellyby's telescopic philanthropy that ignores matters close to home, matters that should be clearly visible to the naked eye; Esther Summerson's domestic philanthropy, limited though it is by her gender and class; and Alan Woodcourt's philanthropy which, like Esther's, is based in genuine charity but, unlike Esther's, is made possible by his mobility. I take Woodcourt to be a particularly interesting case, for he has returned from a shipwrecked Indiaman as a "dark" young surgeon. DeCuir describes Woodcourt's mobility as an ability to go to the "darkest places of Tom-all-alone's." While Woodcourt practices a kind of philanthropic flânerie, Esther is more limited in her movements. She does achieve a modicum of social and philanthropic mobility when she marries Woodcourt, DeCuir argues, but within the continuing and conventionally understood constraints of gender. Her scarred face DeCuir reads as Dickens's mode of conveying Esther's human fallibility. In the union of Alan and Esther we might also imagine the coupling of philanthropic mobility and the mobility of disease. Esther more or less escapes the infantilization of her relationship with Jarndyce by becoming the "the doctor's wife." She has justification for the kind of mobility that has already scarred her. In the darkest places, disease, still, outmaneuvers philanthropy. Like a ghost, upon first recovery from her illness, Esther is scarcely able to recognize herself.

George Eliot's *Romola*, in Chad May's reading, makes exactly this linkage among mobility, philanthropy, and disease. For Eliot's heroine, May suggests, mobility enables both self-actualization and philanthropy, activity on behalf of self and activity on behalf of others. May quotes Eliot's description of Romola's decisive moment, her decision to flee Rome. For Romola, Eliot writes, "there had come one of those moments in life where the soul must dare to act on its own warrant" (quoted in May, 19). Romola in some measure can now act for herself by being, first, adrift in the Mediterranean and then swept ashore to become a ministering angel in a town struck with the plague. But this oddly idyllic interlude must come to an end, for Romola cannot figure for long as the Virgin Mary nor live apart from her own social world. May shows that in the ending of *Romola* the soul's warrant can only be given social form, personal and philanthropic realization, in a domestic space that is clearly marked off from and outside of the "world of men." May draws together various critical approaches to the problematic ending of Eliot's novel, a turn to romance which the novel never finally abandons, and argues that the kind of historical romance Eliot inherited from Walter Scott is here turned to more positive—and I would add to philanthropic—effect. May argues that unlike Scott's Meg Merrilies or his other marginal female figures of romantic suffering, Romola does not disappear; rather her "enclosure within the domestic space" transforms "her own individual suffering to a sympathetic and active strength" (May, 21). The ending of *Romola*, May argues, transforms into social activity the disappearing figures of romantic suffering in Scott's novels. In Scott's fiction by contrast, figures like Meg remain at the novel's "unreadable core."

But in my view, *Romola* too has its unreadable core, its specters of reform. The domestic space, the haven, at the ending of *Romola* certainly entails a political and philanthropic agenda, for the heroine has adopted as her own family her husband's mistress and his illegitimate children. But Romola can only, in the end, inhabit an allegorical space, a space made allegorical because it holds the specters of its own philanthropy at bay. These specters have power insofar as they are animated by passion—the ghost of Tito by erotic passion, the ghost of Savanarola by the passion of self-abnegation. In Romola's world of women we see, not passion of a different order or kind, but passion made safe by being held at bay.

Focusing on the specters in *Romola*, I think, allows us also to read Maria Bachman's and Aria Chernik's essays on Wilkie Collins as commentaries on the process of passion made safe. For Collins (as for his co-author Dickens) making passion safe within the contradictions of Victorian gender codes gave rise as in Eliot to the specters of reform. Bachman provides a fascinating reading of Collins's relatively neglected contributions to Dickens's *Household Words*; she describes the joint work of Collins and his editor as an "assault on the cult of domesticity" (100). Bachman reads Collins's "The Bachelor Bedroom" and "The Cruise of Tomtit" against Dickens's ghastly story, "The Bride's Chamber." Collins's essays celebrate "unprincipled" bachelor life, the bedroom that in Collins's words, "sticks immutably to its own bad character" (quoted in Bachman, 96). The bachelor bedroom puts on notice "the conventionalities of sentimental fiction" (quoted in Bachman, 97). As Bachman points out,

Dickens called on his contributors to embrace "the spirit of reform," but in this case it was not the usual set of social abuses—poverty, neglect, unemployment—but middle class marriage itself that required reform. Here we might argue, Dickens and Collins advocate reform on behalf of themselves, not—as in the cases of Wilberforce and Nightingale or the fictional cases of Esther Summerson and Alan Woodcourt—philanthropy on behalf of others. And yet, if we turn from Collins's glorification of bachelorhood to their critique of marriage, Bachman argues, the consequences for women are less than clear. The dramas of marriage play out in unsettling ways. As long as men are among themselves, as Bachman cleverly shows, we remain in the world of the sitcom. Bachman quotes "The Lazy Tour," jointly composed by Dickens and Collins to this effect: Collins's persona Thomas Idle admonishes the Dickens character Francis Goodchild to avoid falling in love altogether: "It's trouble enough to fall out of once you're in it" (quoted in Bachman, 106, n 81). Falling in love is dangerous. Homosocial harmony is disrupted by heterosexual passion—or, rather, by heterosexual legal and ideological contract.

When women enter the picture, specters arise. Bachman ends her essay with a brief reading of a Dickens story which also appeared in *Household Words*, "The Bride's Chamber." She characterizes this as a "revenge story" "in which a diabolical husband holds his unloved wife hostage in her bedroom...and literally wills her to die until she is no more than a 'white wreck.'" The bride is transformed into the spectral double of the man acting on his own behalf. She becomes a speechless Cassandra. A "white wreck."

Collins's own "white wreck" was the eponymous woman in white. In her essay on Collins's novel, Aria Chernik argues that the woman in white, the ghostly presence / absence of the novel, provides a place of resistance to the inscriptions of gendered identity. It is not that the woman in white, Laura / Anne, is a blank, but that Laura's refusal to sign Sir Percival's nefarious document, which would enable him to control her and her assets entirely, leaves a blank. This blank, Chernik argues, presents the possibility of "ideological reinscription and identity reformation" (147). That is, the blank provides an occasion for the re-formation of identity. The woman in white, on Chernik's reading, is a "place-holder," the "preinterpellative subject, the possibility for resistance and reform, the possibility of being written into an existence that provides the richness of a blank space to reinscribe a counterideology in the form of radical narrativism" (148). And yet, the question remains, in *The Woman in White* as in *The Moonstone*: is a single subject position adequate to a meaningful narration? I would argue that blank space in *The Woman in White* is alternately positive and negative, potentially reformative and potentially terrifying. If the activity on behalf of the self, the critique of marriage (which we might read, mutatis mutandis in Eliot, Dickens, and Collins), is a reinscription of identity, a re-form of the meanings of the self and the self-in-relationship, nonetheless the blank on which this writing is to occur is figured as a ghost. The place of reform *is* the specter of reform. The sensation novel itself becomes a specter of reform, half way between the realist novel and gothic tales of the supernatural.

It is hard to see a ghost, or to explain what one has seen if one claims actually to have done so. The issue of seeing dominates the last section of this collection, as it does Eric Lorentzen's essay on visual literacy in Charlotte Bronte's *Shirley*. Lorentzen argues for what I would call the double heroines' efforts toward reform on their own behalf. He argues that Bronte creates both a "self-fashioning pedagogy" and a critique of traditional patriarchal pedagogy. Caroline actually is in danger of becoming like Dickens's "bride" or Collins's ghostly figure—a woman in white, a woman in danger of losing her life. She pales and pines, but eventually she is rescued by variety of factors—her rediscovered mother's love, her friend Shirley's spirited resistance to her own exclusion from reformist projects, her own growing ability to read against the grain or, in Lorentzen's words, to read "from the margins." If we take this literally, of course, the margin is the blank space, the white space, the ostensibly empty space. In reading from the margin, however, Caroline is in danger of being reduced to the margin. Far from enacting a self-fashioning pedagogy, she is nearly reduced to discarded blank edge on which little learning is inscribed.

The complexity of Caroline's reading from the margin, Lorentzen shows us, is made clear in Caroline's and Robert Moore's controversy over *Coriolanus*. In this famous scene of instruction, Caroline turns the tables on Moore; she instructs him about social duty, laments the reform he cannot or will not undertake in his current circumstances, and accuses him of hauteur toward those to whom he should feel warmer connections (implicitly his workmen and Caroline herself). As Margaret Mitchell argues, however, in the other essay on *Shirley* in this volume, the happy ending, which unites domesticity and reform, is in fact dependent not upon a moral victory for reform or altruism but upon a foreign policy decision, the repeal in 1812 of the Orders in Council, which had restricted trade to by blockading continental ports (158). Once the Orders are repealed, "reform" is possible. Or to put it another way, Caroline's marginal reading does not directly empower her. The effort at action on behalf of oneself is subject to economic and political interests over which one has no control.

At the end a different specter of reform emerges. Robert first proposes and then delights in telling Caroline his plans to double the size of his mill, to cut down the copse and build cottages, to make a broad highway of ash and cinders of the lane between, to see to it that Caroline has a Sunday school larger than she can imagine. Caroline reacts in horror: "Root up the copse?" But yes, Robert answers. And more, and worse, he hopes to enclose the common as well. The narrator does not comment, save indirectly, on Roberts' words. But she allows a dialect voice, the voice of an old housekeeper, to comment in the end. Years back, the housekeeper says, her mother encountered the "last fairish" that ever was seen in the hollow. Thus Caroline's self-pedagogy, her reform on her own behalf and her Sunday school philanthropy for cottagers is shadowed by an evanescent form—not even the last fairy herself, the ghost of nature gone, but only the tale of a tale of a fairy. If we read the hollow allegorically, as we might read the Red Deeps in Eliot's *The Mill on the Floss*, as a female body, even the heroine's female body, the disappearance of the "last fairish" is the disappearance of a passionate connection to one's own being; the "last fairish" being gone, one is dissociated from the flesh itself.

As the "last fairish" or the woman in white show us, fictions are subject to haunting; they evoke even in a resolutely industrial novel like *Shirley* specters which disrupt and dismay. The essays here that detail historical rather than fictional dimensions of reform—Daniel Siegel's discussion of the "Bible-Woman," Maggie Atkinson's discussion of Suffragette jewelry and medals, and Loretta Clayton's discussion of aesthetic dress—make clear the ways reform marked and was marked by social class. And yet even history itself is haunted in peculiar ways. Siegel discusses the "Bible-Woman," the working class woman who serves as the bridge between the middle class and the poor; in the words of the Bible Mission's founder, the Bible-Woman was the "missing link." Siegel argues that Ellen Raynard's memoir the Bible-Woman becomes "perfectly natural and utterly monstrous." This creature, who negotiates class divides, is perhaps a domestic and poorer version of Thomas Babington Macaulay's English educated Indian who was to mediate between the British and their subject. Both the "babu" and the Bible-woman were perceived as somehow monstrous, moving between what was understood by Macaulay and by Raynard as immutable class (and racial or racialized) divisions. The Bible-Woman as Raynard describes her becomes a kind of specter herself. As Siegel puts it, she "becomes the sign, both among her philanthropic colleagues and among her destitute neighbors, of the other" (5).

At the end of the century and at the other end of class relations, aesthetic dress reform brings to the fore analogous anxieties. Aesthetic dress reform, as recommended to the readers of *The Woman's World,* drew upon preceding styles—the Bloomer and Turkish trousers. Proponents of dress reform approached it as a kind of self-fashioning, and a self-fashioning that Loretta Clayton argues, for Oscar Wilde at least, had democratic overtones. Wilde aimed at a wider audience than the socialites who first adopted aesthetic dress. A few years later, as Maggie Atkinson shows, the Suffragettes sold trinkets in their stores at a wide variety of price points, attempting similar to cross class barriers. In both cases, self-fashioning or reform on behalf of oneself cannot occur outside the exchange of commodities. Commodities come to indicate reform, to stand in for reform. Perhaps if we emphasize the *fashion* in self-fashioning this notion needs no further explanation.

Is it possible that by the century's end, reform could not escape the commodity? That "reform" must be understood to be formed by circulation of commodities? In the 1840s the Bible-Woman sold testaments, clothes, and a reformation of life and behavior to her compatriots; in the 1880s Wilde sold magazines aimed at encouraging women to fashion themselves; in the 2008 election, the Obama campaign supported a "progressive agenda" a "reform" agenda by asking supporters to purchase signs, bumper stickers, t-shirts, and other goods. In all three cases, "reform" was literally commodified.

In the Victorian examples cited here, the more philanthropic the object of reform, the more monstrous the *distribution* or *distributor* of the commodity appeared. Perhaps "reform" can never escape the specter of commodities. Jacques Derrida derives specters of Marx from the beginning of *Capital.* We have met several of them here—the "fairish" of Hollow's Mill, the woman in white, the bride in her "chamber." In the theater of commodities, Derrida writes:

> Men no longer recognize in it the *social* charter of their *own* labor. It is as if they were becoming ghosts in their turn. The "proper" feature of specters, like vampires, is that they are deprived of a specular image, of the true, right specular image (but who is not so deprived?). How do you recognize a ghost? By the fact that it does not recognize itself in a mirror. Now that is what happens with the *commerce* of the commodities *among themselves.* These ghosts that are commodities transform human producers into ghosts. And this whole theatrical process (visual, theoretical, but also optical, *optician*) sets off the effect of a mysterious mirror: if the latter does not return the right reflection, if then, it phantomalizes, this is first of all because it naturalizes." [Jacques Derrida, *Specters of Marx: The State*

of the Debt, the Work of Mourning, and the New International, trans. by Peggy Kamuf (New York: Routledge, 1994), pp. 155-56].

Telescopic philanthropy, after all, is a matter of mirrors, mirrors in which Mrs. Jellyby cannot see her own reflection, telescopes in which she cannot see what or who is under her own nose. Reform on behalf of others creates monsters like Mrs. Jellyby, a "missing link" selling Bibles, a woman in white who cannot be singularly named. As it turns out, reform on behalf of oneself is equally dangerous, for to "re-form" one must first dissolve or deform. Caroline and Laura / Anne become white wraiths, only to be given temporary shape in marriage.

This brings us to the point Wordsworth describes in the preface to *Lyrical Ballads* a moment that prefigures the Marxist theater of commodities, the moment of political and literary discouragement marked by the very success of the culture of sensation. Wordsworth laments the success of hourly news and cheap German tragedies; sensation has trumped poetry, news declares the sensational failures of Revolution. To believe that fleeting news, fleeting sensation (the products of Fleet Street) is all that is possible, Wordsworth writes, is to succumb to "idleness" and "unmanly despair."

Where, then, is the outside of the theater of commodities? How to drive a stake through a specter's heart? If all reforms have their specters, where does justice lie? As Laura Rotunno shows in her essay here, Elizabeth Barrett Browning—in her own rewriting of Wordsworth's *Prelude*—suggested one answer: a utopian future, a visionary future made possible by the union of art and social justice. Aurora asserts at the end of Barrett Browning's poem that poetry—that is, passion—and reform can join. The poem performs this conjuncture as it brings together Aurora and her (reformed) lover Romney. Aurora describes their union this way:

> I flung closer to his breast,
> Is a sword, that after battle, flings to sheath;
> And, in that hurtle of united souls,
> The mystic motions which in common moods
> Are shut beyond our sense, broke in on us.
>   (quoted in Rotunno, 65)

Aurora herself becomes the stake, the sword. In a double reversal, she assumes the masculine role while the now blind Romney is feminized. Like Cassandra, however, Romney is given the poem's long concluding speech if not quite its last words, quoting the book of Revelation, Romney imagines a new world, with new churches, new economies, new laws, new societies. And finally Aurora chimes in and finishes this long poem with the jeweled imagery of the New Testament.

But Aurora's speech, too, is theater, theatrical in the extreme, a visionary poetics that declares itself to be also a politics. If a specter remains, it is Marian Earle, the raped virgin, the redeemed working class woman—whose mother was a monster and whose father a drunkard. Marian, Mary, now inhabits the wings of the theater, the margins of the poem, with her illegitimate son. Aurora Leigh's staging and its staginess, like Marx's theater of commodities, leaves us with the persisting question: can there be justice without an imagination of utopia? How else can we escape the theater of commodities among themselves?

BIBLIOGRAPHY

GENERAL WORKS ON VICTORIAN REFORM, GENDER,
AND LITERATURE

Armstrong, Nancy. *Desire and Domestic Fiction: A Political History of the Novel.* New York: Oxford University Press, 1987.

Bodenheimer , Rosemarie. *The Politics of Story in Victorian Social Fiction.* Ithaca, NY: Cornell University Press, 1988.

Booth, Alison, ed. *Famous Last Words: Changes in Gender and Narrative Closure.* Charlottesville: University Press of Virginia, 1993.

Case, Alison. *Plotting Women: Gender and Narration in the Eighteenth- and Nineteenth-Century British Novel.* Charlottesville: University Press of Virginia, 1999.

Dickerson, Vanessa D., ed. *Keeping the Victorian House: A Collection of Essays.* New York, London: Garland Press, 1995.

Elliott, Dorice. *The Angel out of the House: Philanthropy and Gender in Nineteenth-Century England.* Charlottesville: University Press Virginia, 2002.

Flint, Kate. *The Woman Reader*, 1837-1914. Oxford: Clarendon Press, 1993.

Gilbert, Sandra M. and Susan Gubar. *The Madwoman in the Attic: The Woman Writer and the Nineteenth-Century Literary Imagination.* 2nd. ed. New Haven: Yale University Press, 2000.

Goodlad, Lauren M. E. "Beyond the Panopticon: Victorian Britain and the Critical Imagination." *PMLA* 118 (2003): 539-556.

—. *Victorian Literature and the Victorian State: Character and Governance in a Liberal Society,* Baltimore: Johns Hopkins University Press, 2003.

Hall, Catherine, Keith McClelland, and Jane Rendall. *Defining the Victorian Nation: Class, Race, Gender and the British Reform Act of 1867* Cambridge University Press, 2000

Hall, Donald E., ed. *Embodying the Victorian Age.* Cambridge: Cambridge University Press, 1994.

Kent, Susan Kingsley. *Sex and Suffrage in Britain*, 1860-1914. Princeton: Princeton University Press, 1987.

Litvak, Joseph. *Caught in the Act: Theatricality in the Nineteenth-Century English Novel*. Berkeley: University of California Press, 1992.

Losey, Jay and William D. Brewer, eds. *Mapping Male Sexuality: Nineteenth-Century England*. Madison: Fairleigh Dickinson University Press, 2000.

Maitzen, Rohan Amanda. *Gender, Genre, and Victorian Historical Writing*. New York: Garland Publisher, 1998.

Koven, Seth. *Slumming*. Princeton: Princeton University Press, 2004.

Nathan, Rhoda B., ed. *Nineteenth-Century Women Writers of the English-Speaking World*. New York: Greenwood Press, 1986. Princeton University Press, 1987.

Poovey, Mary. *Uneven Developments: The Ideological Work of Gender in Mid-Victorian* England University of Chicago Press, 1988.

Showalter, Elaine. *Sexual Anarchy: Gender and Culture at the Fin de Siècle*. New York: Viking, 1990.

Stanley, Mary Lyndon. *Feminism, Marriage, and the Law in Victorian England, 1850-1895* Princeton University Press, 1989.

Surridge, Lisa. *Bleak Houses: Marital Violence in Victorian Fiction*. Athens: Ohio University Press, 2005.

WORKS ON SPECIFIC AUTHORS OR REFORM MOVEMENTS
IN VICTORIAN ENGLAND

Blanchard, Mary Warner. *Oscar Wilde's America: Counterculture in the Gilded Age*. New Haven: Yale University Press, 1998.

Bonaparte, Felicia. *The Gypsy-Bachelor of Manchester: The Life of Mrs. Gaskell's Demon*. Charlottesville: University Press of Virginia, 1992.

Burton, Antionette. "Fearful Bodies into Disciplined Subjects: Pleasure, Romance, and the Family Drama of Colonial Reform in Mary Carpenter's "Six Months in India"" *Signs,* Vol. 20, No. 3 (Spring, 1995), 545-574

Butler, Judith. "'Conscience Doth Make Subjects of Us All.'" *Yale French Studies* 88 (1995): 6-26.

Cayleff, Susan E. *Wash and Be Healed: The Water Cure Movement and Women's Health*. Philadelphia: Temple University Press, 1987.

Cervetti, Nancy. *Scenes of Reading: Transforming Romance in Brontë, Eliot, and Woolf*. New York: Peter Lang, 1998.

Craik, Wendy. "Lore, Learning and Wisdom: Workers and Education in *Mary Barton* and *North and South*." *Gaskell Society Journal* 2 (1988): 13-33.

Donegan, Jane B. *Hydropathic Pathway to Health: Women and Water-cure in Antebellum America.* New York: Greenwood Press, 1986.

Fascik, Laura. "Dickens and Diseased Body in *Bleak House*," in *Charles Dickens: Bloom's Major Novelists*, edited by Harold Bloom (Broomfield, PA: Chelsea House, 2000), 65-68.

Houston, Gail Turley. "Gender Construction and the Künstlerroman: David Copperfield and Aurora Leigh." *Philological Quarterly* 72 (1993): 213-36.

Lansbury, Coral. *Elizabeth Gaskell: The Novel of Social Crisis.* New York: Barnes and Noble, 1975.

McGavran, Dorothy. "Ruthless for Reform: Language, Lying, and Interpretation in Elizabeth Gaskell's *Ruth*." *Postscript* 12 (1995): 39-49.

Mitchell, Judith. *The Stone and the Scorpion: The Female Subject of Desire in the Novels of Charlotte Brontë, George Eliot, and Thomas Hardy.* Westport: Greenwood Press, 1994.

Mota, Miguel M. "The Construction of the Christian Community in Charles Dickens's *Bleak House*," *Renascence: Essays on Values in Literature* 46, no. 3 (1994): 187- 198.

Mullenix, Elizabeth Reitz. "So unfemininely masculine": Discourse, true/false womanhood, and the American career of Fanny Kemble." *Theatre Survey* (Nov. 1999): 27-42.

Richardson, LeeAnne M. *New Woman and Colonial Adventure Fiction in Victorian Britain: Gender, Genre, and Empire.* Gainesville: University Press of Florida, 2006.

Robbins, Bruce. "Telescopic Philanthropy: Professionalism and Responsibility in *Bleak House*," *New Casebooks: Bleak House*, edited by Jeremy Tambling (New York: St. Martin's Press, 1998), 139-162.

Sanders, Lise Shapiro. *Consuming Fantasies: Labor, Leisure, and the London Shopgirl, 1880-1920.* Columbus: Ohio State University Press, 2006

Schor, Hilary M. *Scheherezade in the Marketplace: Elizabeth Gaskell and the Victorian Novel.* Oxford: Oxford University Press, 1992.

Shuttleworth, Sally. *Charlotte Brontë and Victorian Psychology.* Cambridge University Press, 1996.

Stone, Marjorie. "Bakhtinian Polyphony in *Mary Barton*: Class, Gender, and the Textual Voice." *Dickens Studies Annual* 20 (1991): 175-200.

Stoneman, Patsy. *Elizabeth Gaskell.* Bloomington: Indiana University Press, 1987.

Torrens, Kathleen M. "Fashion as Argument: Nineteenth-century Dress Reform." *Argumentation and Advocacy* (fall 1999): xxx.

Uglow, Jenny. *Elizabeth Gaskell: A Habit of Stories.* London: Faber and Faber, 1993.

Walkowitz, Judith R. *City of Dreadful Delight: Narratives of Sexual Danger in Late-Victorian London.* Chicago: University of Chicago Press, 1992.

Wilde, Oscar. "More Radical Ideas Upon Dress Reform." *Complete Writings of Oscar Wilde.* New York: Nottingham Society, 1907.

CONTRIBUTORS

Maggie Atkinson is an Assistant Professor at Sir Wilfred Grenfell College where she teaches Art history and feminist theory, focusing on modern and contemporary Visual culture. She specializes in nineteenth- and twentieth-century art. She is currently completing a book-length study entitled *The Fringe of Immortality: Fantasy, Memory and Spirituality through Visual Culture 1885-1930*.

Maria K. Bachman is Professor of English at Coastal Carolina University in Conway, South Carolina. She has edited scholarly editions of Wilkie Collins's *The Woman in White* (Broadview Press, 2006) and *Blind Love* (Broadview Press, 2004), as well as a collection of critical essays, *Reality's Dark Light: The Sensational Wilkie Collins* (University of Tennessee Press, 2003). She is currently working on a book project on embodied consciousness and the novel.

Aria F. Chernik is a candidate for a Ph.D. in English at the University of North Carolina at Greensboro. She specializes in nineteenth-century British literature and is working on her dissertation on William Blake and the literary and cultural production of communal subjectivity in the early Romantic period.

Loretta Clayton is an assistant professor of English at Macon State College in Macon, Georgia. Her primary areas of scholarship are Oscar Wilde and late Victorian discourses of aestheticism and fashion. She has written and spoken on these subjects and recently participated in an NEH seminar at the Wilde archive at UCLA's William Andrews Clark Memorial Library.

Andre' L. DeCuir is an Associate Professor of English at Muskingum College and specializes in Victorian Literature. He has published and presented articles on George Eliot, Mary Shelley, Thomas Hardy, Charlotte Bronte, Elizabeth Gaskell, Charles Dickens, and the Pre-Raphaelites. He is currently writing on the influence of nineteenth-century painting on selected Victorian novelists.

Laura Fasick received her doctorate in English Literature and her certificate in Victorian Studies from Indiana University in Bloomington. She is currently a professor in the English Department at Minnesota State University Moorhead. Professor of English, University of Minnesota Moorhead and is the author of *Professional Men and Domesticity in the Mid-Victorian Novel* (2003) and *Vessels of Meaning: Women's Bodies, Gender Norms, and Class Bias from Richardson to Lawrence* (1997) and numerous articles on nineteenth-century literature.

Audrey Fessler is an Assistant Professor of Literature and Women's Studies at the University of Wisconsin, Eau Claire

Chris Foss is Associate Professor of English at the University of Mary Washington, where he specializes in Nineteenth-Century British Literature. He is the author of three other scholarly articles and papers focused upon Toru Dutt. He also has edited two of her poems for the Colonial Poetry Anthology in the Poetry and the Colonies special issue of *Victorians Institute Journal* (2004), and more recently he self-published an annotated on-line critical edition of Dutt's 1882 posthumous volume of poetry, *Ancient Ballads and Legends of Hindustan,* at http://foss.elsweb.org/toru_dutt.

Mary Ellis Gibson is a professor of English at the University of North Carolina at Greensboro, where she works in Victorian and modernist literature, feminist theory and southern literature. She is author of *History and the Prism of Art: Browning's Poetic Experiments* (Ohio State University Press) and *Epic Reinvented: Ezra Pound and the Victorians* (Cornell University Press) and editor of *Critical Essays on Robert Browning* as well as two collections of short stories, *New Stories by Southern Women* and *Homeplaces.* She is a past president of the Victorians Institute.

Eric G. Lorentzen is an Assistant Professor of English at the University of Mary Washington in Fredericksburg, Virginia, where he teaches a wide variety of courses on nineteenth-century British literature and culture, cultural studies, narrative theory and the novel genre, critical pedagogy and theories of literacy, and the multi-national short story. His publications have appeared in *Dickens Studies Annual, The Review of Education, Pedagogy and Cultural Studies, Victorian Newsletter,* and *Virginia Woolf Miscellany.*

Chad May is an assistant professor of English at Kansas Wesleyan University where he teaches British and World Literature. His research interests include the nineteenth-century historical novel, Sir Walter Scott, and the French Revolution.

Dorothy H. McGavran is Professor of English at Queens University of Charlotte North Carolina where she also directs the interdisciplinary Core Program in the Liberal Arts. Her scholarly interests focus on lying in Victorian fiction particularly in the works of Elizabeth Gaskell.

Margaret E. Mitchell's work on Victorian literature and gender has appeared in *Studies in the Novel, Women's Studies, Gissing and the City* (ed. John Spiers), and elsewhere. She is coeditor of *LIT: Literature Interpretation Theory*, a journal of literary criticism, and an associate professor of English at the University of West Georgia.

Anita Rose is an Associate Professor of English at Converse College in Spartanburg, South Carolina, where she is currently department chair. Her research interests include Victorian utopian literature and popular culture. She has published essays on feminist utopias and the reimagining of the Romantic heroic ideal in *Buffy, the Vampire Slayer*. She was the local coordinator for the Victorians Institute Conference in 2006.

Laura Rotunno, Assistant Professor of English at Penn State Altoona, specializes in the nineteenth-century British novel. Her "The Long History of 'In Short': Mr. Micawber, Letter-Writers, and Literary Men," published in Victorian Literature and Culture, won the 2005 Interdisciplinary Nineteenth-Century Studies Essay Prize. She has also published essays in *Browning Society Notes* and *a/b: Auto/Biography Studies*. She has recently completed a book-length manuscript that investigates reading habits, literary professionalism, and the novel's popularity through the lens of the radically changing nineteenth-century British Post Office.

Daniel Siegel is Associate Professor of English at the University of Alabama at Birmingham, where he specializes in nineteenth-century British fiction and Victorian cultural studies. He has published essays in *Victorian Literature and Culture, Dickens Studies Annual, and Novel: A Forum on Fiction*, and is currently completing a book on condescension and philanthropy in the Victorian imagination.

INDEX